VOL. 3

Quicknotes

SIMPLIFIED BIBLE COMMENTARY SERIES

1 samuel
THRU 2 kings

WHO RULES YOU?

CON

ROBE   , Th.M.

CONSULTING EDITOR:
DR. TREMPER LONGMAN

ISBN 978-1-59789-769-3

Produced with the assistance of Christopher D. Hudson & Associates. Contributing writers include: Elizabeth Arlene, Stan Campbell, Anita Palmer, Jane Vogel, and Carol Smith.

Published by Barbour Publishing, Inc., P.O. Box 719, Uhrichsville, Ohio 44683, www.barbourbooks.com

Our mission is to publish and distribute inspirational products offering exceptional value and biblical encouragement to the masses.

Member of the
Evangelical Christian
Publishers Association

TABLE OF CONTENTS

1 SAMUEL

INTRODUCTION TO 1 SAMUEL

The book of 1 Samuel is best understood after a thorough review of the book of Judges. This was a dark era of history for the nation of Israel. God had delivered the Israelites from slavery in Egypt to the promised land in Canaan. The transition had not been a smooth one, yet under the leadership of Joshua the people had done reasonably well. However, after the death of Joshua, Israel went through repeated cycles of blessing and discipline—the result of their obedience or rebellion. Judges ends with the bleak statement: "In those days Israel had no king; everyone did as he saw fit" (Judges 21:25 NIV). That is the situation as 1 Samuel begins.

AUTHOR

What we know as 1 Samuel and 2 Samuel were originally a single book (along with 1 and 2 Kings in its final form), and Jewish tradition credits Samuel as the author. But since Samuel's death is included halfway through the (combined) book, other sources clearly were involved. Several resources were available to other authors at that time, which are mentioned in Samuel and related passages (1 Samuel 10:25; 2 Samuel 1:18; 1 Chronicles 29:29). Even assuming that Samuel made a major contribution to the book that bears his name, no one can state with certainty who authored the other portions. The date of writing is also questioned. Some suggest that since David's death is not included in 1 or 2 Samuel, the writing may have been concluded prior to that time. Others believe Samuel could have been written considerably later—after the kingdom was divided (based on clues such as "kings of Judah" in 1 Samuel 27:6).

PURPOSE

The books of Samuel deal with the transition between Israel's judges and their kings. This was a period when word from the Lord was rare (1 Samuel 3:1). Samuel was just the leader the nation needed to remind them of their spiritual commitments and help them move forward. Even though they would eventually reject Samuel's advice regarding their leadership, he continued to faithfully mediate between the people and the Lord.

OCCASION

The books of 1 and 2 Samuel were recorded to provide historical accounts of a crucial period of Israel's past. The book of 1 Samuel spans Samuel's life from birth to death, chronicles Saul's entire reign as the first king of Israel, and reveals the lengthy transition David underwent from shepherd boy to heir to the throne.

THEMES

Numerous times throughout 1 Samuel, the significance of *obedience* is emphasized, as are the consequences of disobedience. The Israelites would reject both Eli's sons and Samuel's sons as leaders because they did not obey God. We are also shown Saul's recurring tendency to be almost (but not quite) obedient. Closely related is the issue of *receiving guidance from God.* Some of the improper methods attempted include using the ark of God like a good luck charm (4:1–11) and seeking spiritual advice through a medium (28:4–25). In contrast, we see Hannah's fervent prayer (1:1–20), Samuel's ability to discern God's voice (3:1–21), the use of the priestly ephod with the Urim and Thummim, and other methods not fully explained (14:18–19).

HISTORICAL CONTEXT

The previous era of Israel's judges had been a downward spiritual spiral as Israel's numerous enemies dominated them until the people repented and God responded with a leader who would free them (temporarily). As the people moved from judges to kings, the reign of Saul wouldn't be much better. The rules of David and Solomon were, in part, bright spots of repentance, spiritual renewal, and prosperity. But the series of kings would soon drift away from God (with only a few exceptions), resulting in eventual capture and captivity for Israel and Judah.

CONTRIBUTION TO THE BIBLE

The book of 1 Samuel contains some of the favorite stories familiar to children's Sunday schools and Bible story books: Hannah and the boy Samuel, Samuel hearing God speaking to him, Israel's first king, and David and Goliath, to name a few. It is also enlightening to reflect on the stories of people who come into contact with the ark of the covenant when it is not in its traditional location in the tabernacle (or temple). Both the Philistines and the Israelites learn some hard lessons about misusing the holy things of God in this book. Additionally, it is in 1 Samuel where we find an explanation of the cryptic line in the older versions of the hymn, "Come Thou Fount of Every Blessing." When we sing, "Here I raise my Ebenezer," it is a reference to 1 Samuel 7:12–13.

OUTLINE OF 1 SAMUEL

1 SAMUEL 1:1–2:10

THE SON AND THE PSALM OF HANNAH

Setting Up the Section

The book of 1 Samuel is known for its grand accounts of Samuel (the great prophet, priest, and judge), Saul (Israel's first king), and the rise of the great King David. But it begins with the story of a humble and burdened young woman. Hannah's story is a model of the value of ongoing faithfulness and prayer, even when life's circumstances seem overwhelming.

📖 1:1–8

HANNAH'S DILEMMA

Hannah is one of two wives of a man named Elkanah, the other being a woman named Peninnah. Elkanah is a godly descendant of Levi, designated as an Ephraimite because of his place of residence. Peninnah had borne a number of children to Elkanah, but Hannah was barren.

Each year the family traveled some twenty miles or so north of Jerusalem to Shiloh, where the tabernacle was stationed. Three annual feasts (with required attendance for Jewish males) attracted many visitors. The event referred to in this passage may have been the Feast of Tabernacles (Leviticus 23:33–36), a time to rejoice and recall the Exodus from Egypt.

Critical Observation

It is unlikely that Hannah and Peninnah would have had much contact on a daily basis. They probably lived and ate in separate tents, well distanced from each other. But on journeys they would be thrown together, and Hannah would be forced to endure Peninnah's provocations.

1:9–20

HANNAH'S DESIRE

Hannah's inability to conceive a child is bad enough, but traveling with Elkanah's taunting wife makes things worse. On arrival at Shiloh, Hannah hurries off to the tabernacle, where she pours out her heart to God. Eli, the priest, sees her distressed body language but hears no verbal prayer, and jumps to the conclusion that she is drunk (which suggests incompetence on his part). He has no idea she is making a solemn vow to God as she pleads for a son.

After a short conversation, however, Eli sends her away in peace with his endorsement of whatever she has been praying for. Immediately Hannah is able to eat, and she feels much better (1:18). Meanwhile, Elkanah is consistently attentive to Hannah's feelings, and before long she conceives and has a son whom she names Samuel.

1:21–2:10

HANNAH'S DEDICATION OF SAMUEL

The year after Samuel's birth, Hannah doesn't go on the annual trip to Shiloh. Her child is still weaning, and she is not yet able to honor her promise to God. But after Samuel is weaned, and still quite young (1:24), she takes him to Shiloh and presents him to God, leaving him in the care of Eli.

Despite knowing that she will give up her long-desired firstborn son, Samuel's birth gives Hannah great joy. Her prayer (2:1–10) in response to his birth has a number of features worth noting. It employs parallelism and symbolism, indicative of the format of a psalm. Like other biblical psalms, Hannah's prayer is addressed to God and reflects her praise and thanksgiving. What began as her personal expression of gratitude has become part of scripture for all to read and repeat as edification of the soul. Her words of praise seem to reflect Israel's past experiences, particularly the Exodus. (Note her use of *rock* in 2:2 [Deuteronomy 32:30–31] and *horn* in 2:1 [Deuteronomy 33:17].) Hannah's psalm does not concentrate on her sorrow, her suffering, or even her blessings. Rather, it focuses on her God who is holy (1 Samuel 2:2), faithful (2:2), omniscient (2:3), gracious (2:8), all-powerful (2:6), and a sovereign reverser of circumstances (2:6–10). Hannah's is a magnificent expression of faith at a time when she is giving up her (at the time) only child.

Hannah speaks of God giving strength to His king (2:10), although Israel had never had a human king at this time. In this sense, her song is prophetic. Her son, Samuel, will eventually anoint the first two kings of Israel.

The positive, righteous example of Hannah (and Elkanah) stands out in contrast to the sad spiritual state of Israel during the time of the judges as well as the state of the priesthood at that time, as will be seen in the next section.

Take It Home

When it comes to responding to criticism, jeers, and similar unpleasant circumstances of life, it would be difficult to find a better example than Hannah. We find no evidence that she retaliated toward Peninnah in any way. Though hurt and humiliated, she remained hopeful and faithful. In God's timing, her sorrow is turned to joy, and her son will be instrumental in turning Israel from its self-indulgent mentality into a powerful nation that once again has a godly leader and receives abundant blessings of God.

1 SAMUEL 2:11–4:22

THE RISE OF SAMUEL

Setting Up the Section

After the birth of Samuel, it doesn't take long for Eli and the people of Israel to see that he is a special person with a rare (in those days) call from God. As Samuel moves into the office of the priesthood and the role of a prophet, his spiritual integrity is clearly evident in contrast to those around him.

📄 **2:11–26**

A CONTRAST OF LEADERSHIP

Eli had committed to raising Hannah's child, Samuel, but he already had sons of his own. Eli's sons, Hophni and Phinehas (1:3), are wicked men who have no regard for the Lord (2:12). Their priestly responsibilities should include maintaining the tabernacle (Exodus 27:21; Leviticus 24:1–7; Numbers 18:1–7) and the altar (Leviticus 6:8–13). They should also set good examples by avoiding strong drink when serving in the tabernacle (Leviticus 10:8–11), maintaining sexual purity (Leviticus 21:1–9), and remaining ceremonially clean (Leviticus 21:10–22:9). But these sons of Eli do not take their service or responsibilities seriously. They are greedy and insensitive, and they regularly take advantage of others.

Critical Observation

Hophni and Phinehas should have known better than to abuse their sacred positions. The sons of the first high priest, Aaron, had acted improperly and had been judged and killed as a result (Leviticus 10:1–3; Numbers 3:4; 26:60–61).

The maturity of Samuel—physically and spiritually—is seen in stark contrast to Eli's sons. It is worth noting that each year Hannah makes not just clothes to take to Samuel, but she makes *priestly garments*. It might be presumed that she and Elkanah continue to have a positive influence on their son, even as he is growing up in the shadows of Hophni and Phinehas. Their offenses (detailed in 1 Samuel 2:17, 22–25) go beyond the liturgical abuse of the priesthood into moral corruptions. Their disregard for God's law is blatant.

Samuel's first assignment as a prophet is to tell Eli something that isn't pleasant to hear (3:17–18). Yet it seems that his mentor Eli cannot do the same with his own sons. If he attempts to rebuke them, he lacks force and authority. Eli learns of everything they are doing, yet allows the problem to continue. Again, Samuel is a direct contrast (2:26).

2:27–36

A GRIM PROPHECY

The situation with the priesthood is, of course, evident to God. He makes known His displeasure and intent by sending a prophet to Eli—a rare event (3:1). The prophet addresses the priesthood in a proper historical and theological perspective. He first recalls the Exodus, when the Aaronic and Levitical priesthood had been established and respected. Then he looks to the future, when God will build a new house of priests. As for the present, judgment is in store for Eli and his sons—they will all die on the same day, after which God will establish a faithful priest (2:34–35). (The accusation that the priests are fattening themselves on the offerings [2:29] may have hit home with Eli; he is later described as a heavy old man [4:18].)

The problems with the priesthood will be resolved with a new dynasty of priests. The house had been strong under Aaron, but it is crumbling under Eli. Samuel will begin to restore the integrity that has been lost. It will become an enduring house (2:35) that will continue under Zadok, the high priest during the reign of David. Then, ultimately, the fulfillment of this prophecy is found in Jesus. No other priest in Israel's history is worthy to serve as priest eternally.

THE VOICE OF GOD IS HEARD AGAIN

In this passage Samuel is called a *boy*—a term flexible enough to refer to a newborn or a young man. Most likely, several years have passed between chapter 2 and chapter 3, and Samuel is probably entering his teen years.

During this period in Israel's history, the people have stopped listening to God, so God does not communicate with them very often. Therefore, when God speaks to Samuel, the youngster assumes the voice is that of his mentor, Eli. It takes three times before the more experienced priest suspects what is happening (evidencing again his incompetence) and instructs Samuel to reply directly to God.

The lamps burn throughout the night in the temple (2 Chronicles 13:11) and burn out around daybreak. So this setting, where the tabernacle residents are sleeping while the lamps are burning, suggests the early morning hours.

When Samuel finally acknowledges God's voice, God gives him a solemn message concerning Eli. God is about to bring judgment on Eli and his house because Eli has done nothing to hinder the offensive behavior of his sons. Judgment is now imminent. No longer will sacrifice or atonement set the record straight (1 Samuel 3:14).

Demystifying 1 Samuel

Some Bible translations say that Eli does not *rebuke* his sons (3:13), yet it certainly appears that he verbally reprimands them (2:22–25). Other versions offer the translation that Eli does not *restrain* his sons, which seems to be a better word choice. In either case, the result is that Eli and his sons have passed the point of no return.

SAMUEL'S ACCREDITATION AS A PROPHET OF GOD

Not surprisingly, the young Samuel is reticent to approach Eli with the message he has received from God. He doesn't bring it up until Eli confronts him. (Eli, of course, has already heard a similar message from a different prophet [2:27–36].) When pressed by Eli, Samuel reluctantly tells him the entire message.

Eli's response to the prophecy is disturbing. Even after hearing of the impending judgment of God, he doesn't repent of his own sin of neglect. His words have a pious ring of submission to the sovereign will of God, yet are actually an expression of fatalism couched in religious terms.

God continues to speak to Samuel (3:21) and Samuel speaks for God. The people soon notice his evident call as a true prophet (Deuteronomy 13:1–5; 18:14–22; 1 Samuel 3:19). As Samuel continues to listen and respond, the young prophet will soon become a righteous priest and judge as well.

4:1–22

ISRAEL'S DEFEAT

At this point the Philistines have dominated the Israelites for some time (4:9). In a previous battle, Israel lost 4,000 soldiers (4:2), after which they questioned why God would allow such a thing to happen. But rather than consulting God and praying and fasting, they decide to carry the ark of the covenant into the next battle, assuming it will guarantee God's presence with them.

When the ark first arrives at the Israelite camp, a great shout goes out. The soldiers are confident and assured of victory. In fact, the cheering is so loud that it is heard in the Philistine camp. After the Philistines discover the ark has been summoned, they presume that they will be doing battle against Israel's gods as well as their soldiers. (They are well aware of Israel's past victories where the ark is prominent.) But rather than causing them to cower, the news motivates the Philistines to fight harder and die like men, if it comes to that. As fighting ensues, the tragedies accumulate for Israel: They lose the battle, 30,000 men die (including both of Eli's sons), and the ark is captured and carried away by the Philistines.

The news is equally grim on the home front. Eli has stationed himself by the road, anxiously awaiting word. A Benjamite who had escaped eventually comes by. His clothes are torn and he has dust on his head—signs of mourning and defeat. Eli's vision is poor and he may not have detected the visible signs, but he could certainly hear the commotion (3:11). When the messenger confirms the worst, the news is more than Eli's 98-year-old body can handle. He collapses and breaks his neck. As had been foretold, he and his sons die on the same day.

In addition, tragedy also strikes Eli's pregnant daughter-in-law (the wife of Phinehas). The deaths of Eli and her husband, Israel's defeat, and the loss of the ark all hasten her labor. She refuses comfort or help from others, and dies during the delivery. But before she does, she names her son Ichabod ("no glory"). She comments that the glory of God departed with the capture of the ark. In reality, due to Israel's ongoing problematic spiritual condition, God's presence had not been felt by Israel for a long time.

Take It Home

This section of scripture describes three different responses the people had toward God, which are still evident today. The Israelites callously act as if God is their servant, rather than vice versa. But God is not a good luck charm. Eli responds with fatalistic resignation. At least twice God speaks to him through other people, but in spite of the repeated warnings, he does absolutely nothing. Samuel, on the other hand, responds in faith to God's call. He did nothing to prompt God's appearance yet does not take for granted the grace and sovereignty of God. Every Christian is called to faith in Christ and called to proclaim the Word of Christ to others. May we respond as Samuel does—immediately, faithfully, and continually.

1 SAMUEL 5:1–7:17

THE PHILISTINES ENCOUNTER ISRAEL'S GOD

Setting Up the Section

The Israelites appear to be in a bleak situation. The Philistines have just routed the army, with thirty thousand casualties. Their priests are among the dead. Worst of all, the ark of the covenant was captured. But as will become evident in this section, God is still in control and remains active on behalf of His people.

📄 5:1–12

THE CONSEQUENCES OF CAPTURING THE ARK

As the Philistines carry off the ark of the covenant, it may appear to the Israelites that their God is being held hostage. But they—and the Philistines—are in for a few surprises.

The Philistines first take the ark to Ashdod, the northernmost of their five principle cities, where they place it in a temple before one of their primary gods, Dagon. Imagine their surprise the next morning as they come to celebrate Dagon's victory, only to find his image fallen and prostrate before the ark of God. They reposition Dagon and return the next day. The situation is even worse. Dagon has fallen again, and this time its hands and head have broken off. The ark of God may be in Philistine hands, but the god of the Philistines is in the hands of the only true God, the God of Israel.

Prior to the battle, the Philistines had been fearful of Israel's God because they knew He had inflicted the Egyptians with all kinds of plagues (4:8). After the incident in Dagon's temple, a plague begins to spread throughout Ashdod. The local citizens quickly reason that the only way to be rid of the plague is to get rid of the ark, so they send it on to another of their cities, Gath.

Demystifying 1 Samuel

The exact nature of the plague is unknown. Some people have suggested the outbreak of tumors was a widespread bout of severe hemorrhoids, although the number of deaths might indicate something more serious. Since the tumors and deaths appear to be associated with rodents, another likely possibility is that the epidemic might have been a manifestation of the bubonic plague, or something similar.

The citizens of Gath immediately experience the same plague faced by the Ashdodites, and they attempt to forward the ark on to the city of Ekron. By then the Philistines have determined that the plagues seem to be directly associated with the presence of the ark. They strongly suspect that their trouble is the result of God's judgment on them and their god, Dagon. Yet they make no effort to renounce Dagon, cease their idolatry, or worship the God of Israel. Instead, they simply want to distance themselves from Israel's God.

▤ 6:1–7:2

THE RETURN OF THE ARK

After seven months of plagues, the Philistine priests are more than ready to discuss the best way to return the ark to Israel. In their eagerness to be rid of the ark, they still want to exercise caution. They fashion a guilt offering of five gold tumors and five gold mice to send back with the ark. They transport the ark on a cart pulled by two milk cows, whose nursing calves have just been separated from them. The mother cows should not be willing to leave their calves under any circumstances, so when they pull the cart straight toward Israel without turning aside, it is a clear sign that the plagues are no coincidence. The Philistines follow at a distance and see the cart and its cargo come to a halt in Israel.

If the Philistines are glad to be rid of the ark, the Israelites of Beth Shemesh are ecstatic when they realize it has returned. The people reaping in the fields use the wood from the cart as fuel and the cows as an offering. But what begins as a festive occasion quickly comes to an end when some of the people look into the ark—a serious violation of the law. As a result, a plague breaks out and a significant number of people are struck dead.

The ark is transferred to Kiriath-jearim, where it remains for twenty years. David eventually arranges for its transport to Jerusalem.

▤ 7:3–17

POSITIVE CHANGE BEGINS

Samuel is strangely absent from the accounts in 1 Samuel 4–6. But while the ark is set aside for two decades, Samuel is an essential part of Israel's spiritual revival. With the absence of the ark as a "security blanket" (as Israel had attempted during the battle), the people have to look elsewhere for security.

They gather with Samuel at Mizpah, where Samuel promises to pray to the Lord on their behalf as the people fast. While they are there, the Philistines prepare to attack. Samuel offers a burnt offering to God and asks for His deliverance. In response, God sends thunder that creates great confusion among the Philistines and enables the Israelites to overcome them.

Critical Observation

After the Israelites chase the fleeing Philistines, Samuel erects a stone between Mizpah and Shen. He calls it *Ebenezer* ("stone, rock of my help"). It served as a lasting commemoration that the battle had been won with God's help.

After the battle, the Philistine domination over Israel ends for a while. Peace is also established between the Israelites and Amorites, all largely because of the influence of Samuel. From his home in Ramah, he will travel throughout Israel as a kind of circuit rider, fulfilling the roles of priest, prophet, and judge.

Take It Home

The account of the Philistine god Dagon falling before the ark of God is almost comical. But the story quickly turns tragic as the Israelites—people who should have known better—disregard the holiness of the ark. It is a reminder to regularly evaluate the way we approach the holy things of God. Some, like the Philistines, treat holy things almost as superstitions. Others are far too familiar with things that should be regarded with great respect. We can be sure that God invites us to come boldly to His throne (Hebrews 4:16), but we should never take for granted His grace and mercy that allow us to do so.

1 SAMUEL 8:1–11:13

ISRAEL INSISTS ON A KING

Setting Up the Section

In spite of Israel's recurring tendency to fall away from God, He has faithfully called a series of judges to free them from the oppression of various enemies. Now, even though the people have been pleased with the leadership of Samuel, they want to have a king like the nations around them. Samuel will be specific about the potential drawbacks, but the people are insistent.

📄 8:1–22

THE DEMANDS OF A KING

Considerable time has passed as 1 Samuel 8 begins. Samuel has adult sons and is old enough that the people are already beginning to discuss who will replace him. He has gained the respect of the Israelites, but his sons are corrupt. Perhaps Samuel deals with his dishonest offspring because the problem is never mentioned again, yet the Israelites are unwilling to support them as leaders of the nation. Since all the other nations around them have kings, the Israelites want one, too. They don't just make a request to Samuel—they *demand* a king. The people's desire for a king is not only equivalent to firing Samuel as a judge; they are also firing God as their king.

Samuel is disappointed in the people, not because of the personal affront, but because their request is wrong and sinful. But rather than spout off a quick retort to the elders of Israel, he affirms his godly character by turning to God in prayer. God's response confirms Samuel's assessment of the situation.

Critical Observation

The Exodus from Egyptian bondage demonstrates that God is truly the King over Israel. . .or is supposed to be (Exodus 15:16–18). God had allowed for the possibility of a human king—with clearly stated expectations—in the Mosaic Law (Deuteronomy 17:14–20), but that does not negate the fact that the Israelites' demand is from evil intent, rooted in idolatry. During the leadership of previous judges, the people had at least waited until after the death of the judge to revert to their disobedient and rebellious ways. But with Samuel, they seem eager to see him step aside. They had not properly valued the ark, and had lost it. They didn't respect Samuel and his close connection to God. What makes them think anything will be different if they place their trust in a human king instead?

In response to the people's demand for a king, Samuel is explicit about the demands a king will place on the people (8:10–18). Clearly, a king will require a costly and demanding government. Everyone will feel the effects. But the Israelites will not be dissuaded (8:19–22).

9:1–10:9

A KING IS CHOSEN

Oblivious to the seriousness of their sin and all related warnings, the Israelites remain ecstatic about their future king. Yet while Israel is being granted its request, their first leader will not be chosen in the same manner as other human kings. Israel's king is supposed to be a person of God's choosing (Deuteronomy 17:15). Since Samuel has a spotless record in speaking for God, all eyes are on him to see whom God will select.

The events of 1 Samuel 9 bring Saul into contact with Samuel in a manner that makes the prophet certain that Saul is God's choice for Israel's king. Saul's father, Kish, is a Benjamite of some reputation. A "mighty man of valor" (9:1 ASV) can refer to courage, military skill, success, or even wealth. Saul is physically impressive, but many other qualities are yet to be determined.

Saul is sent off with a servant to find some lost livestock. After covering a lot of ground on an unsuccessful three-day search, the servant realizes they are near the home of a man of God. Neither of them appears to have known Samuel by name, but the servant, at least, is aware of his reputation as a prophet. They ask for directions and some young women tell them they have arrived at an opportune moment. From the women's point of view, Saul and his servant are lucky, but the biblical account makes it clear that Saul was expected at Samuel's—even after three days of aimless wandering.

Samuel has been told to anticipate the person God will choose as Israel's first king, but Saul has no such knowledge. As Saul sits down to eat, Samuel even sends for a choice piece of meat that has already been set aside for the guest of honor (9:22–23). The next morning Samuel assures Saul that his father's donkeys have been found. He then has Saul send the servant ahead, and he anoints Saul as ruler over Israel (10:1). He also gives specific instructions and tells Saul exactly what to expect on his way home, including where he will find provisions for the journey.

THE KING IS CONFIRMED

Samuel's words and actions must have been affirming to Saul. Moreover, as soon as Saul leaves Samuel to return home, God changes him (10:9). Upon meeting a group of prophets along the way, Saul joins them in prophesying, giving rise to a new proverb (10:11–12).

Demystifying 1 Samuel

The significance of Saul's prophesying with the prophets is to publicly demonstrate that God has empowered him to judge the nation. When Moses had appointed seventy judges to share his workload (Exodus 18), all of them prophesied before the eyes of the nation, demonstrating that the Spirit of God was upon them (Numbers 11:16–17, 24–25). Saul's similar experience is the first public indication that he is to be Israel's king.

When Saul arrives home, people naturally want to hear about his journey. His uncle seems especially interested to learn that Saul had an encounter with Samuel. Saul provides only sketchy details about the trip, focusing on the search for the donkeys rather than his being anointed. Saul's silence is telling. He was probably supposed to attack the Philistine garrison. Instead, when the Spirit comes upon him, he simply returns home. It will be Samuel who publicly introduces Saul as Israel's king.

Samuel summons all of Israel to Mizpah—the location where they had repented and turned to God at the beginning of his ministry (chapter 7). His audience is enthusiastic and optimistic, eager to hear the coming announcement. But first Samuel reminds them once more that their demand for a king is a manifestation of unbelief and disobedience. No human king will deliver them from their difficulties. Their source of deliverance has always been God, and always will be. Yet God is graciously giving them the king they have demanded.

Although Samuel already anointed Saul, God's designation of Saul is confirmed through the casting of lots. But when Saul's name is chosen, he is nowhere to be found. Further inquiry of the Lord reveals that he is hiding among the baggage. He is then brought forward to the acclaim of (most of) the nation. From a merely physical perspective, Saul is an impressive king.

Samuel presents Saul to the nation, clarifies all the ordinances that pertain to kingly rule, and then sends the people home. One group of valiant men accompanies Saul, not unlike a secret service unit. Another group, however, voices disdain for Saul and refuses to offer gifts. Saul chooses to remain silent and do nothing for the moment.

THE KING'S FIRST TEST

What the Israelites really want is a king who will deliver them from their enemies. The immediate threat is from Nahash, the king of the Ammonites (12:12), who had besieged the Israelite town of Jabesh-gilead. He had told the city's men that they could avoid all-out conflict only by agreeing to lose their right eyes (both humiliating them and rendering them unable to fight effectively).

When Saul is informed of the situation, he takes immediate (and attention-getting) action to recruit an army (11:6–7). He soon has 330,000 soldiers, whom he leads to deliver a crushing defeat of the Ammonites.

Saul becomes an instant hero. His qualifications of being among the prophets and chosen by lot have certainly been impressive proofs of his designation as king. But his ability to rally the nation and defeat an imposing enemy really gets everyone's attention. In fact, the majority want to execute the group of naysayers who have refused to support Saul from the beginning. But Saul earns even more credibility and respect by giving God credit for the victory and granting amnesty to those who opposed him.

Take It Home

This text is a remarkable demonstration of the wonderful grace of God. On a personal level, it shows what can happen when someone is going about mundane, even irksome, tasks. Saul goes out looking for lost donkeys and is anointed king by the time he returns home. Who knows to what end God will use someone's daily tasks? And on a larger level, we see how much more God provides beyond what is requested. The Israelites wanted a king like the kings of other nations. But the person of God's choosing was *unlike* other kings—an exemplary human, transformed in heart and supernaturally empowered by God's Spirit (at least, for the time being). God regularly provides more for us than we ask or imagine (Ephesians 3:20).

1 SAMUEL 11:14–12:25

RENEWING THE KINGDOM

Setting Up the Section

The Israelites have asked for a king in spite of Samuel's clear warning about what their request would eventually entail. In essence, the people are rejecting the leadership of both Samuel and God. As Saul assumes leadership of the nation, Samuel gives his farewell address and offers a final challenge for the Israelites.

📄 11:14–12:5

SAMUEL'S INNOCENCE AND ISRAEL'S GUILT

Saul's impressive victory over Nahash and the Ammonites is hardly concluded when Samuel summons the people to Gilgal to renew the kingdom (11:14). Saul is confirmed as king, sacrifices are offered to God, and there is much rejoicing (11:15).

Samuel had previously summoned people to Mizpah, and the shift to Gilgal is significant. Gilgal is located just west of the Jordan River where the people had camped before entering the promised land. It's where the second-generation Israelites were circumcised and had renewed their covenant with God, and where Joshua erected a memorial of twelve stones. It was also one of the cities on Samuel's circuit (7:16) and the place where Saul was to wait for Samuel (10:8). The city of Gilgal is closely related to God's covenant with Israel.

Samuel is in a potentially uncomfortable, perhaps embarrassing, situation. Israel had previously implied that his leadership was not sufficient, and they had demanded a king (8:1–9). Rather than tiptoe around their charges, Samuel brings them out in the open. He publicly challenges anyone to accuse him of wrongdoing, especially in regard to his official duties.

He begins by pointing out that he had listened to them and granted their request, but they should not expect the same compliance from a king. He then makes a reference to his age (12:2). The Israelites' implication had been that he was too old to judge the nation. But as is true with many Supreme Court justices, age carries with it much experience. Samuel is not "over the hill"; he will continue to serve the people for a long while.

Demystifying 1 Samuel

The Israelites' accusations against Samuel's sons were true (8:1–5), but Samuel could not be accused of such behavior (12:3–5). In addition, it appears that Samuel may have attended to the problem with his sons. Unlike his predecessor, Eli, there is every indication that Samuel is without fault in the discipline of his children.

The people agree that Samuel has done nothing improper (12:4–5). Since Samuel is found not guilty of the charges, then the Israelites' accusations must have been false. Consequently, Samuel is still qualified to judge Israel, and he continues to confront them and call the wayward nation into account for the sin of rejecting him and God.

12:6–18

LESSONS FROM HISTORY

Israel's history as a kingdom began at the Exodus. Samuel points out that their present demand to have a king like the rest of the nations is just one more instance of their rebellion against God. He emphasizes that it had not been Moses and Aaron who had delivered Israel from Egyptian bondage—it was God (12:7). God works through human leaders, but He is the one who delivers His people.

So Samuel summons the Israelites to take their stand before God (12:8). In a sense they are on trial and he is their prosecutor. History is a witness to the fact that the blessings they have received are not the result of their own righteousness. Rather, history shows that the nation's deliverance has been achieved thanks to God's righteous deeds, performed on Israel's behalf, and always in context of their sin. Repeatedly, God has graciously delivered the people from their enemies, but the people persistently forget the Lord and turn to other gods.

Samuel briefly scans Israel's history, citing illustrations from the major periods (the Exodus, the wilderness wanderings, the possession of the land under Joshua, and the periods of the judges) to demonstrate a consistent pattern. Then he links Israel's past with their current situation. Like the Israelites of old, they are once again oppressed by a neighboring nation. Yet while previous generations had realized that outside oppression was a result of sin and had repented before crying out to God for deliverance, this time they have not acknowledged their sin or repented. Instead, they have blamed their circumstances on bad leadership and demanded a king so they will be like all the other nations.

Critical Observation

Notice that Samuel tells the people that this will be *their* king—not God's king. God is giving them what they asked for (12:13). With or without a king, they will suffer the consequences if they rebel against God. The king is not the key to the success of the nation; the key is Israel's trust in and obedience to God.

Samuel underscores the importance of what he is saying with a sign of divine intervention. It is not the rainy season. The people have no reason to expect showers, much less storms. Yet in response to Samuel's prayer, a great thunderstorm immediately blows in—right at harvest season. This would have frightened the people because it would have threatened to destroy the crop. The unexpected rain reminds Israel that both calamity and blessing come from the Lord (Isaiah 45:5–7).

📖 12:19–25

THE PEOPLE'S RESPONSE

Samuel's message—punctuated by the sudden storm—results in great fear among the people. They are beginning to comprehend the severity of their sin in general and their demand for a king in particular. They want no further discipline, and they plead with Samuel to pray for them. Suddenly they are looking not to a king for deliverance, but to Samuel (12:19).

Yet Samuel is not holding grudges. He tries to assure the people with words full of mercy, grace, and hope. Without minimizing the magnitude of their sin, he gives them good reason for faith, hope, and endurance. It is not wrong, per se, to have a king, but it *is* wrong to trust any human for salvation and deliverance from the guilt of sin.

Samuel never suggests that Israel's salvation is based on faithfulness or good works. Nowhere does he tell the people to try harder in order to receive God's blessings. Israel's obedience and service to God is spoken of as the *result* of God's grace, not its *source*.

Like the Israelites, many in today's society—and even within the church itself—may have become accustomed to defining sin in secular terms and then looking for the solution through human means. Individually and corporately, believers may be swayed by secular methods of giving (fund-raising), evangelism (marketing), counseling (psychological methodology), and such. May Samuel's words to Israel be a reminder to us as well that we have a gracious and merciful God. When we sin, He disciplines us so that we might once again turn to Him in faith, obedience, love, and gratitude.

1 SAMUEL 13:1–23

THE BEGINNING OF THE END FOR SAUL

The Battles Begin	13:1–7
Saul's Act of Desperation and Its Consequences	13:8–23

Setting Up the Section

Most of what has been written about Saul so far has been quite complimentary. He has displayed physical strength, spiritual experience, and military skill. He has the full support of the people. But soon things begin to go wrong for Saul—not in major ways, but in numerous little situations where he doesn't quite obey God as he should.

📄 **13:1–7**

THE BATTLES BEGIN

Saul's first battle against Nahash and the Ammonites had resulted in an inspiring victory, but this section reveals that Israel is by no means free of its enemies. The Israelites remain under Philistine control. In fact, it appears that the Philistines have no intention of wiping out the Israelites, who are positioned as a buffer between the Philistines and other more aggressive nations. So even though Saul has a standing army of three thousand soldiers (13:2), Israel remains in subjection to the much larger Philistine force. (The Philistines regulated the number of Israelite weapons by controlling the blacksmith trade [13:19–22].)

Demystifying 1 Samuel

Portions of this passage are incomplete in the original text, which creates some variation in interpretation. For example, 13:1 in the original language reads, "Saul was a year old when he began to reign, and he reigned two years over Israel"—obviously, this was a textual error. The New King James Version interprets: "Saul reigned one year; and when he had reigned two years over Israel, Saul chose for himself three thousand men of Israel." Other translations attempt to fill in the blanks with logical estimates. For example: "Saul was [thirty] years old when he began to reign, and he reigned [forty-] two years over Israel" (NASB), or "Saul was [thirty] years old when he became king, and he reigned over Israel for [forty-] two years" (NIV). The number of Philistine charioteers is also questioned. Some scholars suggest the thirty thousand quantity should actually be three thousand, but the larger number makes more sense in conveying the hopelessness of the Israelite situation.

The delicate détente between the two nations ends when Saul's son, Jonathan, attacks a Philistine garrison without his father's permission. Jonathan's reasoning is not provided, though it is logical to assume from other passages that he is acting on faith, believing that God still wants His people to drive out the nations inhabiting the land He has given Israel.

Regardless of Jonathan's motivation, the Philistine response is predictable. Perhaps Jonathan both expected and desired to provoke a conflict. But the result is an angry swarm of 30,000 chariots, 6,000 horsemen, and countless Philistine foot soldiers bearing down on Saul and his relatively miniscule army.

The scene in 1 Samuel 13 is much different than the one previously described in 1 Samuel 11. Before, Saul was Spirit-empowered and forcefully summoned 330,000 soldiers. Here, however, nothing is said about God's Spirit, and it appears that the number of fighting men is much lower. The soldiers who *do* show up are tentative at first and then terrified when they discover the size of the opposing force. They begin to desert, hiding in caves, thickets, cliffs, cellars, and pits.

Saul has specific instructions from Samuel: Go to Gilgal and wait seven days for the prophet to arrive. When he arrives there, Samuel will offer sacrifices to God and provide further instructions (10:8). But as the seven days go by, Saul agonizes while he watches his army shrink. Some flee across the Jordan River (13:7) while others join the Philistines (14:21). Those who remain are trembling with fear.

📄 13:8–23

SAUL'S ACT OF DESPERATION AND ITS CONSEQUENCES

Saul manages to make it through six days and most of the seventh. But when Samuel still hasn't shown up, Saul calls for the burnt and peace offerings. It appears that he makes the offerings himself. No mention is made of a priest.

Saul may have recalled the previous instance when Israel was gathered to repent and renew their covenant to God. The Philistines had perceived the gathering as a military threat and prepared to attack (7:7). On that occasion Samuel had presented a burnt offering to God as the Philistines approached, and God had sent great thunder that confused the Philistines and allowed Israel to rout them.

Critical Observation

Perhaps Saul perceived that the offering itself had been the means to Israel's deliverance (in much the same way the Israelites had believed taking the ark into battle would ensure God's blessing). If so, it is no wonder Saul is so determined to get the sacrifice offered—with or without Samuel.

Yet it appears that just as Saul makes the offering, Samuel arrives—in plenty of time to have made the offerings himself. Rather than Saul being able to rebuke Samuel for being late, it is Samuel demanding an explanation from Saul. Saul's excuse falls flat.

Samuel's response is direct and stern. Saul's actions are foolish and willfully disobedient to Samuel's instructions. If Saul had obeyed the command of God, his kingdom would have endured forever. But his disobedience costs him a dynasty. God has already sought out and chosen another leader whose heart is in tune with His. Although Saul's kingdom will last for a number of years, it will end with him.

Samuel departs without giving Saul any guidance for how to handle the Philistine threat (10:8). Saul takes a count of his troops and discovers he has only six hundred men ready for battle. In addition, of all the Israelites, only Saul and Jonathan have a spear or sword. The Philistines control all the ironwork in the territory, keeping more sophisticated weapons out of Israelite hands.

And if the difficulty with the main Philistine army isn't enough of a challenge, the Philistines are sending raiding parties in various directions throughout the land. Those destructive raiders appear to be a special force of troops whose task is to destroy human life, cattle, buildings, and crops. If the Philistines are not soon defeated and driven out of the land, much trouble is ahead for Israel.

A shift in power is about to take place, but the motivating force this time will not be Saul. It will be someone who is able to exhibit more faith.

Take It Home

It may appear from a casual reading that Saul makes one little mistake and loses his kingdom as a result, which could infer that God is vindictive or petty. But it was Saul's duty as king to know God's laws and carefully observe them (Deuteronomy 17:18–20). He ignores those general commands along with the very specific instructions of Samuel (1 Samuel 10:8). Like Saul, if we have no sense of our calling, we are headed for trouble. The emergencies of life are not excuses to disobey God's commands; they are tests of our faith and obedience. God often works through less-than-perfect people like Saul—and like us. If we can learn from Saul's mistakes to be more obedient throughout our own difficulties, we can become much more effective in our individual ministries.

1 SAMUEL 14:1–52

JONATHAN'S DISPLAY OF FAITH

Setting Up the Section

Outnumbered and without a plan of action, the Israelites are facing the Philistines. Driven by desperation and self-interest, Saul has made an offering to God, and Samuel has rebuked him and left. But Saul isn't the only leader of Israel's army. His son, Jonathan, is also in charge of some troops. In this section the emphasis shifts to him.

📄 14:1–14

A SIGN THAT INSPIRES ACTION

This account of Jonathan should be considered in light of the preceding actions of his father. Saul has been chosen by God to be the king the Israelites demanded. He is divinely enabled to serve as king by God's Spirit who came upon him (10:5–10). Israel's decisive victory against the Ammonites was hardly initiated by Saul; it had been accomplished by the Spirit of God. Then two years passed with no mention of action on Saul's part, although a later summary of Saul's reign suggests he had a rigorous military career (14:47–48).

It seems that Israel had demanded a king in hopes that he would deliver them from their enemies as the judges had done. As long as Saul trusted God and obeyed His commandments, God would give him victory. The Spirit of God initially came upon Saul as He did upon Samson and other judges, enabling Saul to lead the Israelites victoriously against their enemies.

Yet Saul doesn't appear to be a particularly spiritual man. His hometown (Gibeah) is only three miles from Samuel's hometown (Ramah), yet he has apparently not heard of Samuel when the prophet first approaches him. One also wonders why, after Saul recruits an army of 330,000 and defeats the Ammonites (11:1–11), he doesn't continue on to battle the Philistines. Instead, he sends most of the men home and keeps a standing army of only 3,000. It seems that Saul might have been satisfied with the status quo, not wanting to irritate the powerful Philistines.

It's no wonder that Samuel goes to such great lengths to remind Israel that it has always been God—not their human leaders—who has delivered them from their enemies. Saul may have been slow to comprehend this simple truth, but his son, Jonathan, certainly seems to understand it.

Quite a contrast of these two leaders is shown in this passage. With Israel at war, desperately outnumbered, and miserably equipped, Saul is seen under a pomegranate tree—out of the sun and safely out of reach of the Philistines. Samuel has given him no guidance after his disobedience at Gilgal (13:1–14), but he has with him a priest wearing the ephod—one of the means of determining the will of God (see 23:9–12; 30:6–8). Yet Saul never inquires of God what he should do.

Jonathan, on the other hand, has a definite sense of God's will that prompts him to take action. He is troubled by the influence the Philistines hold over Israel, and he is eager to do something about it. He recruits his armor-bearer to go out on a mission with him. He neither asks permission from nor informs his father. While Saul doesn't want to cause trouble with the Philistines, Jonathan wants to be troubled by them no longer.

Jonathan appears to know much about the will of God from Israel's history and from the nature of God Himself. His words to his armor-bearer (14:6) are filled with a sense of faith and duty. The question in Jonathan's mind is not whether God can deliver the Philistines into the hands of the Israelites, but whether it is God's intent to do so at the time. So he determines another way to discern the will of God.

Critical Observation

Jonathan's reference to the Philistines being uncircumcised (14:6) means that they do not have a covenant relationship with God as the Israelites do. In fact, the Philistines were one of the few people groups in this Old Testament time period that did not practice circumcision. Their uniqueness as an uncircumcised people highlighted Israel's uniqueness as a circumcised people.

Because of the Philistines, the Israelites are not experiencing the freedom from surrounding nations they should. Jonathan realizes that Israel's victory will not be limited by the number of their troops or the kind of weapons they possess if it is God's will to prevail.

A group of Philistines is stationed at Michmash, atop a very narrow pass. Jonathan's plan is to make his presence known, risking the possibility that the Philistine soldiers will come down and fight. But if they invite him to climb up to where they are, he will take it as a sign that God will give him victory.

After approaching with only his armor-bearer, the Philistines do indeed tell the two of them to come on up. Imagine the soldiers' surprise when Jonathan begins wielding his sword as soon as he has climbed to the top. Before long twenty Philistines are dead, and the Michmash pass is opened, allowing the Israelites to pursue the fleeing enemy.

Demystifying 1 Samuel

Why would the Philistines ever invite enemy soldiers into their camp? Why not kill the two Israelites with boulders while they are climbing up? Perhaps it was a boring night and they wanted a little excitement. But more likely, maybe the Philistines were so confident of their superiority that they expected the two Israelites to defect. Either way, Jonathan doesn't conform to their expectations.

GOD JOINS THE BATTLE

A close reading of 1 Samuel 13–14 reveals an interesting wordplay. In 13:7 we read that the Israelites are trembling because of the Philistines. But by 14:15, the *ground* is trembling beneath the Philistines as God sends an earthquake. Their smug sense of security on top of the Michmash pass must have quickly disappeared when that former position of safety became the most dangerous place in the area.

To describe the confusion among the Philistines, the NIV calls it "a panic sent by God" (14:15). The Philistines are disabled and terrified, but the Israelites are also confused at first. They may not have known about the earthquake, since it seems to be limited to the places where the Philistines are stationed, but they can see and hear that something marvelous is happening.

Saul does a quick inventory of his army and discovers that, sure enough, Jonathan and his armor-bearer are missing. It doesn't appear that Saul is happy to confirm this fact. Previously, Jonathan had attacked the Philistine garrison at Geba (13:3), upsetting Saul's tentative truce with them. As the two armies were encamped and at war with each other, Saul was positioned under a pomegranate tree (14:2), managing to avoid further action. But then Jonathan again initiated conflict involving the entire army.

At long last, Saul decides to consult God. Apparently the method involves the ark of God and the outstretched hand of Ahijah the priest, and it seems as though the process is time-consuming. However, as has already been seen, Saul is not a patient person. The commotion in the Philistine camp convinces Saul to act right away, so he instructs the priest to withdraw his hand.

The Israelite army goes in pursuit of the panic-smitten Philistines, with Jonathan and his armor-bearer leading the charge. The ranks of Israel's army swell that day as the six hundred soldiers are joined by the deserters who had been hiding and the Israelites who had previously gone over to the Philistines (14:21).

SAUL'S FOOLISH OATH

Even though the Israelites are taking advantage of the situation, their victory is not what it could have been. Their soldiers are hard-pressed that day, largely because of Saul. He had long been intimidated, if not humiliated, by the Philistines. When he sees his enemies begin to suffer defeat, he determines to make them pay. He places his soldiers under an oath, forbidding them to eat until evening. His reasoning appears to be to avoid wasting valuable time and daylight by stopping for a meal. (The action had begun suddenly and spontaneously, so neither he nor his men are prepared.)

But Saul is wrong on two counts. If he hoped to maximize daylight to kill Philistines, the battle doesn't conform to his expectations. The fighting spreads eastward, first to Beth-aven (14:23) and then to Aijalon (14:31). The Israelites have to pursue the Philistines over twenty miles of mountainous territory. Without food, they become weary and weak. Second, Saul assumes there will be no food for his soldiers. But God has provided the fastest food available—a reserve of honey. A soldier could have dipped his staff into the honey and transferred it to his mouth for a boost of energy in no time at all. There was no faster or finer food around.

Jonathan benefits from the honey because he hasn't heard his father's prohibition. He says what many other soldiers must have been thinking: Saul is not the source of Israel's military successes, but a hindrance to them.

The other Israelites comply with Saul's senseless order not to eat until evening, but fewer Philistines are killed as a result. Additionally, the Israelites are famished. When they come upon the Philistine cattle that evening, they kill them and eat the meat while it is still dripping with blood, in clear defiance of the Mosaic Law (Leviticus 17:10; 19:26). It is unfortunate that they fear disobeying Saul's commands more than breaking God's law.

When their grievous behavior is brought to Saul's attention, he self-righteously points an accusing finger at his famished men (1 Samuel 14:33). Saul's foolish demand has initiated the damage, and now he attempts damage control. He builds an altar of stone where the soldiers can sacrifice their offerings. Yet this can hardly be considered sincere worship. It is merely an attempt to sanctify the appetites of the soldiers so they do not sin further.

Ironically, this is the first altar Saul builds. Did it take a crisis for him to seek to worship his God? This is not exactly a holy moment in Israel's history. In addition is the irony that Saul had forbidden eating in the attempt to save time. Yet to correct the situation, Saul takes the time to build an altar and then ensure that each person's sacrifice is properly slain and prepared.

📄 **14:36–52**

JONATHAN'S CLOSE CALL

At long last the meal is over and Israel is again ready to fight. But when the priest tries to get direction from God, the Lord provides no answer. Saul immediately jumps to a number of conclusions: that someone has sinned, that the sin is the violation of his (foolish) order rather than God's law, and that the sin is worthy of death. Perhaps it is no coincidence that he singles out Jonathan (14:39). It seems he feels that in the area of war, Jonathan is a nuisance at best and a liability for sure. It also appears that Saul *expects* Jonathan to be selected by lot, and perhaps he even feels the situation is perfectly suited to do away with his son.

After Jonathan is identified by the casting of lots he confesses that he has indeed eaten a bit of honey. Although Jonathan had no knowledge of his father's command and had not affected the army in any negative way, Saul supposes that he is the reason for Israel's failure to finish the battle. He feels it is better to kill his son than to admit his own sin and foolishness. Jonathan makes no excuses for himself or any indictments against his father.

With great flair, Saul pontificates about the certainty of Jonathan's death (14:44). But the other soldiers recognize the foolishness of Saul's actions and are unwilling to let him put Jonathan to death. It is Jonathan, not Saul, whom they credit with their deliverance (14:45). Clearly Jonathan has been working *with* God, not against Him. So Jonathan is allowed to live, and with this incident the battle with the Philistines ends—sooner and less decisively than it should have. But the war continues. For the rest of Saul's life, Israel and the Philistines will be in conflict (14:52).

Despite Saul's shortcomings exposed in this passage, he has a reputation as an excellent fighter. Like Samson and other judges, God's chosen leader over Israel could be a moral and spiritual failure, yet still be a great military leader. God is not restricted to using godly people to accomplish His promises and purposes. In addition, from a historian's point of view, all Israel's victories are credited as Saul's victories. For example, he received credit for defeating the Philistine garrison when it had been Jonathan's doing (13:4). This and other victories are by the grace of God, and often in spite of the inaction and foolishness of Saul.

Take It Home

Saul had the title of king and the responsibility for leading the nation, but it was Jonathan who consistently demonstrated faith and character. With this early insight into Jonathan's qualities, it should come as no surprise later on to discover Jonathan's powerful and almost immediate bond with David. Contemporary Christians may find themselves in similar positions—lacking official power or control of a situation, yet in a position to act faithfully and exert a godly influence. Perhaps taking appropriately bold actions in such circumstances will have surprisingly beneficial results.

1 SAMUEL 15:1–35

THE CONSEQUENCES OF PARTIAL OBEDIENCE

Setting Up the Section

Saul got off to a pretty good start as Israel's first king. But as time passed, he began to make some poor decisions, including issuing a foolish oath that almost resulted in the death of his son, Jonathan, and overseeing an offering that Samuel should have made. In this section he again is given some specific instructions to follow, but he doesn't quite obey them fully. The results will be worse than he ever anticipated.

📄 **15:1–3**

THE AMALEKITE PROBLEM

Saul had done battle against the Ammonites, Philistines, Moabites, Edomites, and others (14:47). This time God instructs him to attack the Amalekites, a group dwelling in the southern part of Canaan. Saul is to render God's judgment in return for the hostility they had shown toward Israel during the Exodus.

Critical Observation

Israel already had a lengthy history with the Amalekites. In addition to the conflict that took place under Moses' leadership (Exodus 17:8–13; Numbers 14:25, 43, 45), the Midianites and Amalekites had joined forces to plunder Israel during the time of Gideon (Judges 6:3, 33; 7:12). Later they would create problems for David as well (1 Samuel 27:8; 30:1, 18; 2 Samuel 1:1).

God's instructions to Saul appear harsh to modern sensibilities. But Saul, and anyone familiar with the history of Israel, would have had a different perspective. The law provided the reasoning behind the intentional deaths of entire nations, and even their cattle (Leviticus 27:28–29). Joshua had the same instructions as Saul after the walls of Jericho fell. Not long afterward, as a result of failing to fully eliminate the inhabitants of the promised land, the Israelites found themselves regularly in subjection to other powers.

When a predominantly sinful nation is not totally destroyed, the native peoples would usually teach the Israelites their sinful ways and thus bring them under divine condemnation. In cases such as this one with the Amalekites, the annihilation is retribution for not only the sinful condition of the current generation, but also for their predecessors who had sinned greatly (1 Samuel 15:18, 33). Those who cursed Israel were to receive a curse in return (Genesis 12:1–3). The Amalekites had already been singled out to perish (Numbers 24:20). God had not forgotten what the Amalekites had done, and Israel was not to forget either (Deuteronomy 25:17–19). If we are unsettled by the just wrath of God, we should also note that God takes no pleasure in meting out punishment (Jonah 4:9–11).

📄 15:4–9

SAUL'S DISOBEDIENCE

Saul has specific instructions to attack and destroy the Amalekites without sparing anyone or anything. He doesn't fully comply with the order, and we might be tempted to excuse his disobedience because of the harshness of the order. But that is not the case.

He cannot be faulted for warning the Kenites ahead of time to detach themselves from the Amalekites. The Kenites, closely associated with the Midianites, had an ongoing association with Israel. Moses' wife was from a Kenite family, and some Kenites had traveled to Canaan along with the Israelites (Judges 1:16).

But as for the Amalekites, Saul slaughters everyone there except their king and some of their best sheep and cattle. His disobedience to God's command, therefore, appears to be self-serving rather than mercy-based. He would have gained a measure of popularity among the Israelites—they could use Amalekite animals for their sacrifices (without killing their own), and they could feast on the meat. Meanwhile, Amalekite king Agag would have been a living trophy of Saul's prowess and power.

Saul will defend his partial obedience to Samuel, attempting to justify his actions as doing what God had instructed. Samuel (and God), however, will interpret Saul's partial obedience as disobedience.

📖 15:10–26

SAUL LOSES HIS KINGDOM

God speaks to Samuel before dealing with Saul, expressing disappointment in Saul's performance as king. From God's perspective, Saul has turned away from Him and has not followed clear instructions. Samuel is so troubled that he cries out to God all night. He gets up early the next morning to deal with Saul, who can't be found at first because he is busy setting up a monument in his own honor. When Samuel finally catches up with him, Saul speaks first, proudly affirming that he has carried out God's instructions.

Samuel's reply is classic: "Then what is all the bleating of sheep and lowing of cattle I hear?" (15:14 NLT). It is hard for Saul to claim that he has killed all the flocks and herds of the Amalekites when the best of the bunch are standing there making noise.

After Saul discovers his level of obedience is unacceptable to God, he first tries to blame the soldiers of Israel (15:21). But Samuel is hearing no excuses. God prefers obedience to sacrifice. Saul's lack of obedience is tantamount to arrogance and rebellion (15:23). It is severe enough for God to reject Saul as king of Israel.

Saul next tries a brief (and unconvincing) confession of sin and attempts to quickly guide the discussion back to the blessings of God. He is looking for an ally in Samuel, but the prophet will have nothing more to do with Saul. He is emphatic that God will not change His mind about Saul's ability to rule as king.

Demystifying 1 Samuel

Saul's earlier sin of making the offering himself instead of waiting for Samuel (13:11–14) resulted in Samuel's warning about Saul's losing the kingdom. At that point, God's proposed action might have been conditional (see Jeremiah 18:6–8). If Saul had sincerely repented at that point, perhaps his story would have had a different ending. But in this second similar offense, Saul's motives and attitudes are more clearly exposed. In 1 Samuel 13 God decides not to grant Saul a dynasty, and in chapter 14 He decides to send Samuel to anoint David and bring Saul's reign to an end.

It is sad to read the biblical account of Saul's disobedience. His concern is not that he has sinned against a righteous God, but that his public image will be damaged if Samuel openly severs his relationship with Saul. He lacks a deep conviction concerning the vileness of his sin; he only fears that he will look bad if the situation is not handled properly.

📖 15:27–35

SAUL LOSES HIS MENTOR

When Samuel turns to leave, Saul grabs the hem of the prophet's robe, and it tears. Samuel uses the incident as an illustration of how God had torn the kingdom away from Saul. It will soon be given to another.

And rather than attempting to mollify Saul, Samuel turns his attention to finishing what Saul started by calling for Agag. The Amalekite king is confident that since he has not been executed by now, the danger is over. But if God's command had been to annihilate the Amalekites, how could the one spared be the one who had led them in their wickedness? Samuel kills him on the spot. The text doesn't say, but it is likely that Samuel also saw that all remaining Amalekite cattle were also put to death.

We are not informed that Saul ever truly grieved over his sin, or even this final separation from Samuel. But God was grieved that He had ever made Saul king. Even though Samuel never goes to see Saul again, he continues to mourn for him. The cost of Saul's disobedience will continue to be felt for the rest of his lifetime.

Take It Home

The plight of Saul in this passage is a reminder of the danger of stratifying sins. Many people tend to strongly condemn sins that don't pertain to them, while downplaying their own transgressions. (Telling "little white lies" sounds much better than being a chronic liar.) But to know what God commands, and then to disobey, is to willfully rebel against Him—regardless of the "level" of the sin. Saul's story also reminds us that spiritual leaders must first and foremost be followers of God, determined to please Him before worrying about whether or not they are pleasing other people.

1 SAMUEL 16:1–17:58

THE RISE OF SAUL'S SUCCESSOR

Setting Up the Section

In the previous section, Samuel walks away from Saul, never to visit him again.

But it isn't long until God sends Samuel on another assignment, this time to anoint Saul's replacement as king of Israel. Samuel will follow God's instructions, but this time he isn't told in advance exactly who the person will be. And although it isn't emphasized, this section begins with a lot of fear and nervous tension.

📄 16:1–13

THE CEREMONY OF SELECTING A KING

It isn't long after God has rejected Saul as king that He sends Samuel to anoint the next ruler of Israel. The Lord has narrowed His choice down to a certain family—the sons of Jesse of Bethlehem—but does not designate a specific individual.

However, Samuel isn't particularly eager to take on this assignment. He fears that Saul will kill him. After all, Saul has just annihilated (nearly) all the Amalekites, and previously had been willing to put his own son to death. (Saul's future behavior will demonstrate that Samuel's concerns are well-founded.) To make things more interesting, Samuel will have to travel through Saul's hometown of Gibeah to get from Ramah to Bethlehem. Saul may not know exactly what Samuel is doing, but it is logical to assume that if God had rejected Saul as king, then Samuel would be assigned to designate his replacement.

God gives Samuel a legitimate reason to travel to Bethlehem. He tells the prophet to take a heifer, offer a sacrifice there, and invite Jesse's family to the dinner that follows. When Samuel arrives, it is the townspeople who are frightened. When a prophet shows up unannounced, he doesn't always have good news. The elders are trembling, and they want to know if Samuel has come in peace. He assures them that everything is fine and has them prepare for the sacrifice.

When he had been instructed to anoint Saul, Samuel knew exactly what to expect (9:15–17). This time, however, he has no idea which of Jesse's sons God will choose. The oldest, Eliab, appears to be an ideal candidate, but is not chosen. Neither are the next six sons who stand before Samuel. It is the youngest, the one out doing the childish, mundane chore of shepherding, who is chosen. It is David. Samuel (and all those present) would have chosen someone else. But God wasn't looking at outer qualities; He was looking at David's heart. If David's heart is right, God will provide everything else Israel's king will need. When Samuel anoints David in the presence of his other family members, God's Spirit falls powerfully upon him.

📖 **16:14–23**

TWO PATHS BEGIN TO MERGE

In terms of logistics, how does a young unknown shepherd even begin to replace an established and paranoid king? It will be a lengthy and difficult transition, but this section explains how God providentially begins to bring about the change. With Samuel no longer available to the king, Saul is at a loss for spiritual guidance. And it is at this point when an evil spirit begins to terrorize Saul.

Demystifying 1 Samuel

Not only does God remove His Spirit from Saul, but He also sends an evil spirit that torments the king. God is sovereign, and nothing can take place without His permission. After God sends the spirit to Saul, He sends David to serve as a court musician to provide Saul some relief.

One of Saul's attendants knows of David's musical ability and arranges to have him come to the royal court on a regular basis. In addition to being a gifted musician, David is already a courageous warrior (against bears and lions [17:34–35]) and a person of godly wisdom. The same characteristics that enable David to serve the king are traits that qualify him to serve *as* king. So ironically, David's initial contact with Saul is made in response to Saul's personal request (16:19–22). Before long, he is one of Saul's armor-bearers—someone with a close and trusted relationship with the king.

BIG TROUBLE IN THE VALLEY OF ELAH

Jesse's three oldest sons join the Israelite army, and occasionally David delivers things from home for them (17:13–15, 17–19). The Philistines are still the primary threat to Israel, and one particular Philistine is especially threatening. Twice a day for forty days, a towering individual named Goliath has challenged Israel to send someone out to fight. The winner of the one-to-one combat will determine which nation will serve the other.

Forty days seems like a lengthy standoff. Saul and his army don't really want to fight, and they seem content with the stalemate. But the Philistines aren't in an ideal position for battle either. Their chariots work well on level ground, but not on mountain slopes. Both sides apparently want to avoid a full-scale battle.

Yet the Israelites are growing more and more intimidated by Goliath. He stands between nine and ten feet tall, and his armor seems impenetrable. It gets to the point where, when the Israelites see him, they run in fear (17:24). Their lack of faith is reminiscent of former generations who had sent spies into the promised land and had been fearful of the giants there (Numbers 13:27–33).

Note what a contrast is made when David is introduced to the story. Goliath is described in physical terms: appearance, weaponry, aggressiveness, and so forth. But nothing is said of David's stature, strength, or weapons. Rather, he is introduced in the context of his family. One reason has already been mentioned: David was chosen because of his *heart*, not his outer physical qualities (1 Samuel 13:14; 16:7). Another reason is that the Messiah will come from the tribe of Judah and from Bethlehem (Genesis 49:8–12; Micah 5:2). Jesus will eventually trace His human ancestry back to David.

DAVID VS. GOLIATH

David, as the youngest son of Jesse, is still doing the shepherding and errands. Jesse is quite old at this point (17:12) and surely doesn't intend to place David in harm's way. Most likely he expects David to arrive while the soldiers are encamped rather than when they are rushing toward the battle line a few miles to the west.

Critical Observation

In 1 Samuel 16, David is summoned to work in Saul's court, yet in 1 Samuel 17 he is back with Jesse, and Saul even inquires about his identity (17:55, 58). Various solutions have been proposed to resolve this apparent discrepancy. Perhaps David has grown considerably. Saul might have had a poor or disturbed memory. Or upon a closer reading, we see that Saul asks about David's *father*, not David himself. Also, with Saul and the army off at war, it is likely that David might have taken a break as court musician.

David witnesses Israel's army shouting a war cry while running toward the Philistines (17:20), but then running away as soon as they get close to Goliath (17:24). He keeps asking why someone doesn't do something about Goliath. He learns that Saul has issued a call for a volunteer to fight the Philistine and has offered a number of substantial rewards for any takers. David's oldest brother overhears David talking to the soldiers and rebukes him with a series of false accusations (17:28). No doubt Eliab still feels the sting of rejection from seeing his youngest brother anointed in front of him (16:13). David pays Eliab little mind, responding with a short defense, and goes to ask King Saul's permission to fight Goliath.

Fortunately for Israel, David is neither devastated nor deterred by Eliab's sarcastic retort. He is acting like the king of Israel should act. He trusts God, inspires his fellow Israelites to do likewise, and takes action to defeat the enemies of God. Saul gives David every opportunity, first to excuse himself and go back home, and then to arm himself before fighting, but David has a faith-based confidence. His faith is contagious. Somehow Saul believes there is a good chance David will prevail over Goliath, and he gives him permission to fight. So David takes his shepherd's staff and his sling, and he picks up five smooth stones from the stream on the way to face the giant.

The next section (17:40–50) contains one of the best-known stories in the Bible—the confrontation between David and Goliath. Goliath first tries to intimidate David verbally, but his empty boasts do not faze David. The young shepherd speaks right back to the giant. David understands it will not be his own strength that will win the contest, but God's strength. His faith is rewarded. Although Goliath is armored from head to foot, protected by shield and armor-bearer, he still needs an opening around his eyes so he can see. David's accuracy with a sling sends the first stone into Goliath's exposed forehead, and the giant falls. David, who had no sword, uses Goliath's own weapon to cut off his head.

There must have been a silent and still moment in time as both Philistines and Israelites slowly comprehend what has just happened. With the loss of their champion, the Philistines lose all courage and will to fight, and they turn and run. The Israelites, in pursuit, are able to kill many more of their enemies.

Saul immediately wants to find out more about David's family (17:55, 58). He should have known David, who was one of his armor-bearers and musicians (16:21, 23). But perhaps Saul is interested in knowing exactly where David acquired the wherewithal to face off against Goliath as he had done. One might raise the question, however, of why Saul (the king) and Abner (the commander of the army) are standing around discussing genealogy while the rest of the soldiers are in pursuit of fleeing Philistines.

This is a big day for Israel and the first introduction to David for most of them. But David's instant popularity will soon create problems for him.

Take It Home

The account of David and Goliath is always a graphic reminder of how God has promised to care for and protect His faithful people. When Saul's fear became evident, Israel's soldiers were also frightened (13:5–8; 17:11, 24). But after David stood up to Goliath, the other troops became courageous. It shouldn't matter how large (or numerous, well-armed, mean, etc.) our enemies are. If we remain in a proper relationship with God, He will continue to go before us as He has always done (Deuteronomy 20:1–4). And as we learn to demonstrate faith, it may indeed inspire others.

1 SAMUEL 18:1–20:42
DAVID AMONG SAUL'S FAMILY

Setting Up the Section

David's courageous defeat of Goliath is an impressive moment that changes the course of Israel's history as well as the dynamic within Saul's family. David's instant fame creates jealousy in Saul, even as his display of faith cements a bond between David and Saul's son, Jonathan. After David becomes a member of Saul's family, loyalties change and rivalries intensify.

📖 18:1–5

THE DAVID/JONATHAN CONNECTION

Previous passages have shown that Jonathan has an outstanding faith and eagerness to serve God (13:2–3; 14:1–14), so it should come as no surprise that he is impressed with David's stand against Goliath. He overhears David's conversation with Saul, and an immediate bond forms. We aren't told exactly what it is about David that affects Jonathan so greatly, whether it is David's humility, his willingness to give God credit for the victory, his concern for the people of Israel, or a combination of things. But for some reason, David and Jonathan become kindred spirits from this point onward.

The depth of Jonathan's commitment to David is demonstrated by Jonathan's gift of clothing and armor. A similar transfer of clothing might be made in the transfer of authority from one priest to another (Numbers 20:25–29) or one prophet to another (1 Kings 19:19–21; 2 Kings 2:7–14). Jonathan's symbolic gesture may have demonstrated his awareness that David is the person God has chosen to be Israel's next king—and his personal endorsement of God's choice.

Jonathan isn't the only one intrigued by David. From that day onward, Saul does not let David return home. David will have other things to do besides tend sheep and make deliveries. In fact, David excels at whatever assignment Saul gives him, which impresses both the army officers and the people of Israel (1 Samuel 18:4).

📖 18:6–19

THE DAVID/SAUL SEPARATION

David's heroism is soon depicted in song. Women come out to greet the returning army singing, dancing, and playing instruments. But the lyrics (18:7) are irksome to Saul. Most likely the singers have no intent to compare Saul with David. They are simply elated that

David and Saul have rid the nation of so many of their enemies. Yet Saul interprets their comments literally and becomes jealous of David (18:8–9).

Saul's envy grows quickly. The inspired writer of scripture alerts the reader to Saul's thoughts and motives, which probably aren't as apparent to onlookers at the time. But what began as subtle hypocrisy (chapter 18) soon becomes outright hostility (chapter 19).

When God once again sends a spirit that troubles Saul, David returns to playing the harp with the intent of soothing the king as before (16:23). But this time, Saul attempts to kill David with his spear. David twice escapes without harm (18:10–11). Then Saul's strategizing becomes more subtle. He gives David a big promotion, placing him over 1,000 soldiers. The battlefield is a dangerous place where Saul hopes David will meet his death and be forgotten. But God is with David and gives him great success in all he attempts, which increases David's popularity with the people even more.

Saul even offers David one of his daughters in marriage, on the condition that David continues to fight (18:17). Whether or not this is intended as part of the reward for fighting Goliath (17:25) is uncertain. But Saul is not prepared for David's response. David rejects Saul's offer, not because he is reluctant to endanger himself in battle, but because he is a truly humble man who considers his station in life unworthy of such a gift. After David declines the offer, Saul allows that daughter to marry another man.

📄 18:20–30

THE DAVID/MICHAL CONNECTION

But another of Saul's daughters, Michal, loves David. Saul takes the opportunity to offer David another deal. If David feels he lacks the wealth or social status to be the king's son-in-law, Saul will consider another dowry altogether: one hundred Philistine foreskins. Saul sends word of this offer to David, who responds with enthusiasm. Saul's stated intent is to take revenge on his enemies, but his real desire is to have David killed by the Philistines (18:25). Saul's hopes are dashed again as David returns with twice the dowry Saul had demanded.

Everything Saul attempts backfires. Jonathan has made a covenant of love and friendship with David (18:3), and now Michal is united with David through the covenant of marriage. And the more David goes out to fight the Philistines, the more successful and famous he becomes (18:30).

📄 19:1–24

SAUL'S HOSTILITY INCREASES

When Saul's subtle attempts to kill David continue to fail, the king tries to recruit help from others. He instructs his attendants to kill David, but he also tells Jonathan, who immediately warns David. Rather than openly defy his father, Jonathan wisely sets out to convince Saul to rescind the order. He has David lie low while he tries to reason with his father. Jonathan's plan works (this time), and Saul again welcomes David (19:1–7). But Saul's tolerance doesn't last long.

If Jonathan had any desire to set himself over David as the next leader of Israel, this would have been the ideal time to do so. Yet he willingly subordinates himself and his own personal interests to those of David. He remains a faithful and submissive son to his father, yet is courageous enough to confront Saul when it was not always safe to do so. Saul quickly reverts to his hatred of David, but the incident says much about Jonathan's character.

Scripture provides no indication that Saul is going out to do battle against the Philistines. Yet when David goes out to fight and comes back a hero, Saul is overcome with jealousy and anger. Perhaps Saul's powerful negative emotions are somehow connected with the arrival of the evil spirit that came upon him (19:9). As David is attempting to minister to Saul by playing the harp, Saul again tries to kill him with a spear, and again misses.

This time, however, Saul follows up by ordering a stakeout of David's home. Soldiers are ordered to kill David when he comes out in the morning. But Michal knows her father well and emphatically urges David to escape during the night. Her instincts are good. After David leaves, she uses a household idol and some goat hair to make it appear that David is sick in bed. By the time Saul's soldiers question her, hear her cover story, report to Saul, and return to find they have been deceived, David has had plenty of time to escape.

David goes to Ramah, where he finds Samuel and informs him of his experiences with Saul. The two of them then go to nearby Naioth, where apparently a number of prophets gathered. The king soon learns of David's whereabouts and sends three successive groups of soldiers to retrieve him. But each time, as soon as the group of soldiers approaches the group of prophets, the Spirit of God causes the soldiers to begin to prophesy. After three failed attempts, Saul decides to go in person to get David. But as he approaches, he too begins to prophesy, lying naked half the day and through the night. What had originally been a sign of God's endorsement of Saul as king of Israel (10:9–13) had become God's method of protecting His new choice of king. (We aren't told *what* Saul is prophesying, but could it possibly have included godly insight into Israel's next king?)

DAVID AND JONATHAN RECONNECT

David leaves Naioth and goes to see Jonathan. After a short initial conversation, the two friends discover that Saul is not being completely honest with either of them. To David's credit, he assumes potential blame for the problem with Saul. Jonathan can hardly believe his father was so intent on doing harm to David, but is immediately convinced by David's urgent persuasion.

Demystifying 1 Samuel

One might wonder why David flees from Naioth at Ramah (20:1). He had been pursued by three squads of Saul's soldiers, and then Saul himself. Yet while in the environment of Samuel and the other prophets, he appears to be untouchable. So it seems likely that rather than fleeing *from* Samuel, he is fleeing *to* Jonathan. Perhaps he simply needed a friend at this point in his life.

David also has a plan to confirm that what he is telling Jonathan is true. On the next day is a special festival (Numbers 10:10; 28:11–15) that David will be expected to attend with the members of Saul's family. He plans to be absent. If Saul asks why he isn't there, Jonathan will say that David's family in Bethlehem is making a special annual sacrifice and that David asked to be excused to be with them. It should be no big deal to Saul. If the king is to get angry, it is likely because he has malicious intent. Twice already David has dodged Saul's spear. He had escaped from Saul's soldiers, both in his own home and in Ramah with Samuel. It is only natural to be suspicious that perhaps Saul is looking for yet another opportunity to kill David.

Of course, if Saul does turn out to be angry, Jonathan needs a way to inform David. The gravity of the situation seems to register with Jonathan at this point. Before even answering David, he waits until the two of them have gone to a nearby field, out of range of curious eyes and finely tuned ears. In the field, Jonathan can also point to landmarks as he explains what he intends to do. After speaking to Saul, Jonathan will shoot three arrows. If he yells to his assistant that the arrows are short of the mark, then all will be well and David will be safe. But if he remarks that they are beyond the mark, David needs to leave for his own safety (1 Samuel 20:18–23).

The first day of the festival goes by without incident. David isn't there, but Saul assumes he might be ceremonially unclean—unable to participate for some reason. But when David is gone again the second day, Saul asks Jonathan directly where David is. Jonathan gives Saul the excuse he and David had rehearsed. It is a reasonable, logical reason for David to be absent, but Saul goes into a rage, with his anger focused on Jonathan. He starts with offensive name-calling (20:30). Next he tries to enlist Jonathan's help in finding and killing David (20:31). And when Jonathan tries to reason with him instead, Saul hurls a spear at his own son, attempting to kill him (20:32–33). Saul's aggressive behavior removes any doubt Jonathan might have had about his intentions.

Jonathan's emotions reflect his maturity. He is supposed to be enjoying a feast, but has completely lost his appetite (20:34). He isn't feeling the humiliation his father had tried to heap on him or fear because of his father's rage. Instead, Jonathan is angry and grieved on David's behalf.

The next morning Jonathan goes out with a young boy to the place where he knows David is hiding and watching. He shoots an arrow and gives the verbal signal that lets David know Saul indeed wants him dead. The young lad retrieves the arrow, and Jonathan sends him back to the city.

Most likely, the plan had been for David to escape unnoticed into the forest, but both friends realize their lives will never be the same. If they ever see each other again, it will have to be in secret, and for only a brief time. So David comes out of hiding to say goodbye. Both are sorrowful, but David weeps more than Jonathan.

David's fleeing from Saul had always been temporary. But from this point on, he will never again sit at Saul's table, never play his harp to soothe the king's troubled spirit, never again fight for Saul in the Israelite army. David will be a fugitive constantly on the run. Yet he will know that the friendship he and Jonathan had forged will be ongoing, extending to their descendants forever (20:42).

Some people attempt to read more into this account than mere friendship between David and Jonathan, but there is no justification for doing so. David and Jonathan are two men who love each other as friends and brothers. There is no cause to suggest a relationship that is romantic, sexual, or homosexual.

Take It Home

In this section, Saul tries about a dozen times to kill David, including the times he throws his spear at him, sends soldiers out to get him, and sends him into dangerous battle conditions. If Saul had worked as hard to kill Israel's *enemies*, he would have been a much better military leader and king. But David was so devoted to serving God that he escaped every incident unscathed. While believers should never presume to have any kind of special protection from worldly pains and problems, an ongoing closeness to God can have a remarkably calming effect during hard times. God can provide a peace that transcends all understanding (Philippians 4:7).

1 SAMUEL 21:1–23:14

DAVID THE FUGITIVE

Setting Up the Section

At one time, Saul had felt very warmly toward David, but the closeness ends soon after David's victory over Goliath. Saul's jealousy of David's instant fame creates a rift between David and Saul. Envy soon gives rise to outright hostility, with Saul attempting to kill David a number of times. David has become a fugitive, and this section describes a number of events that take place as Saul pursues him, still hoping to end his life.

📄 21:1–9

PRIESTLY SUPPORT

David is a political refugee, a man without a country. He feels the pain of separation from his wife, from his position in Saul's administration, and from his friend, Jonathan. He is in continual danger, yet he maintains faith in God. It is a time of growth and preparation that will help prepare David for the day he will rule over Israel as God's anointed king.

He travels a few miles north and east of Jerusalem to Nob, the city of the priests. Ahimelech, the high priest, is no fool. He does not know about the schism that has formed between David and Saul, but he does know David is supposed to have a number of troops. When he sees David coming alone, he is troubled. But David has a story prepared. Aware of Saul's influence and potential for violence, David does not disclose all the details of his sudden appearance, perhaps hoping to avoid involving the priests in his feud with Saul. Instead, he tells Ahimelech he is on a secret mission for Saul, and that his men are hidden nearby. If Ahimelech doubts David's cover story, he has the tact not to say anything.

David then comes to the reason for his visit. First, he needs some provisions. The only food available is the showbread (Exodus 25:30)—sacred bread normally eaten only by the priests. Ahimelech is willing to share the bread with anyone who is ceremonially clean, and he gives David what is available. The gift is witnessed by the chief of Saul's shepherds, an Edomite named Doeg.

Next David asks Ahimelech for a weapon, which again may have raised the priest's eyebrows. What kind of soldier on a special mission would be without a sword or spear? At the time few weapons could be found in the entire kingdom—much less in the city of the priests. In fact, the only sword on the entire premises is the sword of Goliath, a trophy/memorial of the victory God gave Israel through David. It belongs to David anyway, so Ahimelech willingly gives it to him. David takes the sword and bread and promptly leaves.

📖 **21:10–22:5**

LIVING ON THE RUN

David's next move is a bold one. He leaves Israel and goes into Philistine territory. In fact, the city of Gath is Goliath's hometown, and David boldly enters carrying Goliath's sword. The Israelites had recently pursued fleeing Philistines right up to the cities of Gath and Ekron (17:51–52), leaving bodies in their wake, but this time David is a political refugee seeking asylum from King Achish. The fact that David is willing to take such a risk illustrates how strongly Saul desires to kill David. Yet whatever David's reasons for going to Gath, it becomes quite obvious that God doesn't want him there. It is not unusual for kings to receive political refugees from nearby nations (1 Kings 11:40; 2 Kings 25:27–30). If they are given sanctuary, they might become grateful allies, if not loyal subjects. But if those are Achish's thoughts, his servants quickly bring him back to reality. David has killed the Philistine hero, Goliath, and people have written songs about him (1 Samuel 21:10–11).

Critical Observation

In both 21:10–15 and chapters 27–29, the Philistine leader Achish is presented as gullible and less than astute. Somehow, he takes a liking to David. He seems overly confident of David's loyalty to him and of his value as an ally. He does not willingly entertain thoughts that David may still be a loyal Israelite, soon to take the throne of Israel.

While Achish begins to rethink his offer of sanctuary, David also gives some thought to *his* predicament. If Achish takes the advice of his people seriously, he might have David put to death. So David feigns madness, slobbering and scribbling on the gates.

Achish is convinced. He hadn't wanted to kill David in the first place, and if the Israelite poses no threat, there is no need to do him harm. The Philistines are glad to get rid of David, and by then David appears ready to leave. He escapes with his life, but not with his dignity.

David leaves Philistine territory and goes into Judah, but just barely. The exact site of the cave of Adullam (22:1) is unknown but appears to have been a safe, secluded hideout not too close to either Gath or King Saul. Word begins to spread that David is there. Among the first to find him are his family members. They are soon joined by Israelites who are in distress, in debt, or out of favor with Saul. They come to David as their new leader, despite the danger of being associated with him. He soon has a band of about four hundred people.

His next stop is the territory of Moab, where he arranges for his elderly parents to stay. Moab is out of Saul's realm of influence, and it had been the homeland of Ruth, David's great-grandmother (Ruth 1:4; 4:13–17). The move appears to put David's parents out of harm's way during the years he is fleeing from Saul.

A prophet named Gad then directs David back to Judah from the land of Moab. The location of the forest of Hereth is not entirely clear, but forests could be dangerous and forbidding places, especially for soldiers (2 Samuel 18:8).

📄 **22:6–23**

SAUL'S WRATH INTENSIFIES

Word of David's movements are bound to reach Saul eventually. The scene in this passage is a somewhat sinister one, with Saul seated under a tree in his hometown, spear in hand and ranting to nearby officials. He blames them for everything. He had found out too late about Jonathan's covenant with David. Even worse, he accuses them of conspiring against him.

But Saul's chief shepherd, Doeg, speaks up with some information that Saul might find useful. He had seen David in Nob, receiving help from Ahimelech and the priests. Doeg tells Saul that he had seen Ahimelech equip David with provisions and Goliath's sword. These things are true. And from Doeg's observation that David had inquired of the Lord (22:10), it would seem that the reason David went to Nob was primarily to seek God's will by using the Urim and Thummim in the priest's ephod (Exodus 28:30).

But what Doeg *doesn't* say (and perhaps he does not know) is that David never informed the priests that he was fleeing from Saul. Neither David nor the priests had ever said or done anything to conspire against the king. But Saul's blinding jealousy and devotion to protecting his throne took precedence over getting the facts straight.

Saul doesn't even need to move; he has all the priests summoned to appear before him. In his mind, Ahimelech and all the other priests are already guilty of conspiracy.

It should have been the responsibility of the priests to enlighten Saul and others in Israel about the judgments of God. But here it is Saul who presumes to pass judgment on the entire priesthood. The king had shown little respect for the priesthood in the past when he offered sacrifices himself instead of waiting for Samuel (13:7–14). Here he shows outright disdain by not even using the priest's name in the conversation (22:12). He doesn't even ask *if* Ahimelech has betrayed him, but *why*.

With remarkable poise, Ahimelech speaks on David's behalf, reminding Saul that David is the king's most faithful servant, honored by the people, the one whom Saul had appointed to positions of authority, and, in fact, Saul's son-in-law. Ahimelech also speaks in his own defense. Yes, he had assisted David, but it wasn't the first time. Ahimelech knows he has done nothing inappropriate, and he knows Saul has no idea what has actually gone on in Nob.

However, Saul is not listening to reason. His mind is apparently already made up. He commands his guards to kill Ahimelech and all the other priests. But no one moves. As much as these men fear Saul, they are not willing to act on his heinous command. Saul then turns to Doeg, a non-Israelite, who doesn't appear to have the same qualms about killing God's priests. But he and Saul don't stop with that terrible crime. Doeg then travels to Nob where he also kills the priests' families and cattle. Eighty-five priests die that day. And how ironic it is that while Saul had defied God's order to annihilate the people and property of the Amalekites (15:1–3, 7–9), he readily wipes out his own spiritual leaders.

Only one priest escapes Saul's wrath: one of Ahimelech's sons named Abiathar. He runs to David and tells him what Saul has done. David assumes full responsibility. He had seen Doeg at Nob, but who could have predicted how far Saul would go in his hatred of David? David could do nothing more for those who had been killed, but he does offer sanctuary to Abiathar.

📄 23:1–14

DAVID SAVES A CITY

David learns that the Philistines are looting a town near their border called Keilah. The problem *should* have been Saul's concern (9:16), but David is already thinking like the king of Israel. Thankfully, when Abiathar fled from Nob, he had taken the high priestly ephod with him. With a priest and the ephod, David can receive God's direction for what to do. After he gets instructions to rescue Keilah, he asks again to be sure. His men aren't eager to come out of hiding to go fight in the open where they will be targets for Saul's army as well as the Philistines.

Still, they go to Keilah. By now David has six hundred followers—a ragtag group of discontents who have fled from Saul (22:2). They aren't trained soldiers, yet they win a decisive victory.

Their fears about Saul prove to be valid, however. Saul learns of David's whereabouts and is pleased to discover that David is in a city with gates and bars. Those protections won't keep Saul out for long, but they will keep David trapped. When David gets word of Saul's intent, he again has Abiathar bring the ephod to consult God. One would think that the citizens of Keilah would be grateful to David and offer him some protection. But God lets him know that Saul is indeed on his way and that the people of Keilah will turn him over to Saul when the king arrives. So before that can happen, David leaves.

Demystifying 1 Samuel

When David seeks direction from the Lord, the answers he receives are hypothetical. For example, God tells him that he will be turned over to Saul, but that is conditional on his staying in the city. He can take action to avoid that ominous result. After David leaves with his men, Saul doesn't bother making the trip. But if David had remained in Keilah, both of God's messages would have come to pass: Saul would have gone to the city, and the city's inhabitants would have handed David over to Saul. It is overwhelming to consider that God not only knows all things that will be, but He also knows all things that *could* be, under any set of circumstances. He is both in control of every situation (sovereign), and He knows all the options of each one (omniscient).

David takes his troops to the desert where they can hide in various strongholds and hilly areas. Saul keeps looking for him, but God is watching over him, and Saul is never able to find him.

Take It Home

David's world is much like our own in terms of spiritual action and risk. Many people tend to be like David's followers, believing that safety is best achieved by isolation or by hiding out from the dangers of the world. But David knew he could calculate his safety in terms of his nearness to God. Believers should not seek to hide when God calls them to be salt and light in dark places, even though risk is still involved. Believers are not immune to the injustices of the world, as Ahimelech and his priests discovered. However, no one is safer than the believer who trusts and obeys God, even during the most dangerous of circumstances.

1 SAMUEL 23:15–26:25

A FUGITIVE MODELS MERCY, PATIENCE, AND FORGIVENESS

Setting Up the Section

David has been hiding from Saul, moving from place to place to avoid being killed. People are beginning to support his leadership, and he has already freed one city from a threatening Philistine presence. In this section, we see David's faith in God

demonstrated in a number of difficult situations. His dependence on God allows him to show forgiveness to those who offend him and repeated mercy to the person who is most eager to see him dead—King Saul.

📖 23:15–18

A BRIEF REUNION

At this point in David's life, his outlook must have been a bit dark and foreboding. He had gone from the champion who slew Goliath to Israel's most-wanted fugitive. He had recently received help from the high priest, and as a result, eighty-five priests and their families had been killed at Saul's order. He had come out of hiding to save a city from Philistine attack, only to discover that the people were quite willing to turn him over to Saul. While on the run from Saul's forces, he was trying to ensure the safety of his family and followers. It had to be an emotionally and physically challenging time.

David has just gotten word that Saul has again pinpointed his location and is on the way. The location of Horesh is unknown, but the Hebrew word means "forest," so it is presumed that David is in a forested area in the Wilderness of Ziph. With all the bad news he has been receiving and the uncertainty of his day-to-day situation, what a pleasant surprise it must have been when Jonathan shows up unexpectedly. Not much is said of their reunion, but what is said is significant.

Jonathan does all he can to affirm David. It is more than a pep talk; he helps David renew his strength in God (23:16). Jonathan encourages David not to be afraid. Yes, Saul is doing everything in his power to find and kill David. But Jonathan—and even Saul—realizes that God is protecting David because David is certain to be the next king of Israel. Jonathan reaffirms that he is secondary to David—his most loyal servant and supporter.

David and Jonathan conclude their short meeting with another covenant, or perhaps a renewal of their earlier one (18:3; 20:16–17). Then Jonathan returns home while David goes back into hiding.

📖 23:19–29

A NARROW ESCAPE

At this time some of the locals (the Ziphites) report David's location to King Saul. Perhaps they want to curry his favor, or maybe they simply want to avoid his anger. But their willingness to betray David is particularly grievous because they, too, are from the tribe of Judah.

Upon receiving the report from the Ziphites, Saul responds with pious-sounding language (23:21). Yet his holy-sounding words are only a front for the wickedness of his intended actions. Such misuse of God's name is one way of taking God's name in vain—a violation of the third commandment (Exodus 20:7).

This time Saul doesn't go rushing out with his army. David has escaped his efforts several times already, and it won't look good to come back empty-handed. Instead, he instructs the Ziphites to watch David closely, making note of his habits and hiding places. When he feels the time is right, Saul makes the journey himself.

David is told of Saul's intention (1 Samuel 23:25), and he moves on a few miles to the desert of Maon. The situation again looks bleak for David as Saul's forces are coming around a mountain and gaining on him. But Jonathan had been right. Saul will not lay a hand on David (23:17). As it seems that David and his forces have no way of escape, a messenger appears to tell Saul that the Philistines are attacking and his help is needed. Saul responds immediately, allowing David to escape again. This location becomes known as the Rock of Parting (23:28), and David moves on to En Gedi where there are protective strongholds.

📄 **24:1–22**

DAVID'S IDEAL OPPORTUNITY #1

As soon as Saul deals with the Philistines, he returns to his pursuit of David. He takes three thousand trained soldiers to fight David's six hundred men. But before Saul has even found David, he stops at a cave to have some privacy for a restroom break. Little does Saul know that he has chosen the very cave where David and his men are hiding.

Perhaps David's crew grew fearful as the king approached their hiding place because they were trapped and had no place to go. If so, however, their fears are soon alleviated as they discover why Saul has entered the cave. Saul has probably thrown his robe aside for the moment, and David uses the cover of darkness to slip over and cut off a piece of cloth. David's soldiers want to do much more, of course. They are surely weary of being on the run and in perpetual danger, and they interpret the remarkable coincidence of Saul's appearance—alone and defenseless—as God's way of delivering David's enemy into his hands.

Critical Observation

In light of David's subsequent remorse (24:5), some people have interpreted his slashing of Saul's robe as an intentional act of defiance that symbolically challenges or undermines Saul's right to rule. That conjecture doesn't seem to be supported by the facts, however. David has nothing but respect for Saul in this passage. More likely, he came to realize that what had been intended as a trivial action had greater weight because it was committed against his king. By raising his hand against God's king, David feels he has raised his hand against God. To David's credit, he doesn't merely persuade or rebuke his men (24:7) when they want to kill Saul. The original word means "tear apart." David tears into his men (verbally), insisting that none of them will harm the king.

They are surely perplexed when David refuses to take advantage of the situation to kill Saul. Even more astounding is what David does next. All they have to do is keep quiet for a few minutes until Saul and his troops go on their way. But David follows Saul from the cave, out into the light, abandoning all efforts at self-protection or evasion. David addresses Saul first as his lord the king (24:8) and later as father (24:11). He shows reverence and submission to Saul. He appeals to Saul to set aside any rumors he might have heard and to judge David's guilt or innocence for himself, based on David's actions.

Saul must have been shocked to hear a familiar voice from behind. He quickly determines that David is not seeking his defeat or death. David isn't attempting to gain the throne by removing Saul from it. Saul can also see the sliver of his robe in David's hands. His life had been in David's hands, and now David is placing his life in Saul's hands. David quotes a proverb to assure Saul he has no evil intent (24:13), and he likens himself to a dead dog or a single flea (24:24)—no threat at all to Saul and his kingdom. Then David rests his case, looking to God for justice and protection, and waits for Saul's response.

Saul begins to weep, responding to David's affectionate address (my father) by calling him his son (24:16). And for the first time, Saul acknowledges the truth. He had heard from Samuel that his kingdom will not endure (13:14) and that God has rejected him as Israel's king (15:26). He had seen that David's popularity could easily allow David to possess his kingdom (18:8-9). He had privately admitted that as long as David was alive, Jonathan would never become king (20:31). Yet he had resisted all those truths, treating David as a traitor to the nation and pursuing him with the intent of killing him. Here, however, Saul publicly admits that God is taking his kingdom away from him and that David's ascent to the throne is a certainty.

In light of this reality, Saul wants David to swear that he will not kill off all of Saul's descendants. It is common practice of the time for new kings to kill off every other possible heir to the throne—especially descendants of the preceding king. Saul doesn't realize that David has already made that promise to Jonathan (20:14-17, 41-42). Nevertheless, David affirms to Saul that he will not destroy all of his descendants.

Saul goes home, but David returns to his stronghold. He is probably hoping that his troubles with Saul are over, but he knows Saul's previous instances of repentance hadn't lasted long (19:1-7). David will remain at a safe distance to see what Saul's long-term response will be. Then again, David's intent may have been for Saul's benefit as well. If the people are ready to turn to David rather than Saul, David's remaining out of the public eye will not prematurely undermine Saul's popularity.

📖 **25:1**

A GREAT LOSS

The death of Samuel is succinctly summarized at this point—without much fanfare, considering his significance to the nation. He had listened to and followed God from childhood. He had defended the people against the Philistines (7:7-14). He served as judge throughout his life (7:15). He had designated and anointed Saul as Israel's first king. He also spoke with God's authority to inform Saul that his kingship was going to be taken away. He anointed David as Saul's successor and was a source of wisdom and comfort for David during Saul's pursuit (19:18-24). The Israelites mourn Samuel's death and bury him in his hometown of Ramah.

Samuel's death must have been particularly hard on David, who had just said good-bye to Jonathan for the last time (23:18) and had left his parents in care of the king of Moab (22:3). He will eventually discover that while he was keeping his distance from Saul, the king had taken David's wife Michal and given her to another man (25:44). And David is about to encounter other problems.

A RICH FOOL AND HIS WISE WIFE

Since David is going from place to place with a following of at least six hundred (23:13), they can't remain in complete isolation. They are bound to run into various people from time to time, and this passage describes one such encounter. David's group is staying in the desert where they come to know some shepherds in the service of a rich man named Nabal. It is sheep-shearing season, when the work is followed by a time of celebration and relaxation.

David sends ten of his group to Nabal to report that they have been treating Nabal's shepherds with great respect and to ask for any provisions Nabal could spare. However, Nabal refuses to acknowledge that David's men have helped protect his shepherds and their flocks. He doesn't even send a token gift. Instead, he insults David, inferring that he is no better than a runaway slave, and he sends the messengers back empty-handed.

Demystifying 1 Samuel

Nabal's insensitivity to David's crew is made worse in light of some of the facts he reveals. If David were an absolute stranger, Nabal might have been somewhat justified in rejecting his request. But he knew David was the son of Jesse (25:10), and Nabal himself was a Calebite (25:3). Caleb had been from the tribe of Judah (Numbers 13:6), as was Jesse. So Nabal must have realized that he and David were distant relatives, yet arrogantly denied him anything, even though much food would have been on hand for the sheep-shearing celebrations.

When David is told what transpired with Nabal, he becomes irate. David has acted honorably. His men could easily have taken whatever they needed from Nabal's flocks, but had not done so. David expected a positive response in return for his positive actions. When he determines that Nabal is being unjust, David determines to achieve justice himself. He orders his men to arm themselves, and he sets out to kill Nabal and every male in his household (25:12–13, 22).

David had tolerated Saul's mistreatment, but Saul was the anointed king of Israel. David considers himself Saul's servant, in spite of Saul's inappropriate behavior. Nabal is a different story. Nabal is not David's superior, and David does not appreciate the demeaning treatment he has received. Furthermore, David is not thinking or behaving as a man of faith as he sets out to kill Nabal and all the males associated with him. He is eager to take action in response to how he is feeling.

Nabal would have suffered dire consequences had it not been for his wise wife, Abigail. One of Nabal's servants had gone to her with an account of what had happened, including a warning that David is likely to retaliate. She wastes no time gathering generous portions of food (bread, wine, grain, raisins, figs, and sheep), packing everything on donkeys, and sending it ahead to David. (One might wonder how she could gather so much food so quickly. The timing is convenient because Nabal had planned a fit-for-a-king banquet [25:36]. He probably never missed what Abigail sent to David.)

Abigail works her way down the mountain, out of sight of David and his men. David likewise comes from higher ground, still grumbling about Nabal's insults and rehearsing what he will do when he finds the ungrateful despot. Without either party realizing what is happening, David and Abigail converge and suddenly find themselves face-to-face with each other.

Abigail is everything Nabal is not: polite, well-spoken, submissive, honest, and ready to take responsibility and blame. Six times she refers to herself as David's maidservant, and fourteen times she calls David her lord. She doesn't try to cover for her husband; she calls him a fool (25:25), and in doing so she may have saved his life. David knows from experience there is no honor or status in killing fools. Perhaps Abigail's comment prompts him to recall feigning insanity while in Philistine territory, which caused the citizens to perceive him as non-threatening. Abigail isn't attempting to exaggerate her husband's faults through name-calling: *Nabal* literally means "fool," and there is little doubt that he lives up to the name.

Next Abigail tactfully points out how taking vengeance will be detrimental to David. God had prevented him from shedding blood for personal revenge (25:26). Abigail acknowledges the hand of God on David, and she exhorts him to avoid wrongdoing (25:28-31). She pleads with David to accept the gift she has brought and asks him to forgive *her* transgression.

Abigail's words stop David in his tracks. He knows she is right, and he praises her in front of his men. She has literally been a godsend, used by God to prevent David from taking vengeance on Nabal and shedding other innocent blood. Had she not acted so quickly, David would have carried out his plan. He thankfully accepts her gift and sends her home in peace.

David leaves vengeance in God's hands, and it comes rather quickly. Nabal is drunk when Abigail gets home, so she waits until the next morning to tell him about her encounter with David. Upon hearing the news, his heart fails, and he dies ten days later.

David rejoices in the news, not so much that Nabal is dead, but that thanks to Abigail, David hadn't acted hastily and done something he would always regret (25:39). And David wastes no time asking Abigail to marry him. Her action had been selfless, and it is quickly rewarded.

During this time, Saul has a change of heart and is about to take up the pursuit of David once more. He even gives his daughter Michal (David's wife) to another man while David is gone. But David's marriage to Abigail counteracts Saul's action. Whatever Saul attempts to deny David, God will amply provide.

📄 26:1–25

DAVID'S IDEAL OPPORTUNITY #2

The events of this section are similar to those of 1 Samuel 24, so much so that some people have suggested it is an alternative account of the same incident. In both cases Saul is pursuing David after being informed of his location by the Ziphites, and in both instances Saul has three thousand men. These are not unusual repetitions. If the Ziphites gained Saul's favor for giving him David's location once, it shouldn't be surprising if they do so again. And it's reasonable to assume that Saul's army is three thousand strong (13:2). Other details of this second account are quite different from the previous one.

David's first close encounter with Saul had been in a cave where David was hiding. This time David seeks out Saul's position and finds him out in the open, asleep and surrounded by his entire army. Saul and Abner, the commander of his army, are in the center of a large circle. David doesn't realize that the entire army is in a divinely induced slumber (26:12), yet he is willing to approach the king anyway. He and a volunteer, Abishai, walk through the sleeping soldiers, right up to Saul. The king's spear is stuck in the ground nearby, and his water jug is near his head.

Abishai is a stouthearted soldier (2 Samuel 23:18–19). Every instinct tells him to take the spear and do away with Saul with one good thrust. After the cave incident, perhaps Abishai thinks David might be squeamish about killing Saul, and he is more than willing to do the job himself. But David had not spared Saul out of fear, but out of respect for the king's position and reverence for God's right to remove the king whenever He deems that the time is right. In addition, David's recent encounter with Abigail may have strengthened his resolve not to be hasty in bloodshed. He tells Abishai to take Saul's spear and water jug, and they go to a neighboring hillside, within earshot of the Israelite army.

David shouts over, but to Abner, not Saul. As commander of the army, Abner is primarily responsible for Saul's protection. David points out the absence of the spear and water jug, and he makes it clear that if his intent had been to destroy the king, Saul would be dead by now. Indeed, David prevented Saul's murder by Abishai, making him a more reliable defender of Saul than anyone else in Israel.

Still groggy, Saul finally recognizes the voice as David's and calls over to him. David then begins to address Saul, giving a personal defense much as he had done previously (1 Samuel 24:8–15; 26:17–20). In essence, David accuses the king of listening to other people who endeavored to make David serve other gods. (As soon as someone left Israelite soil, he or she was quickly exposed to the various gods of the various peoples of the area, and David was being kept away from his community of worship.)

Saul again is quick to confess and repent. He invites David to return. David arranges for someone to come over and retrieve Saul's property. Then the king goes home as David again goes on his way, no doubt anticipating another encounter.

Take It Home

This section contains repeated illustrations of mercy in light of what many would consider reasonable justice. The most obvious examples are perhaps the two times David spares Saul's life when it would have been just as convenient to kill him. Less apparent, but just as emphatic, is Abigail's confrontation with David. Her example is nothing less than an illustration of Christ's salvation for humankind: She saw that many were about to die, she took immediate action that did not personally benefit her in any way, she took the blame upon herself, and she appeased the wrath of one about to judge. Even David's actions in the final story reflect mercy and salvation. Had Saul been put to death that night, Abner and all the rest would have been guilty of failing to protect their king. In that sense, David saves not only Saul's life, but also those of all the soldiers. Such stories should inspire each reader of scripture to act with greater effort to extend mercy and grace to others in life's everyday encounters.

1 SAMUEL 27:1–31:13
THE FINAL DAYS OF KING SAUL

Setting Up the Section

After Saul is told his kingdom is being removed by God and given to another, a considerable amount of time passes before the prediction is fulfilled. In the meantime, David has already been anointed to take Saul's place. Although Saul is trying hard to put David to death, David has twice had Saul's life in his hands and refused to harm him. But after long months of conflict and turbulence, Saul finally runs out of time—seemingly farther away from God than ever. The book of 1 Samuel concludes with his death and burial.

📄 27:1–28:2

DAVID'S PHILISTINE QUANDARY

David has just gotten a reprieve from Saul's persistent pursuit (26:21), but he knows it will only be a matter of time until Saul renews the manhunt. Until this point, David has been sounding confident and faithful (24:15; 26:23–24), and Abigail confirmed those qualities (25:28–29). David's change of heart (27:1) is not explained.

If David primarily wants to stop worrying about Saul, he succeeds. After he arranges with King Achish to live in Philistine territory, David has no more trouble from Saul. However, the move will soon create other problems.

David had hidden out among the Philistines before (21:10–15). He survived, but left the city perceived as a scribbling, slobbering lunatic. This time he is not alone; he has his six hundred men, their wives and families, and his own two wives. At first their accommodations seem ideal. Achish gives David the city of Ziklag, where his group resides. Ziklag is about twenty-five miles from Gath, so Achish won't be privy to David's every activity.

David and his men regularly fight enemies of Israel, killing all the people (to eliminate any witnesses) and accumulating livestock and clothing. Anytime Achish asks about their raids, David tells him they have been fighting the Israelites. It also appears David may have given Achish a portion of the spoils (27:9). In time, Achish comes to trust David. He assumes that David can never go home again, and it seems that Achish will always benefit from having David as an ally.

During this time David's life is relatively carefree. He goes wherever he wants, he associates with the king, he has no fear of Saul or Israelites who might betray him, he and his men live well on the spoils of his raids, and he keeps reducing the influence of the enemies of Israel. His life is good, that is, until one day when King Achish decides to join a larger Philistine coalition marching against Israel, and he enlists David's help. Though taken by surprise, David tells Achish what he wants to hear, and the king responds by bestowing David an honored position (28:2). How amazing that David has gone from being armor-bearer for King Saul (16:21) to being bodyguard for a Philistine king. Of course, now David has the dilemma of how to keep from actually fighting against Israel without Achish discovering his true loyalties.

28:3–25

SAUL'S PHILISTINE PROBLEM (AND UNUSUAL SOURCE OF ADVICE)

Before the writer of Samuel relates the rest of David's story, he shifts to some problems Saul is having in the meantime. The Philistines have harassed the Israelites throughout Saul's lifetime, but this time they seem determined to break Israel's resolve once and for all. It appears their strategy is to divide and conquer by separating Israel's forces and then focusing on the northern and southern halves independently. The numbers of the Philistine forces are staggering, and Saul may have also heard that David was among them. Samuel is now dead, and Saul receives no guidance from the Lord. God doesn't provide an enlightening dream. He doesn't send a prophet. The priests can't even discern God's will with the Urim and Thummim in the priestly ephod (28:6).

Demystifying 1 Samuel

This account of the story says that Saul inquires of the Lord (28:6); the Chronicles account says he does *not* inquire of the Lord (1 Chronicles 10:13–14). Based on Saul's previous spiritual habits, one has to wonder if this inquiry is less a genuine desire to know God's will than a desperate attempt to get God to bail him out of the trouble he has gotten himself into. Either way, he receives no answer.

Saul's uneasiness progresses from fear to terror to sheer panic, and he doesn't always make good choices when he is under pressure (13:7–14). This time he hits a new low. Even though he has been responsible for removing everyone involved in occult practices (28:9), he decides to find a medium and seek some direction. His prior action had been in compliance with God's law (Leviticus 19:31, 20:6, 27; Deuteronomy 18:10–14), so this decision reflects clear disregard for God's will.

His servants know of a medium, but it isn't easy for Saul to arrange a meeting. Getting to her location requires an eight-mile trek from Gilboa to En-Dor (at risk of encountering the Philistines). Saul's disguise (1 Samuel 28:8) serves a couple of purposes. If he runs into enemy soldiers, he certainly doesn't want to be identified as the king of Israel. Nor does he want the medium to discover who he is. Since she is working undercover, she is already suspicious of anyone she doesn't know—and he is the one who has forced her underground.

But after arriving, his secret identity doesn't last long. Saul asks the woman to contact Samuel, but when she does, she grows alarmed. Her response suggests that this is no ordinary conjuring. She immediately discerns Saul's identity, and she sees Samuel as a divine being (28:13) coming up out of the ground. (Other Bible versions translate the Hebrew word as *spirit* or *god*.)

Saul falls on the ground before Samuel, and the two have a short conversation. Saul wants to know what to do. Samuel has frequently spoken to Saul for God, and his messages have been consistent: Because of Saul's disobedience, he is going to lose his kingdom (13:13-14; 15:27-29). If Saul is hoping for a different message this time, he is sorely disappointed. In fact, Samuel says that the next day the Philistines will soundly defeat the Israelites, and Saul and his sons will be with him (28:19).

Saul hasn't eaten all day, and the news literally floors him. The medium is still worried because her client has been the king, but she musters the courage to offer him a meal. He refuses at first, but his companions convince him to eat before returning home.

📖 **29:1-11**

DAVID'S PROVIDENTIAL SOLUTION

At this point the flow of 1 Samuel returns to David's dilemma. Not only are David and his men marching out with Philistine King Achish to do battle against Israel, but they are honored with the crucial position of rear guard, where the bravest and most highly skilled warriors are placed (29:2). Apparently each of the five key Philistine cities had its own king and troops. But this time the Philistines are combining forces to march against Israel.

When the other leaders discover that King Achish has included David among his troops, they are incensed. They feel that Achish is being deceived (which he is), and that David will be a real threat if the Philistines go into battle and he starts fighting for Israel. They even remind Achish of the song that has been written about David concerning how many people he has killed (29:5), and they insist that David return to Ziklag.

In an almost comical scene, the Philistine king gives David the disappointing news that he will not be allowed to fight against Israel. Achish even invokes the name of David's God (Yahweh) in praise of David. With the matter already settled by the Philistines, David even protests their decision (29:8). In reality, it is the best thing that could have happened to extract him from a delicate situation.

Critical Observation

It might not have been the best idea for David to hide out among the Philistines, especially after his deceit of Achish was about to be exposed. It seems clear that God is working to deliver David from a dilemma of his own creation. Yet it is left to the reader to acknowledge God's deliverance in this situation. The only person who actually talks about God in this passage is the Philistine king (29:6).

📖 **30:1-31**

DAVID AND THE AMALEKITES

David and his men must have celebrated all the way back to Ziklag. But approaching their base city, the group sees, and perhaps smells, smoke. On arrival, they find the city burned. Missing are all their family members and livestock, and many of their possessions. Their initial emotion, naturally, is grief. They all weep until they have no more strength. But the next emotion is bitterness, and they begin to blame David for all that has gone wrong. They even talk of stoning him (30:6).

But this event seems to turn David back to God (30:6). He calls for the priest and the ephod to determine whether God will have them pursue the raiders. God assures him of success in rescuing everything.

The trouble is that David's group had been physically challenged during the almost sixty-mile march from Aphek back to Ziklag. Then the emotional toll of finding their city in ruins and families absent makes things worse. Not everyone is up to marching off with David right away. They all start, but a third of them are too exhausted to continue. The other two-thirds leave some of their gear with the two hundred staying behind in order to move faster (30:24).

The trail is indeed cold. David doesn't even know whom he is chasing. But then his men find an Egyptian slave who hasn't had food or water for three days. They feed him and discover it had been the Amalekites who had raided Ziklag. After being promised protection, the Egyptian even agrees to lead David to the Amalekite camp.

The timing couldn't have been better. When David's men arrive, the much larger group of Amalekites is celebrating their easy conquest—drinking and disorganized. David and his men attack, resulting in a slaughter that lasts many hours. Four hundred young men escape on camels, but every other Amalekite soldier is killed. The next day David recovers *everything* that had been taken from Ziklag—wives, families, animals, and possessions—not to mention plunder from the Amalekites.

When David's fighting men return, there are those among them who don't want to share the plunder they have accumulated with the two hundred men who remained behind (30:22). But David steps in and sees that his soldiers all get equal shares. In addition, David sends some of their new wealth to friends and elders at various places throughout Judah (30:26–31). His decision will have far-reaching effects. Many of the recipients are men of considerable influence who will soon be among the first to embrace David as king.

📄 **31:1–13**

THE DEATHS OF SAUL AND HIS SONS

As has already been shown several times in 1 Samuel, when life is going well for David, it is taking a downturn for Saul. The book concludes with one final, graphic example. At about the time that David is in pursuit of the Amalekite raiders, Saul and the Israelite army are fighting the Philistines. David returns with only good news, but the Israelites are soundly defeated. Among the casualties are Saul and his sons (31:2–3). News of the defeat causes neighboring Israelites to flee the area and allow the Philistines to inhabit their cities (31:7), so the loss of the battle not only reduces the size of Israel's army, but also reduces the size of Israel.

Saul is critically wounded and asks his armor-bearer to kill him so he will avoid any torment by his enemies. His armor-bearer is afraid and refuses, so Saul falls on his own sword. The armor-bearer follows suit. A passing Amalekite later takes credit for delivering the death blow to Saul (2 Samuel 1:8–10), though he might have been lying in hopes of receiving a reward from David.

When the Philistines discover Saul's body, they cut off his head, place his armor in the temple of Ashtoreth, and hang his body on the wall of one of their cities. But the inhabitants of Jabesh-gilead remember how Saul had previously kept them from humiliation at the hands of the Ammonites (1 Samuel 11:1–11). When they hear what has happened to Saul, many of their brave men march through the night, retrieve the bodies of Saul and his sons, and return them to Israel for a proper burial. Saul's boldness toward the Ammonites at Jabesh had been his finest hour, and it was not forgotten by those whom he had saved.

The book of 1 Samuel appears to end rather abruptly at this point, because 1 Samuel and 2 Samuel were originally one single book. So the story will continue as 2 Samuel begins.

Take It Home

The final contrasts between David and Saul in this passage highlight the significance of the daily decisions we make, especially as they pertain to spiritual development. Saul makes a series of choices that are not quite obedient to what God has instructed him to do. He has moments of clarity where he sees that he is wrong, yet he never makes a conscious decision to get back on the right path. Eventually, he turns to the occult for guidance and ends up committing suicide. David, on the other hand, tries to consciously make the right decisions even when it is difficult to do so. Both Saul and David face suffering and difficulty, and both have their failures. But because David is slow to anger, quick to repent, and perseveres in his faith, he and Saul come to quite different ends.

2 SAMUEL

INTRODUCTION TO 2 SAMUEL

AUTHOR

There is no mention of the author in the book of Samuel, though Jewish tradition states that Samuel wrote the first twenty-four chapters of what was originally one book of Samuel. In fact, 1 and 2 Samuel and 1 and 2 Kings are thought to be a single historical work edited by the same theological circle during the exile.

PURPOSE

This book tells the story of how David sets out to establish his throne with God's blessing following King Saul's death. David is a man after God's own heart, but he is still simply a man with real shortcomings, and his sin with Bathsheba has a myriad of truly tragic consequences. The text recounts the events of the second half of King David's life during which his reign unites Israel and testifies to God's faithfulness to His servant David and to all His children.

OCCASION

The book of 1 Samuel ends tragically, with King Saul a virtual madman. He turns against David, his loyal servant and friend, and seeks to kill David as though he is a traitor. He fails to obey God's Word, and so brings about his own downfall and demise. Saul even goes so far as to consult with a medium. The closing chapter of 1 Samuel is the account of his death at the hand of the Philistines and his own hand as well. As sad as it is, we breathe a sigh of relief, for now David's days of fleeing from Saul as a fugitive are over. Second Samuel starts immediately afterward to tell how David will reign in Saul's place.

THEMES

Second Samuel is a study in contrasts—of the blessing and curse of power, of the sinfulness that is present even in God's greatest servants, and of the power that temptation, lust, and covetousness have against even the mightiest kings. In this book we are reminded of how even a man of God can fail in major ways, including adultery and murder. And yet, we are struck again and again by God's forgiveness and grace even in the midst of some harsh consequences from David's sinfulness. The resounding theme of 2 Samuel is that even the greatest world leaders must remember that the kingdom, the power, and the glory belong to the Lord alone.

HISTORICAL CONTEXT

Israel is divided when David first comes to power, thanks to the intrigue of men like Abner and Joab. This division is a foreshadowing of future times for the nation of Israel. It is not without some challenge that David becomes king of all Israel.

CONTRIBUTION TO THE BIBLE

Second Samuel leaves us with an appreciation for the greatness of David and also a realization of his human weaknesses. If there is to be a king who will dwell forever on the throne of David (2 Samuel 7:12–14), it must be one who is greater than David. If David is the best king who ever ruled over Israel, then God will have to provide a better king. And so He will; Jesus is the perfect king that David cannot be.

OUTLINE

PROMISE BREAKERS AND KEEPERS 21:1–22

DAVID'S SONG OF SALVATION 22:1–51

EPILOGUE 23:1–24:25

2 SAMUEL 1:1–27

THE DEATH OF A MENTOR AND A FRIEND

Setting Up the Section

David and his men are certainly grateful for the defeat of the Amalekites and the recovery of their families and possessions. But this victory must be overshadowed by David's concern for what is taking place in Israel. When David left Achish to return to Ziklag, the Philistines had mounted a massive fighting force to attack Israel. David knows very well how awesome this military effort is, because he and his men marched in review at the end of the procession. On his third day back in Ziklag, a young man approaches David with news of Israel's defeat.

📖 **1:1–16**

NEWS OF SAUL AND JONATHAN'S DEATHS

From the time he parted ways with the Philistines, David has been greatly concerned for Saul and his beloved friend Jonathan, not to mention the rest of his countrymen. During his pursuit of the Amalekite raiding party and the ensuing battle, David had little time to think about how things were back in Israel. Now, for three days David and his men have been back in Ziklag, wondering how the war is going, or perhaps, how it concluded (1:1–2).

The Amalekite messenger who brings David the news ran some one hundred miles to reach him at Ziklag. His clothing is torn and dust is upon his head. It is a sign of mourning. Reaching David, this young man falls on the ground before him, prostrating himself as though approaching royalty. He brings David news of the death of many Israelites, including Saul and Jonathan (1:3–4).

Demystifying 2 Samuel

The transition from 1 to 2 Samuel is virtually seamless, which is actually the case in the original Hebrew text. In the original text, both 1 and 2 Samuel were contained in one book. The book was divided by the translators of the Septuagint. Since the division, all subsequent Bibles have followed this precedent, calling these two books 1 and 2 Samuel. It is therefore very natural for us to move from 1 Samuel to 2 Samuel without noticing much change.

David is unwilling to accept this man's report without some verification and immediately begins to question him. The young man explains how he came upon Saul, mortally wounded, on Mount Gilboa. There he obliges the king's request to slay him. The messenger seems to think that David will be ready to reward him, even for his role in Saul's death (1:5–10).

The young man sees Saul as David's enemy, an obstacle to his rise to the throne. He sees Saul's death as good news to David and killing Saul as putting him out of his misery. But David sees it much more simply: This man killed the Lord's anointed. It does not matter that Saul would have died anyway and that he made David's life difficult. It does not matter that Saul was suffering or wanted to die. And it does not matter that the Philistines may soon have been upon him. This man killed the Lord's anointed, and now David wants him put to death.

David's response is quite different than the young Amalekite expects it to be. He is grief-stricken over the defeat of Israel and the death of Saul. He is devastated by the death of his closest friend, Jonathan. Any thought of personal gain at the expense of others is cast aside. David sets the pace in the mourning, and his men promptly follow his lead (1:11–16).

1:17–27

DAVID'S LAMENT

This eulogy, or dirge, is a special labor of his love. David's eulogy is a psalm that mourns the deaths of Saul and Jonathan. It says nothing negative about Saul, but instead honors both Saul and Jonathan as fallen heroes. David not only restrains himself from speaking ill of the dead, he honors Saul and Jonathan as war heroes, as men worthy of respect and honor. David's psalm begins by focusing on Saul and ends with the focus on Jonathan.

David's psalm appears to be an expression and consequence of the covenant between David and Jonathan. We have seen the covenant made between these two men (1 Samuel 18) implemented (1 Samuel 19:1–7) and then extended and reaffirmed (1 Samuel 20; 23). By his eulogy, David is already blessing Jonathan and his descendants. David's psalm has been written for a much wider audience than David and his six hundred men. Not only does David wish to honor Saul and Jonathan, he wants all of the sons of Judah to join him (2 Samuel 1:18), and thus instructs that this song be taught to them.

Take It Home

David sets an example of trusting that God will write history, and as God's servant, he must bring proper honor to Saul and Jonathan. His eulogy reflects the forgiveness that he had already exercised toward Saul. The book of Proverbs teaches that the wise person carefully chooses what to say, and how and when to say it. The New Testament reminds us that we should speak only that which edifies the hearers (1 Corinthians 14:4–5, 17, 26).

2 SAMUEL 2:1–32

DAVID BECOMES KING

David Anointed King over Judah	2:1–11
War with the House of Saul	2:12–32

Setting Up the Section

Now that the grieving is over, it is time for David to take his rightful place as king of Israel. Yet there are some obstacles that still remain in his way, as the next several chapters reveal.

📄 **2:1–11**

DAVID ANOINTED KING OVER JUDAH

David seeks divine guidance and is divinely directed to go up to the city of Hebron. After David, his wives, and the rest of his followers arrive at Hebron with their families, the men of Judah anoint David as king (2:1-4). David's graciousness toward the men of Jabesh-gilead (2:4-7) gives the people of Israel an excellent opportunity to make David their king as well. It seems from Abner's words in 3:17-19 that the men of Israel not only know David has been designated as Saul's replacement, but that they want this. The problem is Abner. This cousin of Saul opposes David's reign in Saul's place and orchestrates events so that Ish-bosheth, a surviving son of Saul, becomes king over the rest of Israel. This delays David's reign for several years (2:8-11).

Demystifying 2 Samuel

Abner is the commander of Saul's army, but even more important, he is Saul's cousin. As Abner has much to gain from Saul's appointment as Israel's king, he also has much to lose if Saul is removed. Abner knows that David is the one Samuel anointed as Saul's replacement. Once Saul is dead, Abner is the one who actively resists David's appointment as king in Saul's place. It would not be a stretch to assume Abner fed Saul false information—information that made David look like an adversary who must be hunted down and put to death. Abner is no friend of David's, nor is he a good friend to his cousin Saul.

📖 2:12–32

WAR WITH THE HOUSE OF SAUL

The rivalry between the Benjamites and the house of David continued to grow. Their military leaders are Abner (Benjamites/Israelites) and Joab (Judah).

In the midst of the fighting, Asahel, brother of Abishai and Joab, is hot on the heels of Abner. Abner does not wish to kill Asahel, but the young man is not willing to give up the chase. Finally, after failing to talk Asahel out of his pursuit, Abner kills him. It is almost an act of self-defense, but Joab will never accept the death of his brother at the hand of Abner. He is intent upon revenge (2:18–25).

Both Abner and Joab pave the way for a future division. This text describes the origin of one of many cracks in the foundation of the united nation of Israel, and this crack will develop over time into a gaping chasm, one which seems almost impossible to bridge (2:26–3:1).

Take It Home

How many relationships are shattered because of ego and competition? How many marriages are ruined and churches split because we fail to be peacemakers? Many times small decisions and actions can lead to major issues down the road. Something initially seems like such a small thing, but it causes cracks that grow and swallow us whole over time. Let us beware of the rifts that appear in our own relationships because of neglect and begin repairs in earnest before it becomes something too big to mend.

2 SAMUEL 3:1–39

KING DAVID'S HOUSE

Setting Up the Section

The conflict between Abner and Joab continues, and David is forced to wait on the Lord to reunite Israel.

📖 3:1–21

TAKING SIDES

God brings blessing on the house of David, and it grows stronger and larger even in the midst of trial and waiting for David to become king of a united Israel. This family register of births also fleshes out what we know of David's household, mentioning (in addition to the two wives he brought with him) four more wives. Also notable is the introduction of Amnon and Absalom, who later play a prominent role in the tumultuous period of David's kingship following his sin with Bathsheba (3:1–6).

David and Abner have a long history together. In 1 Samuel, we are introduced to Abner, who is not only the commander of Saul's army, but also Saul's chief of security. While pursuing David, Saul sleeps in the center of his troops, with Abner right beside him. If anyone attempts to harm Saul, they have to get past his troops and Abner. On one occasion Saul and his men are divinely anesthetized (1 Samuel 26:12), allowing David to obtain Saul's spear and water jug. David specifically calls out Abner and accuses him of dereliction of duty, and thus he is worthy of death (1 Samuel 26:14–16). David's words publicly humiliate Abner.

Despite his role in Saul's army, Abner is not mentioned from 1 Samuel 26 to 2 Samuel 2. Here in chapter 3, however, Abner approaches David with the offer to make him king. He claims that the land is his and that he is in charge. If David will but make a covenant with Abner, Abner will handle the rest. He promises to bring all Israel over to David (2 Samuel 3:6–12). David initially accepts Abner's offer of the kingdom with one condition: that he be given back his wife, Michal. David has loyalty to his wife (1 Samuel 25:44) and regards her return as an important reunion for his household, especially because she is from the house of Saul. Ish-bosheth grants this request to David (2 Samuel 3:13–16).

Before his death, Abner meets with the leaders of both sides. There is an agreement in principle. All that is left to do is finalize it. It seems that if he had lived, he would have done as he promised (3:17–21).

📄 **3:22–39**

JOAB MURDERS ABNER

Joab returns from a raid and discovers that David has formed an alliance with Abner, who he is still angry with over the death of his brother, Asahel. He does not kill Abner in the context of war—which would not be viewed as a murder but a necessary part of war (see 3:28–34; 1 Kings 2:30–33). Instead, Joab clearly believes his own position is threatened and calls Abner back. In a private conversation of which David is unaware, Joab murders Abner to avenge the blood of his brother (2 Samuel 3:22–27).

When David learns of the murder of Abner by Joab, he publicly renounces the actions of Joab as reprehensible. There is no excuse for what he has done. David condemns the murder and calls down divine judgment on Joab and his family (3:28–29). David then mourns the death of Abner, seeing to it that his burial is honorable, even if his death is not (he dies the death of a fool). David not only walks behind the bier, weeping loudly and chanting a lament for Abner, he also refuses to eat all day long. It is obvious to all that David had no part in the death of Abner (3:31–39). David's standing with the people continues to increase.

Critical Observation

God providentially removes Abner so that David will not become king because of him. Abner's reasons for switching his allegiance from Ish-bosheth to David are questionable. Abner's approach to David seems similar to Satan's approach to our Lord in His temptation (Matthew 4:1–11; Luke 4:1–12). Like Satan, Abner claims that the kingdom he offers is really his (compare 2 Samuel 3:12; Luke 4:5–7). Abner wants David to enter into a covenant with him (2 Samuel 3:12), but when David does become king of all Israel, he enters into a covenant with the people with the Lord's favor (2 Samuel 5:3).

2 SAMUEL 4:1–12

WAITING ON THE LORD 4:1–12

Setting Up the Section

As the conflict continues to sort itself out, David exemplifies patience during a tough time of transitioning power.

📖 4:1–12

WAITING ON THE LORD

Although the Lord had anointed David as the next king, Abner had installed Ish-bosheth as Saul's replacement. With the death of Abner at the hand of Joab, Ish-bosheth loses all his courage. He could hardly stand up to Abner, let alone even think about standing up against David. Now Ish-bosheth is on his own, knowing that Abner had already set up David to rule in his place (4:1).

Two men think they are the solution. These men are fellow members of the tribe of Benjamin and commanders of divisions of Israelite soldiers (4:2–3). They take matters into their own hands and proceed to brutally kill Ish-bosheth in his own home while he is lying in bed (4:5–8). They do not understand David's love for Saul or his commitment to protect the lives of his offspring and the honor of his name (1 Samuel 24:16–22). David refuses to look the other way when others do evil to facilitate his ascent to the throne. He understands what being God's king is all about and trusts that God will make him king as long as he honors Him (4:9–12).

Here we are introduced to Mephibosheth, Jonathan's lame son, who will be honored with David's blessing in chapter 9 (4:4).

Critical Observation

David waits fifteen years from the time he is first anointed by Samuel to the time he becomes king over Judah. Even after David is anointed as king of Judah, he must wait a full seven years to be anointed king of all Israel. This means David waited more than twenty years of his life to be made king. How David handled this two-decade delay is the subject of this message. As David waits on the Lord, the divisions around him splinter and crackle relationships even among his closest friends and family. This is a reoccurring theme in his life—how sin can come between even the closest allies to make them enemies. David has gone through many different experiences, all of which will make him a better king for having endured them. He is now much better prepared to reign as Israel's king (5:4–6).

The promise God made to Israel and to David took a long time being fulfilled. David becomes king of Israel after a considerable delay and with a great deal of adversity. This is typical of the way God brings about His promises and purposes. God is not in a hurry. It is in times of waiting for God that many have failed in their faith and obedience. Waiting tests our faith and endurance. Like David, waiting is a significant part of each of our lives, and God will reward us if we are patient and faithful as we await His blessing.

2 SAMUEL 5:1–25

DAVID: KING OF ISRAEL

Setting Up the Section

Ish-bosheth has just been murdered in what concludes a bloody and difficult phase of David's coming to power as king of Israel. Now God has new lessons for the king to learn as he takes over Jerusalem and meets with an old enemy, the Philistines.

📄 **5:1–16**

JERUSALEM: A PLACE OF ONE'S OWN

The Israelites are the ones who come to David in Hebron and the ones who recognize and anoint him as their king (5:1–3). The people are the initiators, just as they were the initiators when Saul became their king. The significance of the submission of the Israelites to David as God's king is best understood in comparison and contrast to 1 Kings 8–12, where the people demand a king, and Saul is given to them as their first king.

In the earlier situation, the Israelites were rebelling against God, demanding a king without being willing to repent (1 Samuel 8). Here, in stark contrast, the Israelite leaders are acting out of obedience to God, not in rebellion against Him. The king they gain in David is, in some measure, the king they deserve. When they approach David, they acknowledge several vitally important truths, which are the basis for David's kingship and thus their submission to him. They recognize that they share a common heritage with David—that they are under the same original covenant with God and that God desires unity for His people. The Israelites also recognize that David has provided leadership for many years now, and they accept David as God's anointed choice for the throne. Thus, David becomes king of all Israel.

At the same time, he finally obtains a place of his own. The place has been known as *Jebus* up to this point in time, and its inhabitants are called the *Jebusites*. But from this text onward, Jebus becomes Jerusalem, and Zion is called the City of David. God continues to bless and increase David's power and his household (5:6–16). In the next chapter, Jerusalem will become the dwelling place of God, as the ark of the covenant is brought to the city where Solomon will later build the temple and where Israel's coming king, Jesus Christ, will eventually ride in triumphantly on a donkey one week before His crucifixion.

Demystifying 2 Samuel

Jebus is first mentioned as a city occupied by true Canaanites (Genesis 10:15–16), the descendants of Canaan, the third son of Ham (Genesis 10:6). It is this Ham who saw the nakedness of Noah (Genesis 9:22) and who brought a curse upon himself and his descendants (Genesis 9:25). Also in Jebus is Mount Moriah, where Abraham offered up his son, Isaac, which is the same mountain on which Solomon will later build the temple (2 Chronicles 3:1). When the Israelites took over the promised land, they failed to completely drive out the Canaanites from Jebus (Joshua 15:63). This leads to a kind of coexistence, which results in the Israelites embracing the sins of the Jebusites and oppression from their neighbors as a divine chastening (Judges 3:1–8).

David recognizes that no kingdom can be viewed with fear (or even respect) if it is not able to expel its enemies from its midst. The Jebusites need to be dealt with, and David knows it. It is time for these enemies of God to be defeated. The defeat of the Jebusites and the taking of Jebus is the first step in Israel's conquest of their enemies—a conquest that is partial in the times of Joshua and the judges. This victory will overshadow the victory of Saul and the Israelites over the Ammonites (1 Samuel 11).

The possession of Jebus as David's new capital will unite Israel. The city is virtually on the border of Judah and Benjamin. It is a city that neither the sons of Judah nor the sons of Benjamin have been able to capture. Thus, taking this city as his capital will not seem to favor either of these two tribes. In addition to all of this, its natural setting makes it difficult to defeat (which is why the Israelites had not taken and held it before). It is in the hill country, on the top of more than one mountain, and is surrounded by valleys. With a little work, it is a virtual fortress (2 Samuel 5:9).

DAVID DEFEATS THE PHILISTINES

The Philistines, unlike the Israelites, will not submit to David as God's king. They attack David, seeking to kill him and to remove the threat that he and a united Israel pose. Not once, but twice, these Philistines come against David and the army of Israel. And twice God gives David the victory over his enemies. Those who receive David as God's king are blessed; those who reject David as God's king are crushed (5:17–22).

It is interesting to note that once David is established as king of Israel, the first enemy he meets is the Philistines. It parallels the first battle that David ever finds himself in after he is anointed by Samuel as the future king—his battle with Goliath, the giant Philistine who had frightened all of Israel's forces (1 Samuel 17). The picture here is of God going ahead of David into the battle—as indicated by the sound of marching in the tree tops—and delivering the victory to His servant (2 Samuel 5:23–25).

2 SAMUEL 6:1–23

GOD RAINED ON DAVID'S PARADE

Setting Up the Section

Some days, no matter how carefully we plan and orchestrate events, things just have a way of going wrong. And sometimes even the most well-intentioned actions can inflict the wrath of God.

THE ARK BROUGHT TO JERUSALEM

God gave very clear instructions about the ark of God. He not only gave specific instructions about how it should be made, He also indicated who should carry it and how it should be transported from one place to another. In Numbers 5, God tells exactly how the tabernacle should be taken down and carried to its next resting place.

No wonder Uzzah is struck dead for having laid hands on the ark. The ark is holy. It is not be touched. By using poles, men could transport the ark without touching the ark itself. And these men, walking in step with one another, give the ark stability. Putting the ark on the ox cart made it susceptible to the movements of the cart and less stable, and thus more likely to fall off the cart. The only way to keep this from happening is to grab hold of the ark, as Uzzah does, and to die. Uzzah is a reminder to us that God's holiness is such that sinful people cannot draw near to Him unless He provides the means to do so (6:1–8).

David is struck with fear of the Lord and decides to let the ark remain outside the city in the house of Obed-edom, the Gittite. God's blessing on the house of Obed-edom, where the ark rests for three months, assures David that the nearness of the ark is a blessing, but that it must be brought to Jerusalem in accordance with God's directions. David resumes bringing the ark into the city—this time being careful to observe God's instructions.

The ark is carried six steps, and then a sacrifice is offered. Those first six steps are no doubt the tensest steps of the entire journey. As the journey continues, the men's courage and joy increase. Soon there is great celebration as they make their way to the holy city.

Along the way, David and his entourage dance and worship God and offer sacrifices as signs of humility before God (6:9–15).

Critical Observation

The ark had accompanied the Israelites wherever they went while they were in the wilderness. It went before the Israelites when they crossed the Jordan River (Joshua 3:14–17). We find the ark mentioned quite often in 1 and 2 Samuel. Samuel sleeps near the ark as a child (1 Samuel 3:3). When the Israelites are being beaten by the Philistines, they unwisely take the ark into battle with them as a kind of magic charm. They not only lose the battle, they lose the ark as well (1 Samuel 4). The next two chapters (5–6) of 1 Samuel are the account of how God plagues the Philistines, and how they finally decide they do not want the ark among them. In Exodus 25, God tells Moses He will meet with him and speak to him from above the ark, between the cherubim (Exodus 25:22). God chose to manifest His presence in the tabernacle, specifically from the ark. When God's glory first filled the tabernacle, even Moses was not able to enter (Exodus 40:34–35). Sinful men cannot get too close to a holy God.

📖 6:16–23

JUDGING JOY

It seems there is only one person in all of Israel who does not and will not enter into the spirit of rejoicing and celebration, and that person is Michal, David's wife. The author of the Chronicles makes very little of this, devoting only one verse to the subject and informing us that as Michal looks on, she despises her husband in her heart for his role in the celebration (1 Chronicles 15:29).

Michal has no intention of being a part of the celebration, and she proceeds to distract from David's praise and blessing. She is not angry with David for doing something wrong and standing out from the rest of the people. She is angry with David for behaving like the common people and not acting like a king as he worships God. He had humbled himself, demeaned himself, and lowered himself. And Michal judges David for his joy (2 Samuel 6:16–23).

David serves as a prototype of Christ in this text and beyond. He is both a king and a priest (he wears a linen ephod). David lays aside his royal robes and humbles himself, just as our Lord lays aside His royal robes and humbles Himself (see John 13; Philippians 2:5–8).

Critical Observation

Michal serves as a kind of prototype of the self-righteous scribes and Pharisees of Jesus' time. As Michal had come to enjoy her position as daughter of the king, so the scribes had come to enjoy their privileged position as religious leaders in Israel. They fear losing their power and status. They challenge Jesus about His authority. They look upon the Lord with disdain because He associates with the lowly. Just as Michal bears no fruit (in other words, children), neither do the scribes and Pharisees. Those who worship God must come to Him in humility, not in pride. Michal is the only person not joyfully worshiping God. No wonder, since she is preoccupied with herself.

2 SAMUEL 7:1–29

BUILDING GOD'S HOUSE

Setting Up the Section

David begins to formulate a plan to build a house for God. However, Nathan reveals that God will build for David, and it surpasses the temple-house David wants to build for God.

📄 7:1–17

GOD'S PROMISE TO DAVID

To the people of Israel (and those outside Israel for that matter), David is the highest authority in the land. But in relation to God, David is merely a servant. David is living in a palace, and God is living in a tent, at least in David's mind. David almost appears to want to give God a helping hand. David has a bright idea, but it does not correspond with God's plan as revealed to Nathan. David is referred to as the *king* (7:1–3), but when God refers to David, He calls him His *servant* (7:5). The question God asks David sets the tone for what is to follow: Are you the one who should build my house?

God gave Israel the tabernacle; the temple is David's idea. God explains that as the Creator of all things, He neither requires nor can be confined by a dwelling made by human hands. In short, God does not need a temple, and He does not ask for one. God reminds David who is taking care of whom. God gently rebukes David for this heady plan. David has taken the wrong posture of helping out God, rather than being the one who has constantly been helped *by* God (7:5–7).

After pointing out all that He has done for David and Israel in the past, God goes on to tell David that he hasn't seen the best of it yet. God promises to appoint a place for His people where they will be planted. They will have a place of their own (as David intended to give God a place of His own), and they will dwell in peace there because the wicked will no longer afflict them. God has been behind all of David's successes, and now He is promising even greater glory. God announces to David that He is going to build a house for him by blessing his descendants and ultimately bringing the Messiah through his bloodline (7:8–15).

David will have sons, and these sons will become sons of God in that they will rule over Israel. But there will be one very special Son, and through Him all of the promises God has made here and elsewhere (pertaining to the kingdom of God) will be fulfilled, either in His first coming or in His return to the earth. It is in this Son that all of David's hopes, all of Israel's hopes, and all of humanity's hopes are fulfilled—this is the essence of what is often called the Davidic Covenant (7:16–17).

📄 7:18–29

DAVID'S PRAYER

David now stands in awe of the fact that God takes him, a man of no status or standing, and makes him king of Israel. This, too, is what God has reminded David through Nathan (7:8–9). David sees his standing and status as Israel's king as the result of God's sovereign grace, and not as the recognition of his potential greatness. It is amazing how pride and arrogance can distort one's thinking. No wonder humility is the starting point, the prerequisite, for wisdom (Proverbs 11:2; 15:33; 18:12; 22:4; 29:23).

God has done great things for David, but these were not done for David alone. God has worked in David and through David to bring about the fulfillment of His promises to the entire nation of Israel. Verses 23 and 24 recount the greatness of God as revealed in His acts on behalf of His people, Israel. The reason for David's confidence is God, not himself (7:18–24).

The presumptuous self-confidence that characterizes David in the early verses of this chapter is gone, replaced by a humble confidence based in the God who made it. God has promised this good thing to His servant (not to the king). The promise is clear, and any promise made by God is a sure thing. Thus David petitions God for its fulfillment (7:25–29).

Take It Home

We need to be on guard against prideful thoughts of our own contribution to the kingdom of God. It is always He who will be carrying us, rather than us carrying Him. How easily we begin to focus on what we have done and can do for God, rather than on all He has done and will do for and through us.

2 SAMUEL 8:1–10:19

WAR AND PEACE

Setting Up the Section

David uses his newfound power at war with the enemies of Israel in chapters 8 and 10. In chapter 9, we learn of how David's kindness toward Mephibosheth allows him to use his power to fulfill his covenant commitment to his beloved friend, Jonathan, and his promise to Saul.

📄 8:1–18

DAVID'S VICTORIES

The Philistines, located to Israel's west, are troublesome to Israel (Genesis 26:1, 8, 14–15, 18), especially from the time of the judges onward (Judges 3:3, 31; 10:6–7). Samson fought with the Philistines (Judges 13–16). It was the Philistines who took the lives of Eli's two sons and indirectly caused the death of Eli, as well as taking the ark of God (1 Samuel 4–7). Jonathan attacked a Philistine garrison in Israel, precipitating another confrontation with the Philistines (1 Samuel 13:3–14).

David killed Goliath, a Philistine, and then led the pursuit of the Philistines (1 Samuel 17). It was the Philistines who eventually defeated the army of Israel and killed Saul and his two sons (1 Samuel 31). It was also among the Philistines that David sought and found sanctuary (1 Samuel 21:10–15; 27). Once David becomes king, the Philistines think it's best to attack quickly in an attempt to nullify the threat he will pose to them. They fail, and now David will subdue them, ending their tyranny for some time. We know from the parallel passage in 1 Chronicles 18:1 that the chief city is actually Gath. No wonder David is able to capture it; he knows it well.

The killing of the Moabites seems amazingly harsh and barbaric. But standard warfare rules during this era usually dictated killing all of one's enemies. So the fact that David spares one-third of the Moabites (2 Samuel 8:2) demonstrates his mercy. As king of Israel, David is God's representative. These Moabites are enemies of Israel, and therefore they are enemies of God. As such, they all deserve to die. The wonder is not that two-thirds of the Moabites are killed, but that one-third is left to live. And in the killing of the two-thirds, any thought of resisting David or rebelling against him is laid to rest.

This is a period for David where Israel celebrates many victories. The outcome of all of David's activities is that he defeats his enemies (8:1–13). Israelite garrisons are found among the neighboring nations (8:14), whereas foreign garrisons had once been in Israel (1 Samuel 10:5; 13:3–4). This means they will no longer be able to resist, harass, or oppress Israel for some time. There will be peace in the land, just as God promised.

All of the success David achieves is from the hand of God (2 Samuel 8:6, 14). David's dominion grows such that he has to add administrative and secretarial personnel to his staff, recorded in verses 15–18. Where David rules, there is justice and righteousness (8:15). As a result, David's name becomes great (8:13), just as God had promised (7:9). In addition, the tribute paid to David is great. He obtains great quantities of silver, gold, and bronze (8:7–12). These riches are stored, and at least some become building materials for the temple that Solomon will construct (1 Chronicles 18:8).

📄 9:1–13

DAVID AND MEPHIBOSHETH

David is a man who makes promises and keeps them. Before he became Israel's king, he made promises to both Jonathan and Saul. To Jonathan, he promised to protect his life and to show loving-kindness to his house forever (1 Samuel 20:12–17). To Saul, he vowed not to cut off his descendants after him (1 Samuel 24:21–22). Now Saul and Jonathan are dead, and David is king.

David not only remembers his commitment to Saul, he goes far beyond it. It seems as though all of Saul's descendants are dead. No descendant of Saul approaches David, seeking his favor. David is now in a position to carry out his promise to Jonathan—all he needs is one of his descendants. David inquires as to whether there is a descendant of Saul to whom he may show kindness for Jonathan's sake (2 Samuel 9:1). David speaks of this act of kindness as the kindness of God (9:3).

Only one of Jonathan's sons is still living—Mephibosheth, who is crippled in both feet. Ziba doubts David will want him to be the one to whom he shows favor. Yet David summons him and promises to restore to Mephibosheth all the land which had belonged to his father, and which he had evidently lost sometime after the death of Saul and his father. Not only will David restore all that to which Mephibosheth is heir, he will make him his regular guest at the palace. Mephibosheth is overcome with gratitude and relief, falling prostrate before David once again, calling attention to the fact that he is a dead dog (9:8). David uses this very expression to refer to himself in speaking to King Saul (1 Samuel 24:14).

Demystifying 2 Samuel

At this time, when one king prevailed over another by winning in battle, he would cut off the thumbs and the big toes of his opponent, and then keep them as a kind of showpiece. These incapacitated kings would sit under the table of the victorious king, getting the scraps, like dogs. These defeated kings were not honored guests; they were trophies of war. David would have none of this with regard to Mephibosheth. He does not want him at his table as a subjected foe, but as an honored guest, the son of his beloved friend, Jonathan. It is an amazing act of grace (9:7–13).

DAVID DEFEATS THE AMMONITES

Hanun is the Son of Nahash, who as king of the Ammonites has been on good terms with David. When David hears of Nahash's death, he sends a delegation to Ammon to convey his respect for Nahash and to mourn his death. The advisors of this newly installed king give him some bad counsel. They assure Hanun that David's intentions cannot be honorable. He is only sending these men as spies to obtain intelligence so that he can attack them, as he has so many other nations. This explanation of events gives Hanun the excuse he is looking for—a reason to break the alliance his father made with David and Israel.

David receives word that his delegation has been abused and humiliated. Their beards are, for the Hebrews, a mark of dignity. Hanun has half of the beard of each man shaved off. In addition, he has their garments cut off to embarrass them. David takes pity on the dishonored delegation. He sends to meet them and then instructs them to wait in Jericho until their beards grow back, and then to return to Israel.

We are not told that David summoned his troops, intending to go to war. We are told that the sons of Ammon recognize that they have angered David (10:6). Rather than apologize or attempt to reconcile with David, the sons of Ammon seek to make an alliance which will strengthen them in their conflict with Israel. Syrians from several regions are hired as mercenaries (10:6). Only after David learns of this military buildup does he call his army into active duty.

David and his forces draw up to battle with the Ammonites and their Syrian mercenaries. This coalition army divides into two groups, intending to attack the Israelites from the front and the rear. When Joab sees this, he divides the army of Israel into two forces. He leads one division, and his brother Abishai leads the other. Joab sets himself against the Syrians, and Abishai is to fight the Ammonites. If either of the two becomes hard-pressed by their opponent, the other is to come to their aid.

Critical Observation

The political and military intrigue in 2 Samuel 8 and 10 are used providentially by God to give Israel the land and the victory God had long before promised His people (Genesis 12:1–3). The tribute that David obtains from his subjected enemies seems to provide the raw materials that will be required for the building of the temple. These events fulfill not only the promise of God made to David in 2 Samuel 7, but also the promises God made long before to Abraham and the patriarchs and to Moses.

Take It Home

In chapters 8–10, David serves as a prototype of Christ. He establishes his kingdom by prevailing over the enemies of Israel, subjecting them to himself. On the other hand, David shows mercy toward Mephibosheth, the son of Jonathan and the grandson of Saul. Mephibosheth is the sole heir of Saul, the last candidate for king. Usually, a king in David's place would kill such potential contenders to the throne, but David seeks this man out and shows mercy to him. This is not because of what he can contribute to David and to his kingdom (he is handicapped, which in those days makes him useless in the eyes of men). It is because of David's love for his friend, Jonathan, Mephibosheth's father. This serves to remind us how the two dimensions of God—sovereignty and grace—combine perfectly. God's grace is sovereign grace, not earned or deserved.

2 SAMUEL 11:1–27

DAVID COMMITS ADULTERY

David with Bathsheba	11:1–4
David and Uriah	11:5–27

Setting Up the Section

The picture of David at the pinnacle of his success in chapters 8–10 sets the scene for David's fall to the depths in chapters 11–12. David's experience is proof that spiritual highs do not assure that we cannot fall, but may in some ways prepare us for a fall.

📖 11:1–4

DAVID WITH BATHSHEBA

Up until this point, David has been leading his men in battle. But here, as spring returns and the Israelites go back to fight the Ammonites, David suddenly steps back from his duty and stays in Jerusalem. David is failing to lead the people in subduing their enemies and instead has become arrogant in his victories. David is starting to become like Saul in that he is willing to let others go out and fight his battles for him. Among those David is willing to send in his place are Joab and Abishai.

Joab is not the commander of the army of Israel by David's choice. David had distanced himself from Joab and Abishai because of the death of Abner (2 Samuel 3:26–30). Joab became the commander of Israel's armed forces because he was the first to accept David's challenge to attack Jebus (1 Chronicles 11:4–6). Suddenly, David is willing to stay at home and leave the whole of Israel's armed forces under Joab's command. David is probably not motivated by trust in Joab as much as he is by his disdain for the hardship of the campaign to take Rabbah (2 Samuel 11:1–2).

A relaxed and aimless King David, shirking his duties in battle, spies a beautiful woman bathing one evening while strolling on his rooftop. He learns that she is married to a Hittite named Uriah, who is a soldier in his army. Bathsheba is perhaps the most famous object of desire in the whole Bible because David, a man after God's own heart, is brought down from a place of glory because of his adultery with her and the resulting cover-up (11:3–5).

Many wish to view this text in a way that forces Bathsheba to share David's guilt by assuming that she somehow seduced him. In fact, when Nathan pronounces divine judgment upon David for his sin, Bathsheba and Uriah are depicted as the victims, not the villains. The tragedies that take place in David's household are the consequence of his sin, just as Nathan indicates (12:10–12).

The root of David's sin is not low self-esteem; it is arrogance. He has come to see himself as better than the rest of the Israelites. They need to go to war; he does not. They need to sleep in the open field; he needs to get his rest in his palace bed. They can have a wife; he can have whatever woman he wants.

David's sin is the abuse of power. In the previous chapters, David employs his God-given power to defeat the enemies of God and of Israel. He uses his power as Israel's king to fulfill his covenant with David and his promise to Saul by restoring to Mephibosheth his family property and by making him a son at his table. Now, David, drunk with his power, uses it to indulge himself at the expense of others. Sexual abuse and sexual harassment are two common ways people, even today, abuse their power, and just as David quickly discovers, they remain some of the most destructive sins.

Take It Home

Prosperity is as dangerous—if not more dangerous—as poverty and adversity. Often when it appears everything is going right, we are in the greatest danger, because we forget that we need God and that we must rely on His power. No longer on our guard, we can easily become drunk with our own power and control. Yet this will backfire just as it does for King David. How can you remember God when times are good? What can we learn from David's sins of omission as well as his sins of commission? (Examine 1 John 1:7–9; 2:1–2; 3:4–9 for some New Testament guidelines for avoiding sin.)

📖 11:5–27

DAVID AND URIAH

One of the tragic aspects of this story is that the sequence of sin in David's life does not end with his adulterous union with Bathsheba. It instead leads to a deceptive plot to make her husband, Uriah, appear to be the father of David's child with Bathsheba and culminates in David's murder of Uriah and his marriage to Bathsheba (11:5–27).

Throughout history, many attempts have been made to cover up incompetence, immorality, and even crimes. In the Bible, cover-ups appear early: Adam and Eve sought to cover their nakedness and to hide from God, not realizing their efforts betrayed their sin and guilt. Second Samuel 11 is one of the great cover-up attempts of all time, and like so many, it fails miserably.

It seems likely that David and Uriah are not total strangers, but that they know each other to some degree. Uriah is listed among the mighty warriors of David (2 Samuel 23:39; 1 Chronicles 11:41). Some of these mighty men came to David early, while he was in the cave of Adullam (1 Samuel 22:1-2), and likely among them were brothers Joab, Abishai, and Asahel (2 Samuel 23:18, 24; 1 Chronicles 11:26). Others joined David at Ziklag (1 Chronicles 12), and still other great warriors joined with David at Hebron (1 Chronicles 12:38-40).

It seems unlikely that Uriah is ignorant of what David has done and of what he is trying to accomplish by calling him home to Jerusalem. Rumors must have been circulating around Jerusalem about David and Bathsheba and could easily have reached the Israelite army which had besieged Rabbah. Uriah not only refuses to go to his house and sleep with his wife, he sleeps at the doorway of the king's house, in the midst of his servants. He has many witnesses to testify that any child borne by his wife during this time is not his child. Bathsheba is not said to have any part in David's scheme to deceive Uriah or to bring about his death, much less any knowledge of what David is doing (2 Samuel 11:6-13).

When the deception of making the child appear to be Uriah's fails, David, instead of repenting, escalates the sin by ordering to have Uriah sent to the front lines of the battle—a virtual death sentence for an innocent man. Certain biblical figures may cause us to question whether they really ever came to faith in God, such as Balaam, Samson, and Saul. But we have no such questions regarding David. He is not only a believer, he is a model believer—a man after God's heart. Nevertheless, David, in spite of his trust in God, in spite of his marvelous times of worship and his beautiful psalms, falls deeply into sin. If David can fall, anyone can (11:14-26). And that is precisely what Paul warns believers about in 1 Corinthians 10:11-12.

Take It Home

Uriah is a reminder to us that God does not always deliver the righteous from the hands of the wicked immediately, or even in this lifetime. In the Old Testament, as in the New, God sometimes delivers His people from the hands of wicked men, but often He does not. Their deliverance comes with the coming of the Messiah, the Lord Jesus Christ. Uriah, like all of the Old Testament saints, dies without receiving his full reward, and that is because God wants him to wait. Uriah is not immediately delivered from the hands of the wicked.

2 SAMUEL 12:1–31

DAVID AND GOD

Setting Up the Section

In this section God sends the prophet Nathan to confront David about his sin.

📄 **12:1–6**

A POWERFUL STORY

Nathan is a prophet and a friend to David. Even one of David's sons is named Nathan (5:14). David informs Nathan of his desire to build a temple in 2 Samuel 7. Nathan will name Bathsheba and David's second son (12:25). He will remain loyal to the king and to Solomon when Adonijah seeks to usurp the throne (1 Kings 2). Nathan does not come to David only as God's spokesman; he comes to David as his friend.

Nathan confronts David about his sin by telling him a story about sheep—one greedy shepherd has taken everything from a lowly farmer who had only one sheep. The story, of course, parallels the actions of David with Bathsheba and Uriah. David, a former shepherd himself, immediately recognizes the wrongfulness of the actions of the greedy murderous shepherd in the story (2 Samuel 12:1–4). David identifies two evils that have been committed by this fictional rich man. First, the man has stolen a lamb, for which the law prescribes restitution (Exodus 22:1). Second, David recognizes what he views as the greater sin, and that is the rich man's total lack of compassion (12:5–6).

David does not see what is coming. The story Nathan tells makes David furious. David is furious because a rich man stole and slaughtered a poor man's pet. He does not yet see the connection to his lack of compassion for stealing a poor man's beloved companion, his wife. The slaughtering of Uriah is most certainly an act that lacks compassion. The crowning touch in David's display of righteous indignation is found in the religious flavoring he gives it by the words, "as surely as the LORD lives" (12:5 NLT).

📄 **12:7–12**

NATHAN'S INDICTMENT

David has just sprung the trap on himself, and Nathan is about to let him know about it. The first thing Nathan does is dramatically indict David as the culprit. In stunned silence, David now listens to the charges against him. Through Nathan, God speaks to David as though he has forgotten all the things God has given him, or rather as though he has come to take credit for them himself. God reminds David that He has given everything he possesses to him. Has it been so long since David himself was a lowly shepherd boy? David is a rich man because God has made him rich. And if he does not think he is rich enough, God will give more to him. David has begun to cling to his riches rather than to the God who has blessed him (12:7–8).

David was thinking only in terms of the evils the rich man committed against his neighbor, stealing a man's sheep and depriving him of his companion. Put another way, David thinks only in terms of crime and socially unacceptable behavior, not in terms of sin. God wants David to understand that David's evil actions violate God's revealed Word (12:9–10). Nathan draws David's attention to his sin against God and the consequences God has pronounced for his sin (12:11–12).

Critical Observation

First and foremost, David's sin is against God. He has ceased to humbly acknowledge God as the giver of all he possesses. He has ceased to look to God to provide him with all his needs and his desires. David has not only stopped relying on God for his needs, he has disobeyed God's commands by committing adultery and murder. David's sin against God manifests itself by the evils he commits against others. Nathan outlines these, employing a repetitive *you* as he speaks to David.

📄 **12:13**

REAL REPENTANCE

Remember that David's repentance is the culmination of a painful process, climaxing in the confrontation of David by Nathan. David's confession follows shortly after the account of his sin. But the text itself indicates that David's sin took place over a considerable period of time, slightly more than nine months by estimation. David knew what he did was wrong, but he chose to persist for a time. He does not confess his sin, and the result is torturous (Psalm 32). While sin has its momentary pleasures (Hebrews 11:25), it eventually grieves the Spirit who indwells us, and thus the believer's spirit can no longer take pleasure in that sin.

Demystifying 2 Samuel

Psalm 32 is one of two psalms (along with Psalm 51) in which David himself reflects on his sin, his repentance, and his recovery. Verses 3 and 4 of Psalm 32 fit between chapters 11 and 12 of 2 Samuel. The confrontation of David by Nathan the prophet, described in 2 Samuel 12, results in David's repentance and confession. But this repentance is not just the fruit of Nathan's rebuke; it is also David's response to the work God has been doing in David's heart before he confesses, while he is still attempting to conceal his sin.

David confesses his sin, without any excuses, without any finger-pointing toward others. He sees that he has sinned against God. Psalms 32 and 51 (both written by David) indicate that David gave his sin a great deal of thought, and the more he reflected on it, the more heinous it became to him. Since these psalms are preserved for worship and for posterity, David's sin and his confession become public knowledge. Ultimately, his sin is against God and God alone. This is not to diminish the evil he had done to Uriah and Bathsheba, but sin is ultimately the breaking of God's law. Crimes are offenses against people, but sin (in this highly specific sense) is only against God, in that it breaks His laws. David had broken at least three laws. He coveted his neighbor's wife, he committed adultery, and he committed murder (Exodus 20:13–14, 17).

David does not presume upon God's grace, expecting to be forgiven and to have his life spared. He knows what he deserves, and he does not ask to escape it. From Psalm 51, we know that David's repentance results in a renewed joy in the presence and service of God, and a commitment to teach others to turn from sin (Psalm 51:8, 12).

Drawing near to God and clinging to Him alone changes David's heart. According to the law, David should have died for his sins. Based upon divine grace through the coming death of Christ, David is forgiven for his sins and assured that he will not die. These words from Nathan must have been a huge relief to David, who knew he did not deserve anything but God's wrath (2 Samuel 12:13).

12:14–31

THE DEATH OF A CHILD

David's sense of relief is short-lived, however, because Nathan is not finished with what he has to say. The child conceived by Bathsheba with David will not live. By taking the life of this child, conceived in sin, God makes a statement to those looking on about how seriously He takes transgression of His law (12:14–15).

In spite of David's sorrow, sincerity, and persistence in petitioning God to spare the child's life, his request is denied. The child indeed dies. David must not have been with the child when it happened, or he would have seen this for himself. David does, however, see his servants whispering to one another, perhaps furtively glancing in his direction as they do so. They are afraid to tell David because they fear he might cause harm. The text is not altogether clear about whom the servants fear David might hurt (12:16–18).

Still David has a remarkable peace about the death of his first child by Bathsheba, a peace which causes those who witness it to marvel and to question David about it. And, as we can see from David's response to the questions posed by his servants, he is able to praise and worship God at a time of loss and sorrow for his child (12:19–23).

Take It Home

The Christian's hope and joy in the midst of trials and tribulations is witness to faith in Jesus Christ. David's servants expect him to react to the death of his son in a very different way. His peace surpasses understanding and his joy and desire to worship God in the midst of tragedy amaze them. David is able to give a reason for his hope (1 Peter 3:15). Even in the worst of circumstances, we must cast ourselves upon the God to whom we have entrusted our souls and our eternal destiny. Our confidence and our joy are in the Lord.

Following the death of their son, David goes to comfort Bathsheba; and as a result of their union, God blesses them with the birth of a second child, Solomon, who will become the next great king of Israel. Nathan prophetically names the son Jedidiah, which means "loved by the Lord." Again, the story of David's life is a study in stark contrasts and how God uses them to teach, train, and refine His servant king (12:24–25). It is significant that the closing action of this section describes David returning to his place as the leader of Israel's army claiming victory over Rabbah of the Ammonites on the people's behalf. This role is the one David had originally shirked when he fell into sin with Bathsheba (12:26–31).

2 SAMUEL 13:1–15:12

TRAGEDY IN THE ROYAL FAMILY

Setting Up the Section

God gives King David power, riches, and prosperity, not because of David's greatness, but because of God's grace. Following the death of David's first son with Bathsheba, David's family continues to experience serious tragedies and trials as a consequence of his sin. Soon, David's sin will divide the nation and deprive David of his throne for a time.

📄 **13:1–36**

AMNON'S SIN AGAINST TAMAR

The character of Amnon warns about the pursuit of fleshly lusts (compare 1 Corinthians 10). Jonadab warns about the danger of using the sins of others to further our own interests, making them a part of our own agenda, rather than paying the price for rebuke and correction. David instructs us concerning passivity toward sin (2 Samuel 13:1–11).

This story of betrayal, lust, rape, and murder demonstrates the divisive power of sin—breaking bonds between individuals, families, and, most seriously, with God. Sin is the root of disunity and division. Amnon has confused his "love" for his sister Tamar with his desire to have sex with her. Obviously, Amnon's love does not stand the test of 1 Corinthians 13. Love is not synonymous with sex. Amnon's brand of love is not at all concerned about respecting the other person or doing what is right, both of which characterize the love that God encourages and prescribes (13:12–16).

Tamar is one of the strongest women in the Bible—and yet she suffers terribly as a result of her brother's sin. She begs him to spare her and still he rapes her and then sends her away to fend for herself. Her brother Absalom takes her in, but because of the sexual crime against her, she remains desolate (13:15–20).

David is furious about the crime committed against his daughter, yet it seems that he does nothing about it. His tangled web of loyalty paralyzes him. David's inaction facilitates the sin of others (13:21–22). Absalom is not willing to deal with Amnon biblically; he wants to get his revenge in his own way. This he does, and in doing so becomes a murderer and a fugitive who will famously challenge his father's throne. From Absalom, we learn the danger of resentment and bitterness even in the midst of righteous anger (13:23–36).

Take It Home

As we examine the tough realities that David's family is dealing with, we are reminded that no one is worthy of eternal life—except Jesus Christ. Every single person is born in sin and fails to live up to God's standard of righteousness (Romans 3:23; 6:23). We all deserve the penalty of death. God, in His mercy and grace, has provided a solution in the person of His Son, Jesus Christ. He came to this earth, adding perfect humanity to His undiminished deity by revealing Himself as God's only way to heaven and eternal life (John 14:6).

📄 **13:37–14:33**

ABSALOM, ABSALOM!

After Absalom murders Amnon, he chooses political asylum in Geshur with his grandfather. David is not wrong to still love this son and yearn to see him. But it would not have been right for David to pardon him so he could return. It would not even have been right to visit him in Geshur. God uses Absalom to continue to draw David closer to Him (13:37–39).

Using trickery and deception, Joab pursues his own self-serving agenda in seeking to manipulate David into bringing Absalom back to Israel. Presumably using Joab's words, a woman from Tekoa is able to get David to commit himself to the safety of her son. Finally, David rules with a divine oath that this son is not to be harmed. Now the woman can appeal to the precedent David has just set (which it seems cannot be changed) and press David to deal similarly with his own son (whose guilt is much more clear [14:1–20]).

David gives in, reluctantly, to Joab's prodding. He tells Joab that he can bring Absalom back to Israel. The assumption is that he will not allow anyone (any avenger) to take Absalom's life. But somewhere along the line, David considers what he has done and makes a change in plans. Absalom is not to be brought back to Israel as though an innocent man, free to come and go as he pleases. Absalom is to be under house arrest, confined to Jerusalem and his own house (14:21–23).

There is a kind of poetic justice in this confinement, as it is Absalom who had confined his sister Tamar to quarters. By confining Tamar to his house, Absalom kept her quiet. He also kept her desolate. All of this enabled him to carry out his evil plan to murder Amnon. Now, David confines Absalom to the same quarters in which he confined his sister.

Absalom has a great deal going for him. He is a good-looking man, without a single flaw. His hair is his crowning glory, and everybody knows it. He has three sons and a beautiful daughter, who also adds to his standing. He is a celebrity of that day. He requests to see the king's face, accepting that the consequence may be death. Even though he is a murderer, his actions prove that he believes he is on the side of justice and that his heart is not repentant (14:25–33).

📖 15:1–12

DAVID HUMILIATED

Absalom is very charming and wins the hearts of the Israelites by promises of justices and displays of affection. Absalom uses his freedom to undermine David's reputation and standing with the people. Absalom's betrayal is the ultimate tragedy—much like Saul's attempts to kill David or Judas's kiss that betrays Christ (15:1–6). Soon, Absalom is in full rebellion, which leads to the division of Israel, and finally the death of Absalom at the hand of Joab. Absalom's life is truly a trail of tears.

We must be careful not to say that God is punishing David for his sins through the suffering of others. Many people will suggest that whenever a person suffers, it is because they are being punished for their sin. Job's friends believed this and continually sought to compel him to repent (Job 4 and 5). Our Lord's disciples assumed the man born blind was this way because of someone's sin (John 9:1–2). There are those whose suffering is the direct result of their sin (Deuteronomy 28:15), but this is not always the explanation for suffering. Sometimes the righteous suffer for being righteous (1 Peter 4).

This text has much to say about parenting. The Bible is amply clear that there are no perfect parents—that nature and nurture are surely two parts of the human condition. Even the godliest men and women parent children who rebel against God (think of Eli, Samuel, Saul, and now David). Obviously, parents honor God by being good to their children and teaching them the way of the Lord, but each person is ultimately responsible for his or her own choices.

Absalom is a man who "bites the hand that feeds him." He lacks any sense of debt to his father, and there is no evidence of gratitude on his part. But more than this, there is absolutely no true submission to his father-king. Absalom sees himself as next in line for the throne. He does not submit himself to his father. Instead he uses his position and power to undermine his father's authority and to disrupt his kingdom. Behind his father's back, he speaks ill of his father, making him look bad in the eyes of others. And all of this is done to get ahead (2 Samuel 14:7–12).

Critical Observation

Through Absalom's rebellion, God allows David to see his own sin from a different point of view. The story provides powerful perspective. Absalom is a warning to us all about submission and its counterpart, rebellion. David cannot save his son Absalom any more than we can save our children. For the appropriate reconciliation to occur, Absalom needs to submit to God in repentance. To be reconciled to God, one must acknowledge his or her sin and rebellion against God and accept the free gift of eternal life that He offers in the gospel of grace.

2 SAMUEL 15:13-16:19

TRAIL OF TEARS

Setting Up the Section

Word comes to David that the people's allegiance has turned to Absalom and that a full-scale rebellion is about to occur. It is at this point that David decides to flee from Jerusalem, along with many of his followers. Those who will be numbered among his followers (and who will remain behind in Jerusalem) will be determined by whether or not they are true friends of David.

📄 **15:13-16**

AT THE PALACE IN JERUSALEM

Notice that the messenger's report, as conveyed to the reader, does not indicate that Absalom has already sounded the trumpet, declaring himself king (15:10). Nor is it said that Absalom is actually marching on the city. But it is apparent that this is assumed. If it has not already happened, it will happen very soon. This is the time to act.

Instead of giving the order to prepare for battle, David gives the order to prepare to flee from Jerusalem. Here is the man who did not hesitate to stand up to Goliath when no one else was willing to do so, including Saul himself. Here is the man who, when insulted by Nabal (1 Samuel 25), was provoked to anger and set out to kill this man and every male member of his household. Why is David so eager to flee rather than fight?

It is important to understand that in fleeing from Jerusalem, David has not indicated his intention to abdicate the throne. This is why he leaves ten concubines behind to keep his house (2 Samuel 15:16). He is leaving town, but he is not leaving his throne. Absalom may seize it, but this will not be because David has handed in his resignation. The concubines are a symbol of David's continuing reign over Israel.

There are a number of reasons David makes the decision to flee. First, David knows that God will bring about troubles in his kingdom from within his own family. If the rebellion of Absalom is a part of the divine discipline he has brought upon himself, David is not sure whether he should resist it. If this is of God, will David be fighting against God to fight against this rebellion? David clearly indicates his intention to wait until he has a sense of certainty about what he should do.

Additionally, David loves Absalom. He does not want to precipitate a fight with him because he does not wish to kill him (chapter 18). Why start a fight you are not willing to win? And so it is that David chooses flight over a fight.

📄 **15:17–22**

AT THE LAST HOUSE

David pauses at the last house and allows those going with him to pass him. This last house may refer to the last of the houses that his wives and children inhabit in Jerusalem, but it appears to be the last house they come to before leaving the town. David stops at the outskirts of Jerusalem, pausing as those fleeing with him pass by. This gives David the opportunity to allow some to accompany him and to encourage others to turn back.

Demystifying 2 Samuel

The first major group of those loyal to David, who will accompany him as he flees from Jerusalem, are loyal foreigners—Gentiles. These all seem to be men whose association with David goes back to his days spent hiding out from Saul in the land of the Philistines. Among these are the Cherethites, Pelethites, and Gittites. The Cherethites and Pelethites are mentioned earlier (8:18) and later (23:22–23) in 2 Samuel. They are foreigners led by Benaiah. These men were probably a kind of honor guard for David who protect his life. Many kings had foreign mercenaries who served as their personal bodyguards.

A Gittite is a person from the Philistine city of Gath. Goliath was probably the most famous Gittite (21:19).

In addition to this larger group of faithful Gentiles, there is one who is a relative newcomer: Ittai the Gittite (15:19–22). This man must have been both loyal and capable for David to make him commander of a portion of his troops in chapter 18. There are a number of reasons why Ittai should have felt little obligation to follow David. He is a foreigner—it isn't his fight. He is a relative newcomer. He is accompanied by a number of children, who will certainly be a burden and be in danger if Absalom pursues David. So David pulls him aside to suggest that he turn back. Ittai responds with an outpouring of loyalty—in a speech that is notably similar to the response of Ruth to Naomi (Ruth 1:16–17).

📄 **15:23–29**

JUST OVER THE BROOK KIDRON

David demonstrates that he has learned something valuable by commanding Zadok to return the ark of the covenant to Jerusalem. He knows that if God is truly with him, then He will bring David back to Jerusalem, back to the place where God has chosen to dwell. If God is not with him, David knows the ark will do him no good.

This is a far cry from the mindset seen in 1 Samuel 4. There, when the Israelites suffer a defeat at the hands of the Philistines, the people fetch the ark, assuming it will somehow magically give them victory. Instead, the Israelites are defeated, Eli's two sons are killed, and the ark is taken by the Philistines. On top of this, Eli falls dead with the news that his sons are dead and the ark is in enemy hands. David does not see the ark as some kind of magic charm that assures him of God's presence or of divine deliverance. Jerusalem is where the ark belongs, and David is not going to attempt to take it with him.

📄 **15:30–37**

THE ASCENT OF THE MOUNT OF OLIVES

David ascends the Mount of Olives, weeping as he makes his way toward the top. His head is covered and his feet are bare, as is the case with all those accompanying him. The report reaches David that Ahithophel has joined Absalom in his revolt. This is a devastating blow because Ahithophel's counsel is so reliable (16:23).

Critical Observation

While the loss of Ahithophel is a devastating loss for David's administration, it should not come as a great surprise because of his relationship to David—Ahithophel is Bathsheba's grandfather (11:3; 23:34). Ahithophel very likely feels toward David as Absalom feels toward Amnon, so it is little wonder that he decides to side with Absalom at this point.

David's response is to utter a prayer that God will somehow thwart the counsel of Ahithophel. The answer to his prayer is not that far off, for David has hardly begun praying when his trusted friend, Hushai the Arkite, arrives. His coat is torn and he has cast dust on his head, both signs of mourning. This is indeed a most terrible thing that has happened. Hushai is ready to accompany David wherever he is going. David changes Hushai's plans. The king informs Hushai that if he does accompany him into hiding, he will only be an added burden. Hushai can perform a much more valuable service to David by returning to Jerusalem and pretending to become one of Ahithophel's loyal supporters. This way, Hushai will be in a position to counter the counsel of Ahithophel. David informs Hushai that Zadok and Abiathar are also loyal supporters. When Zadok or Abiathar hear something from the palace, they can send a message to David by their sons: Ahimaaz, Zadok's son, and Jonathan, Abiathar's son.

📄 **16:1–4**

THE SUMMIT OF THE MOUNT OF OLIVES

David and his followers have just passed the summit of the Mount of Olives. There he is met by Ziba, the servant of Mephibosheth. Ziba was a servant of King Saul. In order for David to fulfill his covenant with Jonathan, he needed to find an heir of Saul to whom he could show favor for Jonathan's sake. He was told of Ziba, who was formerly Saul's servant. Ziba was summoned, and there he informed David about Mephibosheth. When David brought Mephibosheth into his home, to eat at his table, he also restored to Mephibosheth all that was his as the heir of Saul and Jonathan. David also appointed Ziba and his family to serve Mephibosheth as his servant, as they had done before Saul's death.

Now we meet Ziba again. This time Ziba meets David with provisions for the journey ahead. David inquires of Ziba as to why he is bringing these supplies, and Ziba tells him that it is for the king and those with him, since the journey will prove difficult. David then asks Ziba where his master, Mephibosheth, is. Ziba tells David that Mephibosheth has gone to Jerusalem, hoping that his father Saul's kingdom will be restored to him. On the basis of Ziba's account, David gave to Ziba and his sons all that had been given to Mephibosheth.

📄 16:5–14

AT BAHURIM—STONED BY SHIMEI

Bahurim is a small town not far from Jerusalem. This is the place where the two spies, Ahimaaz and Jonathan, were hidden in a well until Absalom's men gave up searching for them (17:17-20). Here, a man named Shimei appears, not to mourn with David nor to provide supplies for his journey, but to mock and curse him, throwing dirt and stones at David and his followers.

Shimei's accusations are interesting. He accuses David of being a man of bloodshed. We immediately think in terms of Uriah and his death, ordered by David himself. But this is not what Shimei mentions specifically. He speaks of David's shedding of blood in terms of Saul and his house (16:8). Abishai wants to shut this man's mouth permanently by cutting off his head, but David refuses permission, convinced of the sovereignty of God in all these matters. He knows that Shimei's actions are wrong, even that his accusations are inaccurate. In spite of this, David believes that it is possible that God is speaking to him through this man, and thus he will not seek to silence him. Instead, he proceeds, looking to God for his vindication.

📄 16:15–19

BACK IN JERUSALEM

David's flight from Jerusalem certainly prompts Absalom's bold advance to the city and his possession of it. Once in the city, Absalom turns to Ahithophel for counsel as to what he should do next. Ahithophel counsels Absalom to symbolically declare himself king in a way that will make a statement to David and to all Israel. Ahithophel recommends that Absalom take the ten wives (or concubines; the terms seem to be used almost interchangeably here) and publicly sleep with them, as a symbol of his possession of the throne (along with the harem). The taking of a king's harem certainly symbolizes the taking of his place. Ruben does this by taking one of Jacob's concubines (Genesis 35:22; 49:4). Adonijah will attempt to do this with Abishag, one of David's concubines (1 Kings 2:13-25).

Absalom's actions regarding David's wives are not only a gesture that symbolically proclaims his taking of the throne; it is also the fulfillment of Nathan's prophetic words (2 Samuel 12:9-12). There is never any doubt that God will bring about that which He had spoken through Nathan. The author of this text does not want us to miss the fact that this event is, in part, the fulfillment of Nathan's words. David sinned with one woman, taking her as his wife when she was the wife of another. Now, Absalom takes ten wives of David and makes them his own wives by sleeping with them.

David sinned in private; Absalom purposely makes a spectacle of his. David's humiliation in this situation is great. Let us never deceive ourselves into thinking that our sin is worth the price. If David could have seen where his sin was leading, he would never have chosen the path he did.

In the tragedies of David's flight from Jerusalem and his son's humiliation of him, we are reminded that people betray one another in terrible ways—even ones bound by bonds of family or friendship. The one friend who does not desert Moses or Joshua or Paul or David is God. He is not intimidated by anyone, nor is He deterred by suffering and sorrow. His love is not based on what we can give to Him or what we have to offer through friendship. His love is unconditional. He is the model, the benchmark, for a true friend, whose life calls us all to go the extra mile and turn the other cheek even for our enemies.

2 SAMUEL 16:20–19:8

DARKEST DAYS

Setting Up the Section

This passage is filled with intrigue and drama and more tragedy for David. David is overwhelmed by sorrow and suffering. Still, there is deliverance and hope for David in these dark hours as he passes through the valley of the shadow of death (Psalm 23).

📄 **16:20–17:4**

AHITHOPHEL'S COUNSEL

Ahithophel's counsel is exceedingly shrewd in several ways. It offers an appealing course of action to Absalom. He, not unlike his father David, can stay home from the battle with his wives while Ahithophel and his army are at war with David (16:20–22). Absalom can quickly enter into his possession of the throne, yet without the dangers or discomforts of going into battle. As an added incentive, he can indulge himself with David's wives in a way that gets back at David and hurts and humiliates his father. Only David, Absalom's real enemy, will be killed.

Ahithophel proposes a quick, easy victory for Absalom. It is almost too good to be true, but Absalom (like his father) believes that Ahithophel speaks wisely (16:23–17:4). The fact is it is a plan that would have worked, but God has other plans for David and for Absalom. These plans are brought to pass through David's friends: Hushai, Zadok, and Abiathar, their sons Ahimaaz and Jonathan, a farmer's wife in Bahurim, and a number of other faithful friends and supporters of David.

📄 17:5–14

HUSHAI'S COUNSEL

Hushai has one great handicap: Absalom and everyone else in Israel know he is David's friend. How can Absalom trust a man who has been David's friend for so long? His counsel must be suspect. Rather than try to avoid this issue, Hushai uses his friendship.

Hushai challenges the assumptions on which Ahithophel's plans are based. He proposes a very different plan. Hushai insists that Ahithophel has dangerously underestimated David and his ability to defend himself and his kingdom. Hushai reminds Absalom and the elders of Israel about the kind of man David is. He is no mental weakling, but a tough and seasoned warrior. Absalom's rebellion will not break David's spirit; it will antagonize him. David will be fighting mad and fighting ready (17:7–9).

If Ahithophel comes into the wilderness to attack David, they will fight him on his turf. After all, David has spent years hiding from Saul in the wilderness. Does Ahithophel really think David can easily be found sitting among the rest of the people? He will be hiding out, and when Ahithophel and his small army arrive, David will pounce on them, giving them a humiliating defeat. It will be Absalom's soldiers who will lose heart and run, not David or his men (17:10).

Hushai's plan brings about a bigger battle, so that not only will many of Absalom's supporters die, but Absalom himself will be killed, thus ending the revolution. In reality, Hushai's plan gives David the time he needs to plan his battle (17:11–13). It allows David to fight on his turf. Hushai's plan makes Ahithophel's counsel seem foolish, which is exactly what David had prayed for (15:31). It brings about the deliverance of David and the defeat of his enemies (17:14).

📄 17:15–29

DAVID'S ESCAPE TO MAHANAIM

As Absalom prepares to cross the Jordan in hot pursuit of David, David and his men flee to the gates of Mahanaim. This is indeed a city with history. It was Jacob who gave this city its name. As he returned to the land of promise, fearful of what would happen when he met his brother Esau, Jacob is met by angels, prompting him to say, "This is God's camp" (Genesis 32:2 NASB). And so it is that Jacob names that place Mahanaim (meaning "two camps").

Is David fearful about meeting up with his son Absalom? We know from later events that he wishes to avoid a confrontation that will end in death. He should have remembered that God always protects His people, His promises, and His purposes, even by the use of angels if needed.

Ahithophel remains in Jerusalem only long enough to be convinced that his counsel is not going to be heeded by Absalom. Once it is clear that Hushai's counsel has prevailed, he knows he is finished. He has gambled everything on the assumption that Absalom will prevail over David. Now he knows that Absalom is destined to be defeated. He makes his way to his own home, sets his business in order, and kills himself. What a tragic end for a man with such great potential (2 Samuel 17:23).

Critical Observation

God provides for David at Mahanaim in more tangible and visible ways as well. When he and his faithful followers arrive, there are those ready and willing to help. Particularly amazing is the help that David receives from Shobi, the son of Nahash, and now king of the Ammonites. David and Nahash had been on relatively friendly terms, but when Nahash died and his son, Hanun, took the throne, he foolishly humiliated the delegation David sent to mourn Nahash's death (10:1–5). This disgrace led to war between Israel and the Ammonites. In fact it is this war with the Ammonites (and specifically the besieging of Rabbah) that David decided to avoid, leaving the battle to the Israelites under Joab's command; and during his stay in Jerusalem David fell into sin with Bathsheba (11:1–5). David finally defeated the Ammonites (12:26–31). Now Shobi is on the throne and eager to come to David's aid when he is opposed by Absalom. The Lord provides allies for David in unusual ways.

The second supporter to come to David's aid at Mahanaim is Machir, the son of Ammiel from Lo-debar (17:27). This is the man who takes in Mephibosheth after the death of King Saul and of Jonathan (9:4–5). Finally, Barzillai the Gileadite, an elderly man of great wealth, brings supplies for David and those with him. We learn even more about this man in 19:31–40. What an encouragement these men and their assistance must be to David.

📄 **18:1–18**

THE DEFEAT AND THE DEATH OF ABSALOM

David is wisely advised—because of his status as the priority target—to stay behind while his men go to battle. As David's men head off to fight Absalom's men, David charges them to deal gently with Absalom (18:5). Everyone hears these words. How different from the advice of Ahithophel, who intends to kill David alone and let the rest of the people live. David allows his men to kill any other Israelite, but not his son, the leader of the revolution. He commands those who are risking their lives for him to fight, but not to fight to win. It underscores how sensitive and loyal David is to the fact that though he is his mortal enemy, Absalom is also his son (18:1–5).

Absalom's forces suffer a great defeat, not only at the hand of David's men, but even from the forest itself. Absalom's men are not cut out for this kind of warfare. A total of twenty thousand men die in this slaughter, which spreads out over the whole country-side, as Absalom's men begin to turn and run for their lives. It is a great victory for David, and a devastating defeat for Absalom (18:6–8).

We do not know whether Absalom is running for his life or not, but he does seem to be alone at the time his mule runs under the branches of a great oak tree and Absalom's head is wedged in the branches. None of Absalom's men seem to be around to rescue him. (They may have been fleeing for their lives.) One of Joab's men comes upon Absalom and mentions it to his commander. Joab is incensed that this young man has not killed Absalom on the spot. Would he not have been rewarded for doing so? The young man is taken back by Joab's rebuke.

He reminds Joab that David, their commander-in-chief, has specifically forbidden anyone to harm his son Absalom. No matter what Joab may promise to do for him, this soldier knows that when David learns he has killed his son, there will be no protection for him.

It is ironic that it is Joab who kills Absalom, since it was Joab who had orchestrated amnesty for Absalom and brought him back to Jerusalem. It was Joab who obtained greater freedom for Absalom and brought him into the king's presence. And yet, for all Joab had done for Absalom, this man set out to take the throne away from his father, and to set another as commander over Israel's forces (16:9–18).

Joab has played a major role throughout the story of David's kingship. It was likewise Joab who, under orders from David, had Uriah killed in battle, without raising a word of protest. And now this military commander, who would kill a righteous man at David's request, kills David's own son in direct violation to his orders. Joab is not averse to doing dirty work. David, who abused his almost absolute authority to take Uriah's wife and have him killed at Joab's command, is powerless to save his own son from death at the hand of Joab (or anyone else).

Demystifying 2 Samuel

Both Absalom and Ahithophel fail to correctly answer the most important question any person will ever answer in their lifetime: "Who will I serve as king?" Absalom and Ahithophel do not want David for their king. Both, in effect, want to be king of their own lives. But in rejecting David as their king, they are rejecting God's king, and thus they are rebelling against God Himself. Both of these men have great ability, but in the end, their talents are of no eternal profit because they refuse to submit to God's authority and His chosen king.

18:19–33

PROCLAIMING THE GOOD NEWS

Joab knows his king well. He knows that David will not take the news of Absalom's death lightly. That is why he is reluctant to send Ahimaaz to David with the news. This is also why Ahimaaz hedges his answer to David's specific question about Absalom's well-being. David has been waiting for news of the outcome of the battle (18:19–28).

There is more space devoted to the messengers who report to David than there is about the war between the two opposing armies, including the account of the death of Absalom (18:28–33). Besides the space devoted to the relaying of the message, the text emphasizes the term good news, using it four times. When the translators of the Septuagint rendered this term in Greek, they used the term that we often find in the New Testament in reference to the proclamation of the gospel. The good news that Ahimaaz proclaims to David is that God has given him the victory by the death of his son. But this news is not good for David. It is a strange parallel to the New Testament gospel, which hinges on the death and resurrection of the Son of the eternal King, God (18:33).

JOAB REBUKES HIS KING

The scene of this victorious army returning to Mahanaim must have been jubilant. There would be shouting and celebration. What a great day of victory. But King David is not with his army. Instead, the triumphant soldiers learn that David is grieving over the death of his son. Now, instead of feeling proud of what they have done, David's men feel ashamed. David's warriors, who risked their necks to save their king, now hang their heads in shame. A day of victory is suddenly transformed into a day of mourning. The soldiers begin to sneak into the city, as though they have done something wrong (19:1–4).

Joab rightly rebukes David for putting everyone who has come with him from Jerusalem to shame, not just his soldiers, but his wives, children, and his concubines as well. By his response to the day's events, David reveals that he loves his enemy more than his friends and family. He loves those who hate him more than those who love him. He has shown total disregard for those who are willing to give their all for their king. Joab puts it as bluntly: David would rather have heard that his entire army was slaughtered and that his son Absalom was alive than to learn that his army had prevailed, but that Absalom was dead (19:5–7).

Take It Home

Many of David's psalms are written in a time of despair, possibly even during this time of exile from his throne and war with his own son. David uses the psalms to express his fears, despair, depression, and to cry out to God for strength. He finds hope and help in remembering the God to whom he speaks. And in the process of writing these psalms, David has also ministered to many people from his own despair. It is often from our times of mourning and sorrow that we begin to see life more clearly, to trust in God more completely, and to recognize our profound need for Him. If this is the case, then suffering and sorrow and even depression may at times be our friend and not our enemy. Anything that draws us more closely to God is something in which we should rejoice (James 1).

2 SAMUEL 19:9–20:26

RETURN TO JERUSALEM

Setting Up the Section

David is about to return to Jerusalem to resume his reign over the nation of Israel. To win the favor of the people (and perhaps to remove a thorn in his own flesh), David removes Joab as commander of his armed forces, replacing him with Amasa.

📄 19:9–18

CONVINCING ISRAEL

The people who had supported Absalom as king and remained in Israel need to be handled carefully in order to convince them to accept David as their king again. Word of their reluctance to accept him reaches David while he is still residing in Mahanaim. He acts in a way that makes it easier for the Israelites to welcome him back. David sends word to Zadok and Abiathar (the priests who were in Jerusalem and had remained loyal to him), instructing them to speak to the elders of Judah. This is David's tribe, the tribe which first anointed David as their king when he was in Hebron. These are David's closest kinsmen. It is logical that they should take the lead in bringing David back to Jerusalem.

David makes it even easier for the people of Judah by announcing that he is firing Joab as commander of his army and replacing him with Amasa. This action on David's part does the trick. Word comes from the elders of Judah, inviting him to return. David and all those with him make their way from Mahanaim to the banks of the Jordan River. The people of Judah assemble at Gilgal to assist David and those with him in crossing the river, and to welcome him back as their king. In addition to the people of Judah, a good-sized delegation of Israelites is present, representing the other tribes as well. Among these are Mephibosheth, Ziba (his servant, along with his sons and servants), and Shimei, accompanied by a thousand Benjamites.

📄 19:19–23

REPENTANCE AND FORGIVENESS

Shimei is no stranger to David. He is the descendant of Saul who harasses David and those with him when they flee from Jerusalem (16:5–14). He hurls rocks, dirt, accusations, and insults at David. Abishai had wanted to shut this man's mouth permanently then, but David refused, assuming God was, in some way, rebuking him through Shimei. Now, on his return, David must pass through Bahurim, Shimei's hometown. Shimei knows he is in serious trouble. David is once again the king of Israel, and he may reasonably view Shimei as a traitor who needs to be removed.

📄 19:24-30

DAVID DEALS WITH MEPHIBOSHETH AND ZIBA

Ziba, his sons and servants, and Mephibosheth are there to greet David and help him on his journey through the Jordan and on to Jerusalem (19:24). While Ziba is somewhere around, the conversation here is between David and Mephibosheth. Ziba is the one who appears to have forsaken David, while Mephibosheth seems to be in good standing. David asks Mephibosheth why he did not accompany him when he fled from Jerusalem. The accounts he receives do not match. Rather than trying to reconcile them, David divides the land he had given to Mephibosheth.

David declares that Mephibosheth's land (which David had given him earlier, and then given to Ziba) will be divided evenly between him and his servant Ziba. Once again, it is a day of rejoicing and reunion. David will give both men the benefit of the doubt and make a judgment that might facilitate their reconciliation.

Mephibosheth acknowledges David's graciousness to him in the past and also that he is unworthy and undeserving of any special consideration from David. He then seems to waive his rights to what David has given him, signing them over (as it were) to Ziba. Whether he actually does this is another matter. But the impression he seeks to give David is that he is more than happy to live in the king's presence and that further benefits are unnecessary and unwanted (19:28-30).

📄 19:31-39

BLESSING BARZILLAI

Barzillai is an elderly man, eighty years old to be precise. He is also a very wealthy man. He must have lived close to Mahanaim, for it is there where this generous old man provides for the needs of David and those with him while in exile. Now that David is going back to Jerusalem, Barzillai goes to great efforts to extend his friendship and hospitality to him on his return. It is some twenty-five miles (approximately—we don't know exactly where Mahanaim was located) back to the Jordan where David will cross, and another twenty to twenty-five miles to Jerusalem. This old man accompanies David to the Jordan and beyond to Gilgal (not far from where ancient Jericho would have been).

David wishes to show his gratitude to this elderly man and invites Barzillai to accompany him to Jerusalem, where the king promises to abundantly provide for him. Barzillai graciously declines David's offer. He is too old, he admits, to appreciate the difference between filet mignon and mush, or between the concert soprano voice of one of David's musicians and his own singing in the shower. David's delicacies would be wasted on him; and besides, he does not have all that much time left. He prefers to stay in his own home, near the place where his parents are buried and where he, before long, will be buried as well.

Barzillai does not wish to personally benefit from the generous offer David makes him, but he does propose an alternative. Barzillai commends a young man, Chimham, to the king, asking David if he will confer his blessings on this lad, as if upon him. From what we are told in 1 Kings 2:7, we know David intends not only to keep his promise to Barzillai in his lifetime but to continue it after his own death. David instructs Solomon to continue to be kind to Barzillai's sons (note the plural). It is assumed that Chimham is a son of Barzillai and that either at this time or later he is joined by another son or more. David generously provides for these men as Barzillai has cared for him.

📄 19:40–20:2

THE GREAT DIVIDE

As David and his men return to Jerusalem, the quarrelling continues between the men of Judah and the other ten tribes of Israel. Petty jealousy and strife prevail, so much so that the ten tribes become angry and embittered toward the men of Judah. Tensions are at an all-time high. Any precipitous action here could cause the situation to ignite.

Something precipitous does happen. There just happens to be a man among the people of Israel whose name is Sheba (20:1). The author makes it known that he is trouble (the text literally reads, "son of belial"). Sheba would not be taken seriously under normal circumstances. But in the heat of this argument, Sheba loses his temper (or sees the opportunity to assume leadership here) and blurts out, "Down with the dynasty of David!" (20:1 NLT). These words are all it takes for these Israelites to turn on their heels and leave with Sheba. And so this once joyful procession turns sour with a bitter debate and now a major schism. One moment these Israelites claim David as their leader; the next they are following Sheba, a worthless man. David has not even reached Jerusalem, and his kingdom is already a divided one. It looks as though he is starting all over again, as the king of the tribe of Judah.

Critical Observation

When the people of Israel are arguing with the people of Judah, the Israelites claim ten times the ownership of David since they have ten tribes. In other words, David is ten times more obligated to them. But when the people of Judah speak of their relationship to David, their claim to him is that he is near kin. Neither the ten tribes of Israel nor the tribe of Judah speak of David as God's anointed king. Both tribes follow David for self-serving reasons. Thus, Judah is hardly better for following David than the men of Israel are for leaving him.

📄 20:3–13

BACK TO BUSINESS

The first thing David does after arriving in Jerusalem is deal with the ten wives (or concubines) he left behind to keep the house. Absalom has slept with these women in public; there is no way David can go back to the way things were. He will never sleep with any of these women again. He appoints a place for them to stay and provides generously for them, but they have been defiled by Absalom.

The next item of business for David is the rebellion that is under way, led by Sheba. For some unexplained reason, Amasa does not assemble the armed forces of Judah in the three-day time frame David sets down. You can imagine how uneasy David must be, knowing that every hour Sheba is free that the threat to his kingdom increases. It must pain David greatly to finally admit Amasa is not coming, at least not for a while, and to call for Abishai, the brother of Joab and a long-time pain-in-the-neck for David (1 Samuel 26:6–11; 2 Samuel 16:9–12; 19:21–22). David would not ask Joab to do the job, for it would appear to be an admission that he has erred in firing Joab and replacing him with Amasa. But when Abishai goes out from Jerusalem, leading David's select warriors (the Green Berets or Navy Seals of his day) in pursuit of Sheba, he is accompanied by Joab.

When Joab and Amasa meet, Joab promptly kills him. It does not seem to be at Joab's initiative that a certain soldier takes it upon himself to address the rest. He is one of Joab's men, so we would expect him to be loyal to Joab and one of his supporters. Seeing Amasa lying there dead, it is obvious to him that there needs to be a new commander of the army. After all, someone needs to give the orders. It seems clear that next in the chain of command is Abishai. He is the oldest son (1 Chronicles 2:16), but most importantly, he is the one David sends to pursue Sheba when Amasa does not return. In spite of this, the young man urges the rest of his colleagues to acknowledge Joab as their new commander, and it seems this is precisely what happens. There is no mention of any protest, and Joab is spoken of as the leader from here on.

📄 20:14–26

THE DEMISE OF SHEBA

Joab and his forces finally track down Sheba at Abel Beth-maacah. When they hear that Sheba has sought refuge in this fortified city, they put the city under siege. A wise woman sizes up the situation and takes the initiative. She goes to the wall, calls down, and asks to speak to Joab. He comes near, and she recounts to him how this city has been highly esteemed as a source of wisdom and counsel. It is a place known for ending disputes. Why then would Joab want to destroy such a place? She goes on to tell Joab that she is among those in the city who are peaceable and faithful in Israel. They have done nothing to deserve what Joab is dishing out. This is a part of the inheritance from God. Does Joab really wish to be responsible for destroying it?

Joab assures the woman that he does not wish to destroy the city. He then informs her why the city is being besieged. They are seeking but one person, Sheba the son of Bichri, who is guilty of rebellion against King David. If the woman will arrange to have this man handed over to them, they will go on their way in peace. The woman assures Joab that Sheba's head will be thrown over the wall to him. The woman then convinces the people of the city to execute Sheba, and his head is thrown down to Joab and his army. With this, Joab blows the trumpet, indicating the cessation of hostilities (20:20–22).

Take It Home

The events of 2 Samuel 19–20 underscore the reality of divine providence. There are times when God intervenes in the lives of His people in direct ways. The roots of division between Judah and the other tribes of Israel run deep in Israel's history, but it is evident that Israel is divided for a very short time in David's day. This division is never completely healed. It lays dormant for the years of Solomon's reign, but it comes to life after his death. In all of this, God is preparing the nation for the division He purposes. We must remember to submit to God's anointed King in our own lives just as the Israelites were called to. In the new expanded kingdom of God's chosen people, God has appointed Jesus as our sovereign King. Let us submit to Him as Savior and Lord, and let us live as His loyal subjects, for His glory and our eternal good.

2 SAMUEL 21:1–22

PROMISE BREAKERS AND KEEPERS

Righting a Wrong	21:1–14
War with Giant Enemies	21:15–22

Setting Up the Section

King Saul had violated a covenant with the Gibeonites that was more than four centuries old. His actions with regard to the Gibeonites bring a famine upon the land of Israel some time after he dies. Now David must deal with Saul's covenant breaking and make things right.

📄 21:1–14

RIGHTING A WRONG

The Gibeonites are an interesting people. Our author refers to them as Amorites (21:2), but they are more technically known as the Hivites (Joshua 9:1, 7; 11:19). These Gibeonites were among those living in Canaan, whom God had commanded Israel to annihilate (Exodus 33:2; 34:11; Deuteronomy 7:1–2). This would have been the case except for a strange turn of events, which is described in the book of Joshua (chapter 9).

Demystifying 2 Samuel

Under the leadership of Joshua, the Israelites had just crossed the Jordan River (Joshua 3) and captured the city of Jericho (Joshua 6) and then Ai (Joshua 7–8). The next city to come under attack by Israel almost certainly would be Gibeon, and the Gibeonites knew it. Gibeon was a great city, and its warriors were among the best (Joshua 10:2). But rather than fighting the Israelites, they were allowed to stay in Canaan as their slaves (Joshua 9:16–17). The treaty the Israelites made with the Gibeonites also assured these people of Israel's protection (Joshua 10:8).

As we come to our text, some four hundred years have passed since the leaders of Israel made their covenant with the Gibeonites. God is angry with Israel because of the sin of Saul and his bloody house against the Gibeonites. Saul and his house commenced a program of genocide against the Gibeonites.

The Gibeonites must bless Israel, the people of God, in order for God to once again bless Israel. It seems to be almost an exact reversal of the Abrahamic Covenant, where God promises to bless those who bless the Israelites. Here the Israelites have violated the Gibeonites, however, which deeply angers God. Being God's chosen people does not give anyone a license to sin. God hears the cries of the oppressed and judges sin, even when that sin is committed by His chosen people.

Critical Observation

This passage emphasizes the importance of covenants. Throughout Old Testament history, God deals with people through covenants (Genesis 9:1–17; 12:1–3; 17:1–22; Exodus 19–20; 31:12–17; Deuteronomy 5; 2 Samuel 7:12–17). Then, in the New Testament, He ushers in the New Covenant by the Lord Jesus Christ through the shedding of His blood (Jeremiah 31:31–34; Luke 22:20; 1 Corinthians 11:25; 2 Corinthians 3:6; Hebrews 9:11–22). God has not dealt with His people capriciously; He has always dealt with them in accordance with a covenant. David's dealing with the Gibeonites, at its roots, is a matter of keeping covenants. Israel had made a covenant with the Gibeonites. Even though this covenant is four hundred years old, it is still to be honored. No matter how good Saul's intentions might have been, the covenant must be kept. The breaking of that covenant had serious consequences.

This passage foreshadows the gospel in so many ways. Not only does it remind us that God relates to His people by means of His covenants, but it speaks to us particularly of the New Covenant. Saul's sins had to be atoned for or God's blessings could not be enjoyed. Saul's sin brought adversity in the form of a famine. Money could not atone for this sin—only the shedding of blood. It is the shedding of this blood that brings about atonement and appeases both God and the Gibeonites. The story of Saul, David, and the Gibeonites reminds us not only that sin must be atoned for by the shedding of blood, but that there is a payday, according to God's timing, for sin.

📄 **21:15–22**

WAR WITH GIANT ENEMIES

This chapter describes the end of David's military career. It is not yet the end of his reign as king of Israel, but it is the end of his military career. David will no longer go out to fight with his men (21:17). David's military career began with a contest with Goliath and a victory over the Philistines (1 Samuel 17). The ending of David's military career is a final battle with one of Goliath's offspring and the defeat of the Philistines.

This is a story of closure and transition. The task of leaders is not to do everything, but to facilitate ministry, to train, equip, and encourage others who will take their place to do an even better job. If this is what Christian leadership is to be, then David is a great leader. Under Saul, not one man is willing to stand up to Goliath. In David's ministry, there are many willing and able to do so. David is now free to step aside (first as commander of the military and later as king) because he has done his job well.

2 SAMUEL 22:1–51

DAVID'S SONG OF SALVATION

Setting Up the Section

This passage records David's reflections, penned at the outset of his reign as Israel's king. The text is virtually identical to (and possibly quoting) Psalm 18.

📄 **22:1–3**

DAVID'S DELIVERER

In the first verse of the psalm, we are given the historical background for this song of David. David wrote this psalm after God delivered him from the hand of his enemies and from the hand of Saul. It would seem then that the psalm was written shortly after Saul's death and at the outset of David's reign as king. David now occupies the throne, and from this vantage point, he reflects on God's gracious dealings in his life to fulfill His promise that he would be Israel's king.

God is David's fortress and his stronghold. He is David's shield and the horn of his salvation. These are not mere images; these are the very means God employed to save David's life from the hand of his enemies. And now, David urges us to look beyond these means which God employed to God Himself. It is God who delivers; He is our place of safety.

📄 **22:4–20**

CRY FOR HELP

David called to God for deliverance, and God responded in a way that signaled His sovereignty over all creation. When God heard David's cry, He responded, as evidenced by all of His creation. God is angered by the enemies who have endangered His anointed king, and all of creation reflects God's anger. This is not just a description of a God who is eager to save His king, but a God who is intent upon destroying the enemies who threaten His king.

God reaches down and plucks His servant from the waters, delivering him from his strong enemy and setting him down in a broad place on solid ground. Though David's enemies are stronger, God delivers him from their hand. He is David's support when they confront him.

DIVINE DELIVERANCE

In the Law of Moses, God made it clear to His people that He would bless them as they trusted in Him and kept His law (Deuteronomy 7:12–16). On the other hand, it was also clear that their righteousness attained by their works was not the basis for God's grace. David understood that God saves the righteous and condemns the wicked. It is for this reason that God hears David's cry for help and comes to his rescue from his wicked enemies. Not only does God save the righteous, but He saves the afflicted, while He condemns the proud.

Very often God will have us play a role in His deliverance. In such cases, it is God who gives us the strength and ability to prevail over our enemies. David stood up to Goliath and prevailed, but it was God who gave the victory. David describes the strength God supplies in terms of waging warfare. God's strength enables him to leap over a wall and to overrun a troop of men (2 Samuel 22:30). Military strength begins in the mind. David had the moral courage to stand up to Goliath as well as the God-given skill to strike him down with his sling.

The basis for this strength of courage (faith) is God's Word. God's Word (both direct and indirect revelation) guides David's actions. He not only sets David on the high places (the place of military advantage), He gives David the sure-footedness that enables him to fight from this position (22:34). God is the one who trains David's hands for battle, who gives him the strength to bend the difficult bronze bow (22:35). He gives him the shield of His salvation, and then gives him firm footing with which to stand and fight (22:36–37).

Reflecting on God's deliverance and enabling strength, David's conclusion is one full of hope and anticipation. David is God's anointed king, but his reign is soon to end. God has proven to be David's deliverer, but it is not over. Because of the covenant God made with David, he will have an eternal throne. David's psalm reminds us that if God is our refuge, there is no need to fear.

2 SAMUEL 23:1–24:25

EPILOGUE

Setting Up the Section

As David continues to reflect on his time as king of Israel, we are reminded to celebrate the greatness of other people.

PROFILES IN COURAGE

David confidently speaks of a reign of righteousness for his house. This is not due to David's merits or self-righteousness, but rather to the grace of God, assured through His covenant with David (7:14). Based upon God's covenant with him, David is assured of an eternal reign of righteousness, signed, sealed, and delivered in the covenant of God as fulfilled (ultimately and permanently) in the person of Jesus Christ. This is David's ultimate salvation and desire, brought about by God, the author and finisher of all salvation. David's song of salvation is centered in God. The message of the Bible is not the promise of salvation and eternal life for all people; it is the offer of salvation to all people. David celebrates God's offer of universal salvation in this passage.

David is a man of courage. When a lion or a bear threatened his father's flock, he refused to allow any losses. When Goliath blasphemed the name of God, David killed him. David constantly proved himself to be a man of courage. Is it any wonder he attracted like-minded men? The man who stood up to Goliath was surrounded by courageous men who would gladly take on Goliath's descendants (21:15–22). Courage inspires courage—it's no wonder we find so many heroes among those closest to him.

Considering the heroes of courage remembered here, we are reminded that God uses an army of followers to accomplish His purposes. The church is the body of Christ, composed of those Jews and Gentiles who are believers through faith. Each member of the body has a unique function, which they carry out by means of their spiritual gifts. No one should think of themselves as independent of the rest of the body (1 Corinthians 12:21–22), nor should anyone think of themselves as nonessential (1 Corinthians 12:14–19).

📄 24:1–25

FIGHTING MEN AND AN ALTAR

Divinely incited, David decides to number the fighting men of Israel and Judah. Numbering is not necessarily wrong. Moses numbered the fighting men of Israel in preparation for battle (Numbers 1:1–4). Moses also numbered the Kohathites (Numbers 4:2) and the Gershonites (Numbers 4:22) for priestly service. Saul numbered the Israelites to defend the people of Jabesh-gilead by fighting the Ammonites (1 Samuel 11:8). David numbered those loyal to him in preparation for defending himself against an attack by his son, Absalom (2 Samuel 18:1). In none of these cases is numbering wrong.

Numbering Israel seems to produce the knowledge that David is forbidden to have, a knowledge of his greatness and military strength (compare Deuteronomy 17:14–20). He wants to see his strength and power, and even though forbidden, it is what his heart desires. The Lord is angry with Israel, and the pestilence which came to His people was justly deserved—not only because of David's sin but because of Israel's sin. How ironic that David seeks to learn how many Israelite warriors are at his disposal, and as a result of his finding out, the numbers are changed by seventy thousand men.

David's faith in God for judgment is well-founded. God had poured out His wrath on His people, but now He takes compassion on them. The angel of the Lord is standing by the threshing floor of Araunah the Jebusite when he was ordered to halt.

1 KINGS

INTRODUCTION TO 1 KINGS

First Kings was originally joined with 2 Kings in one book. The narrative covers almost five hundred years, tracing the history of Israel and Judah from the last days of the monarchy under David to the disintegration and capture of the divided kingdoms.

AUTHOR

The author of this book is unknown. While there is a Jewish tradition that points to the prophet Jeremiah as the author, there is more evidence that the book evolved over a long period of time.

PURPOSE

The purpose of 1 Kings is not explicitly stated. However, the fact that Kings doesn't mention the return of the exiles to Jerusalem suggests that the book is written in order to answer the question, "Why are we in exile?" This book serves as a kind of warning about the consequences of falling away from faith and the practice of that faith. In the same way, it serves as an encouragement toward consistent obedience.

Many scholars believe that the exilic author(s) of Kings is looking at the history of Israel and Judah through the prism of Deuteronomy. They are evaluating how well they have observed the law, and of course the answer is not well at all.

HISTORICAL CONTEXT

While today 1 and 2 Kings appear as two separate yet related books in the Bible, it is important to remember that they are actually two parts of the same book. The date of both should be considered at the same time. The last event mentioned in 2 Kings 25 is the release of Jehoiachin from Babylonian prison during the reign of Evil-Merodach (Amel-Marduk) who reigned from 562–560 BC, thus the book had to be completed in its final form between this date and the end of the exile (which is not mentioned in the book of Kings) in 539 BC.

THEMES

There is no single theme in 1 Kings. It instead offers historical events and theological commentary that continues biblical themes consistent with earlier books. For example:

God in history as sovereign Lord
God in judgment
God as deliverer
God's promise to David
God's prophecy

STRUCTURE

The writer of 1 Kings provides a framework for the histories of each kingship recorded. The beginning resume includes dates, length, place of reign, and theological appraisal (whether the king did right in the eyes of the Lord). The ending may include a citing of sources, additional historical notes, notice of the king's death and burial, and successor. In between is the drama of the reign itself.

1 KINGS 1:1–53

SOLOMON BECOMES KING

Setting Up the Section

The first section begins dramatically in the twilight of King David's glorious reign, with the question of his successor hanging in the air. His oldest living son, Adonijah, wants to reign. But the throne of Israel will not be left to the rules of hereditary succession; God will determine the next king.

📖 1:1–10

ADONIJAH'S BID FOR THE THRONE

In verse 1 we learn that David is now so old that he can't even keep himself warm, much less rule the nation. He seems even older than seventy; but for David, it isn't just the years—it is the mileage.

The selection of a beautiful virgin to warm David up may sound strange or even immoral, but it was a recognized treatment in the ancient world. When Josephus describes this in his *Antiquities of the Jews*, he says that this was a medical treatment, and he calls the servants of 1 Kings 1:2 "physicians."

Also, David almost certainly makes this young woman, Abishag the Shunammite, his concubine, which is not at this time illegal or prohibited by God. Later, in chapter 2, Adonijah will condemn himself to death for asking for Abishag as a wife. His request would only be so outrageous if Abishag had belonged to David as a concubine.

Critical Observation

A concubine in ancient culture was not a simple mistress; she was a wife of secondary rank. Still, David's relationship with Abishag the Shunammite is disputed, and many have associated her with the Shulamite addressed in the Song of Solomon (Song of Solomon 6:13), concluding that she became romantically involved with David's son, Solomon. This is conjecture.

In 1 Kings 1:5–6 we meet Adonijah and his ambitions. In exalting himself, he violates a basic principle in the scriptures: that we should let God exalt us and not exalt ourselves (Psalm 75:6–7; James 4:10).

Adonijah gathers a personal military force of chariots and fifty men to run ahead of him. He may have remembered his charismatic older brother, Absalom, who did the same thing (2 Samuel 15:1) and whose bid for the throne was similarly doomed. In fact, the writer notes that Adonijah is very handsome (as Absalom was) and was born right after Absalom. It seems clear that Adonijah hopes that if he puts forth the image of a king, he will become king in reality.

Critical Observation

Second Samuel 3:2–5 describes the sons of David and lists Adonijah as the fourth son. We know that two of the three sons older than Adonijah are dead (Amnon and Absalom), and we suspect that the other older son (Chileab) either died also, or he was unfit to rule because he is never mentioned after 2 Samuel 3:3. Thus by many customs, Adonijah would be considered the heir to the throne. But it is God who would determine the next king, not heredity.

The writer of 1 Kings observes (1:6) that David doesn't challenge Adonijah on his behavior. Sadly, David did not do a very good job raising his sons.

In 1 Kings 1:7, Adonijah gains the key support of Joab (David's chief general) and Abiathar (the high priest of Israel). It is sad to see these once trusted associates of David turning on him late in his life. Joab may have sought revenge for David's choice of Amasa over him (2 Samuel 19:13). Abiathar might have been jealous of Zadok, the high priest (2 Samuel 8:17).

But some remained loyal to David (and to the Lord's plan for the throne), including his mighty men, or special guard (1:8).

Adonijah throws both a feast and a sacrifice (1:9), inviting all his brothers except for Solomon. The idea is that he will burn the fat of these animals as a sacrifice to the Lord and use the meat to hold a dinner honoring and blessing his supporters.

NATHAN AND BATHSHEBA INTERCEDE FOR SOLOMON

David is clueless to everything going on (1:11). Nathan, David's old friend and prophet, knows that if Adonijah does become king, he will immediately kill every potential rival to his throne, including Bathsheba and Solomon. He instructs Bathsheba what to do.

Nathan knows that David is indulgent toward his sons and finds it hard to believe that Adonijah would act out the way he has. So Nathan (1:13–14) describes a message to be presented in a convincing way—Bathsheba will remind him of a promise.

The specific promise Nathan and Bathsheba refer to is not recorded before, but we know from 1 Chronicles 22:5–9 that David does in fact intend for Solomon to succeed him as king. (It is a remarkable display of grace, really, that a son of the wife David took through adultery and murder in the most infamous scandal of his life should be his heir.)

Bathsheba begins by telling David the facts about Adonijah's actions. Then she uses this tender appeal, reminding David that her life and the life of Solomon are in grave danger if Adonijah should become king.

Critical Observation

The latest mention of the prophet Nathan was in 2 Samuel 12, where he rebuked his friend David over the scandal with Bathsheba and murder of Uriah. Yet now, at the end of his days, David receives Nathan, and it seems he remains a trusted friend. David did not treat Nathan as an enemy when he confronted him with the painful truth, and he responds again when Nathan informs him of Adonijah's rebellion.

SOLOMON IS MADE KING

David finally sees what's happening and moves quickly to confirm Solomon. He calls in Bathsheba, and with a solemn oath (1:28) confirms the previous promise he made that her son Solomon would be the next king.

Bathsheba's response in verse 31 is a customary expression of thanks and honor. Since David knows that death is near, it may have sounded strange in his ears.

David next orders arrangements for Solomon's anointing, calling in three prominent leaders in Israel who do not support Adonijah as king: Zadok the priest, Nathan the prophet, and Benaiah. David knows who is loyal to him.

In the scene of 1:32–35, we have a rare glimpse of all three offices in cooperation—prophet, priest, and king. Each of these offices is gloriously fulfilled in Jesus.

David wants the proclamation of Solomon as successor to be persuasive. He has five points to the plan for Solomon: (1) Solomon is to ride David's own mule; (2) Zadok and Nathan are to anoint him; (3) they will blow the horn; (4) they will say, "Long live King Solomon"; (5) Solomon will sit on David's throne.

Take It Home

Benaiah reacts with an exuberant, "Amen!" (1:36), underscoring an important principle: Unless the Lord God blesses the selection of Solomon, he will not stand. Benaiah senses that this is the Lord's will and offers the prayer that God would in fact declare it. His wish in verse 37, that Solomon's reign would be greater than David's, is on a human level fulfilled. But on a spiritual level, it is not.

Zadok, Nathan, Benaiah, and the Cherethites and the Pelethites (foreign mercenaries who served under David) escort Solomon to Gihon (1:38). Gihon is outside Jerusalem and its major source of water, making it a popular place for the people to gather.

Demystifying 1 Kings

The mule in ancient Israel was rare and expensive. It had to be imported and was ridden only by royalty. (Everyone else rode donkeys.)

No one could use anything owned by royalty without permission. Thus Solomon riding on David's mule was a sign that David had appointed him his successor.

📄 1:41–53

SOLOMON'S MERCY TO ADONIJAH

Adonijah's party is over before Solomon is proclaimed king. Bathsheba and Nathan act quickly and it is rewarded. At the sight of Solomon's anointing, the people rejoice so loudly (1:40–41) that Adonijah and his followers ask what is happening. Despite Adonijah's best marketing campaign, he could not win the hearts of the people. They sense that Solomon is the man, not Adonijah.

The trusted messenger, Jonathan (1:42), reports the events in 1:43–48, including King David's own words of praise to God (1:48). This tells Adonijah that even his father David is completely behind Solomon. There is no hope for his future as king.

In verses 49–50, we see Adonijah's guests scatter, and Adonijah flees to Jerusalem to the altar, a traditional place of refuge. Everyone now knows he fears for his life and is asking for Solomon's mercy. Word gets to Solomon (1:51), who grants amnesty unless Adonijah does evil (1:53). He sends men to get Adonijah, allows him to show allegiance, and then sends him home.

1 KINGS 2:1–46

THE SECURING OF SOLOMON'S THRONE

Setting Up the Section

After his father, King David, bids farewell with final instructions, Solomon takes care of old business as a way to secure his reign.

📖 2:1–12

THE FINAL ACTS OF KING DAVID

In his final charge to his son Solomon, David—Israel's greatest king, apart from the Messiah—acknowledges that he is just a man who shares the common destiny of all the earth. (See 1 Chronicles 28 and 29 for an expanded account of David's last speech, which emphasizes Solomon's duty to build the temple.)

David's advice to be strong was a typical exhortation for new leaders, not just in Israelite literature but more broadly ancient Near Eastern literature. See Joshua in Joshua 1. In verse 4, David alludes to the covenantal promise that as long as David's sons walked in obedience, they would keep the throne of Israel.

Take It Home

God's promise to David is an amazing one. No matter what the Assyrians or the Egyptians or the Babylonians did, as long as David's sons were *obedient* and followed God, He would establish their kingdom. He would take care of the rest. (Unfortunately, they didn't hold up their end of the bargain.) All children of God have a similar promise (Matthew 6:33). God says that if we put Him first, He will take care of the rest.

David wants Solomon to begin his reign in justice. First on the list of actions concerns Joab, his former commander, who was guilty of the murder of both Abner, the general of Israel's army under Saul (2 Samuel 3:27), and Amasa, one of David's military commanders (2 Samuel 20:9–10).

David doesn't mention Joab's killing of Absalom, which David commanded him not to do (2 Samuel 18). Perhaps by this time David recognizes that Absalom in fact had to die for his treason and attempted murder against David.

David charges Solomon to use wisdom but to not let Joab die in peace.

Demystifying 1 Kings

Joab was one of the more complex characters of the Old Testament. He was David's nephew (1 Chronicles 2:16–17), and while fiercely loyal to David, he was not strongly obedient. He disobeyed David when he thought it was in David's best interest, and he was cunning and ruthless in furthering his own position.

Many scholars think that David did not command Joab's execution during his lifetime because Joab knew about the murder of Uriah, the husband of Bathsheba (2 Samuel 11:14–25). Joab may have used this knowledge as blackmail against David. However, it appears others knew of David's sin with Bathsheba and against Uriah also (such as Nathan the prophet and servants in David's court). It would seem that Joab's knowledge would only be effective as blackmail if no one else knew it.

David orders Solomon to show kindness to the sons of Barzillai the Gilead, who supported him when he was fleeing Absalom. In saying that they should be allowed to eat at the king's table, David is providing them the equivalent of having a pension, food and clothing, and a house and land to support him and his family.

But Shimei son of Gera, the angry follower of Saul whom David had vowed not to kill, doesn't fare as well. David orders Solomon to kill the obnoxious rebel (2 Samuel 16:5–13).

In verse 10 the author simply records the end of the earthly life of David. Appropriately, David is buried in the City of David. His tomb is known in the time of Jesus and the apostles, according to Acts 2:29. What is currently labeled in Jerusalem as David's tomb is almost certainly *not* the genuine one known in ancient times.

📄 **2:13–46**

SOLOMON SECURES HIS THRONE

The phrase in 2:12 shows that the establishment of Solomon's kingdom is a fulfillment of the promise made to David in 2 Samuel 7:12–16. That promise is ultimately fulfilled in Jesus, the Son of David; but it also has a definite and partial fruition in Solomon and all of David's heirs down to Zedekiah.

Immediately, the author puts Adonijah back on stage, approaching Bathsheba. She wisely asks if he comes peacefully, since Adonijah has reason to wish revenge.

By claiming that the kingdom is his and all Israel looks to him, Adonijah seems to suffer from delusions of grandeur. In reality, he only has a handful of influential malcontents to support him, and they quickly deserted him when it was evident that David favored Solomon.

His audacious request to take the concubine widow, Abishag from Shunem, as his wife is more than it seems. In 2 Samuel 16:20–23, Absalom—the brother of Adonijah—asserts his rebellious claim on David's throne by taking David's concubines unto himself. Adonijah wants to build a claim to Solomon's throne by taking David's concubine as his wife. Bathsheba agrees to bring the request to Solomon. She may have felt that it is best that Solomon knows what Adonijah wants to do.

Demystifying 1 Kings

Why would Adonijah, knowing the warning Solomon made in 1 Kings 1:52, make the outrageous request for King David's concubine? Perhaps he felt that Solomon was too young, too inexperienced, or too timid to do the right thing. He soon found out that Solomon was a decisive leader.

When she says she has one small petition, she is being at least a little sarcastic to make the request of Adonijah seem even more offensive to the ears of Solomon.

Solomon reacts immediately. Solomon understands that this is Adonijah's attempt to declare claim to the throne of Israel. He is zealous to give justice to Adonijah because he knows that God gave him the throne of Israel.

He acts according to the parole terms granted to Adonijah in 1 Kings 1:52. Adonijah made a wicked, treasonous request and is executed because of it.

Abiathar, the priest who supports Adonijah as the next king, in defiance of the will of God and the will of King David (1:7), deserves death. This is treason against both God and the king of Israel.

Yet Solomon shows wisdom and acts with mercy toward Abiathar in light of his past standing as a chief priest and supporter of David. But Solomon lets Abiathar know that he can still be executed.

When Joab hears of Adonijah's execution and Abiathar's banishment, he knows he's next. Now he imitates Adonijah's attempt to find refuge by taking hold of the horns of the altar (as Adonijah does in 1 Kings 1:50-53).

Although it was almost a universal custom in the ancient world to find sanctuary at a holy altar, Solomon knows that this tradition is not used in Israel to protect a guilty man (Exodus 21:14). Since Joab refuses to leave, Solomon has his rival, Benaiah, execute him right at the altar.

When it comes to the rebellious Shimei, who is associated with the household of the former King Saul and shows himself as a threat to the house of David (2 Samuel 16:5-8), Solomon again shows mercy.

David instructs Solomon to not allow Shimei to die in peace (1 Kings 2:8). Solomon begins dealing with Shimei by placing him under house arrest, perhaps to eliminate any opportunity to plot with others against the throne. Shimei knows that Solomon is being merciful and generous to him. He not only agrees with the arrangement, but he is grateful for it.

However, three years later (2:39-40) he abuses the mercy to retrieve runaway slaves. It seems to have mainly been a matter of neglect or forgetfulness, but it is criminal to neglect a royal covenant. Shimei pays with his life.

1 KINGS 3:1–28

SOLOMON IS GIVEN GREAT WISDOM

God Gives Solomon Wisdom	3:1–15
An Example of Solomon's Great Wisdom	3:16–28

Setting Up the Section

God gives Solomon the opportunity to ask for anything, and Solomon wisely asks for wisdom, even after unwisely bringing a new Egyptian wife into his court. He then famously uses his godly wisdom to decide a conflict between two mothers claiming one baby.

📄 3:1–15

GOD GIVES SOLOMON WISDOM

First Kings 3 opens with Solomon marrying an Egyptian princess, as part of an alliance with the Pharaoh, and bringing her to Jerusalem.

Marriage to fellow royalty was a common political strategy in the ancient world and continues to the modern age. It was not only because royalty wanted to marry other royalty, but also because conflicts between nations were avoided for the sake of family ties.

Demystifying 1 Kings

This is not Solomon's first marriage. First Kings 14:21 tells us that his son, Rehoboam, came to the throne when he was forty-one years old, and 1 Kings 11:42 tells us that Solomon reigned forty years. This means that Rehoboam was born to his mother—a wife of Solomon named Naamah the Ammonitess—before he came to the throne and before he married this daughter of Pharaoh.

Critical Observation

Marrying a foreign woman was not against the Law of Moses—if she became a convert to the God of Israel. Ruth was an example of this. A Moabite, she returned to Bethlehem with her mother-in-law Naomi and adopted Naomi's faith. Ruth then married into Naomi's family (Ruth 1–4).

Solomon eventually collects a thousand foreign wives and concubines, which makes him more than just a bad example. They ruined his spiritual life. First Kings 11:4 says Solomon turns away from the Lord when he is old, but the pattern is set with this first marriage to the Egyptian princess. It perhaps makes political sense, but not spiritual sense.

Nehemiah, five centuries later—after the disintegration and captivity of Israel and Judah—is angry and frustrated because the people of Israel marry with the pagan nations around them. He charges them to remember Solomon's bad example (Nehemiah 13:25–27).

In 1 Kings 3:2–4, we see how the people are making sacrifices at the high places—shrines meant for worship. These shrines are allowed in Israel as long as the altars are built for worship of the one true God and not corrupted by idolatry (as commanded in Deuteronomy 16:21). When the temple is built, sacrifice is then centralized at the temple (Deuteronomy 12). Solomon in 3:3 is described as walking according to God's law, but there is a contrasting "except" when it comes to his sacrificing at the high places.

Solomon goes to Gibeon, where there is a most important high place. He offers a thousand burnt offerings. This huge amount of sacrifice demonstrates both Solomon's great wealth and his heart to use it to glorify God.

This is an important event marking the beginning of Solomon's reign. According to 2 Chronicles 1:2–3, the entire leadership of the nation goes with Solomon to Gibeon.

Critical Observation

What set Gibeon apart was that the tabernacle was there, even though the ark of the covenant was in Jerusalem. How did that come to be? Saul moved the tabernacle to Gibeon (1 Chronicles 16:39–40), but David brought the ark to Jerusalem and built a temporary tent for it (2 Samuel 6:17; 2 Chronicles 1:4).

Why didn't David bring the tabernacle from Gibeon to Jerusalem? There are a few possibilities: (1) He may have believed that if the tabernacle was in Jerusalem, the people would be satisfied with that and lose the passion for the temple God wanted built; (2) it may be that the tabernacle was only moved when it was absolutely necessary, as when disaster came upon it at Shiloh or Nob; (3) or David simply focused on building the temple, not continuing the tabernacle.

Solomon's dream recorded in 1 Kings 3:5–15 is one of the more significant dreams in the Bible. God offers him an amazing opportunity, with an amazing promise. This isn't because Solomon sacrificed a thousand animals; it is because his heart is surrendered to God.

Take It Home

The natural reaction to reading this promise of God to Solomon is to wish we had such promises. We do (see Matthew 7:7; John 15:7; 1 John 5:14).

Solomon praises God before asking for anything, and he remembers God's faithfulness to both his father David and himself. He acknowledges that he comes to God in great humility, and especially considering the job in front of him.

With that, Solomon asks for more than great knowledge; he wants understanding, and he wants it in his heart, not merely in his head. Actually, the ancient Hebrew word translated *understanding* is literally, "hearing." Solomon wants a hearing heart, one that will listen to God.

God is pleased by Solomon's request. God knew his great need for wisdom, discernment, and understanding. God is also pleased by what Solomon does not ask for: riches, fame, or power for himself.

God answers Solomon beyond all expectations (3:11-14). Solomon doesn't ask for riches and honor, but God gives him these things. Solomon experiences God's ability to do far beyond all that we ask or imagine (see Ephesians 3:20).

Then Solomon awakes and realizes it is a dream (1 Kings 3:15). But at the same time he knows it is a message from God. God does answer Solomon's prayer and makes him wise, powerful, rich, and influential. His reign is glorious for Israel.

Critical Observation

We can fairly say that Solomon tragically wasted the gifts God gave him. Though he accomplished much, he could have done much more—and his heart was led away from God in the end (1 Kings 11:4–11).

📖 **3:16–28**

AN EXAMPLE OF SOLOMON'S GREAT WISDOM

One of the most famous stories in the Bible is found in 1 Kings 3:16-28. That Solomon would take the time to settle a dispute between two prostitutes is testimony to his goodness and generosity.

The problem of two mothers claiming one baby seems impossible to solve. It's one woman's word against another's.

Solomon's solution to the problem (a sword) at first seems foolish, even dangerous. The wisdom of his creative approach is only understood when the matter is settled. In the same way, the works and the judgments of God often first seem strange, dangerous, or even foolish. Time shows them to be perfect wisdom.

The true mother's love is revealed in verse 26. She would rather have the child live without her than to die with her. She puts the child's welfare above her own.

Solomon issues his ruling in 3:27, rewarding the baby to its mother, and causing all of Israel to hold him in awe because they know Solomon has wisdom from God.

1 KINGS 4:1–34

SOLOMON'S ADMINISTRATION

Solomon's Cabinet and Governors	4:1–19
The Prosperity of Solomon and Israel	4:20–28
Solomon's God-Given Wisdom	4:29–34

Setting Up the Section

Solomon's leadership is organized, creative, and, initially at least, non-oppressive, perpetuating the prosperity established by his father David.

SOLOMON'S CABINET AND GOVERNORS

Solomon is a leader of leaders. No wise leader does it all himself; he knows how to delegate responsibility and authority and get the job done.

Solomon's great wisdom enables him to see the need to acquire, train, and employ the right people to meet those needs.

In verses 2–6, we learn how the government is structured—much like that in modern nations. There are chief officials who serve as ministers, or secretaries, over their specific areas of responsibility.

Jehoshaphat also served under David (2 Samuel 8:16; 20:24; 1 Kings 4:3). The role of recorder is more than a historian. Scholars say he was like a chief of protocol, or even a secretary of state.

Critical Observation

Abiathar is listed as a priest (4:4). Including him after his exile (2:26) seems to be a problem. But scholars remind us that Solomon could not take away his title as priest, even if he banished him.

In 4:7–19 we learn of Solomon's twelve district governors over Israel. These men are responsible for taxation in their individual districts. The districts are strictly separated by tribal borders, as had been done in the past, but often according to mountains, land, and region. Thus, Solomon's leadership is creative. He is willing to try new things.

Each governor is required to make provision for one month of the year. It doesn't seem too much to do one-twelfth of the work, so each of these governors likely doesn't feel overwhelmed by the burden of raising so much in taxes. Taxes are paid in grain and livestock, which are used to support the royal court and the central government.

THE PROSPERITY OF SOLOMON AND ISRAEL

Under Solomon's leadership, Israel is described as large, happy, and expansive (4:20–21). It is a golden age for Israel as a nation. The population has grown robustly, and it is a season of great prosperity, allowing plenty of leisure time and pursuit of good pleasures.

Solomon's reign encompasses all kingdoms from the Euphrates River to the border of Egypt, well beyond what Abraham was promised. Solomon is not a warrior or a general. This peace was achieved by King David and is enjoyed by King Solomon. It is also assisted—under God's providence—by a season of decline and weakness among Israel's neighbor states.

Such an empire requires a lot. The daily provision described in 4:22–23 is of course not for Solomon only. This is for Solomon's entire household, his royal court, and their families. Some estimate that this much food every day could feed 15,000 to 36,000 people.

Demystifying 1 Kings

The kor, or cor, equaled 220 liters or about 55 gallons. We can accurately picture thirty 55-gallon drums full of fine flour being delivered for every day.

Part of the prosperity encourages Solomon's collection of horses and chariots. His famous stables show what a vast cavalry he has assembled for Israel. Second Chronicles 9:25 is a parallel passage and has 4,000 chariots instead of 40,000: The smaller number seems correct, and the larger number is probably due to copyist error.

Unfortunately, it also shows that Solomon does not take God's Word as seriously as he should. In Deuteronomy 17:16, God speaks specifically to the future kings of Israel about acquiring horses for themselves. One may argue if twenty or one hundred horses violate the command, certainly forty thousand stalls of horses do.

Yet at this point, there is order, and each officer meets his obligation to provide what is expected of his district (1 Kings 4:27-28).

Take It Home

Each follower of Jesus Christ has a charge to fulfill in the kingdom of God, and we should be diligent to perform it—and expectant in being supplied for it.

📖 4:29-34

SOLOMON'S GOD-GIVEN WISDOM

Because of God's gift of wisdom, Solomon becomes a prominent and famous man, even among kings (4:29-34). In a strong sense, this is the fulfillment of the great promises to an obedient Israel described in Deuteronomy 28:1, 10.

Ethan the Ezrahite and Heman are mentioned in 1 Kings 4:31. Ethan is the author of Psalm 89, and Heman is the author of Psalm 88. The other names are only mentioned in this passage.

Only some of Solomon's three thousand proverbs are preserved in the book of Proverbs. He composes songs (1 Kings 4:31), but few psalms.

Solomon's wisdom more so concerns science and nature (4:32-34). He knows much about plant life, animals, birds, reptiles, and fish—the spectrum of created things.

1 KINGS 5:1–18

PREPARATIONS TO BUILD THE TEMPLE

Setting Up the Section

Solomon nurtures his father's friendship with the king of neighboring Tyre, who helps supply him with needed materials and manpower for the building of the temple.

📄 **5:1–12**

SOLOMON'S ARRANGEMENTS WITH HIRAM OF TYRE

Hiram, the king of Tyre, reaches out to Solomon, son of his friend, King David. David was a mighty warrior against the enemies of Israel. But he did not regard every neighbor nation as an enemy. David wisely built alliances and friendships with neighboring nations, and the benefit of this reaches Solomon.

Solomon's reply in verses 3–6 refers to Hiram's knowledge of David's wish to build a temple. This means that David told Hiram spiritual things.

David couldn't build the temple until he had vanquished his enemies and no natural disasters threatened (5:4). Now Solomon enjoys that peace and intends to take advantage of it.

He proposes to build a house to honor God. He wants to show reverence by setting the plan apart from pagan practices, as Solomon notes in 2 Chronicles 2:6, where builders construct actual residences for their gods.

So Solomon begins to obtain the materials needed for the temple. He doesn't start from scratch, though. David had already gathered some supplies (2 Chronicles 22:4).

The cedar trees of Lebanon were legendary for their excellent timber. This means Solomon wants to build the temple out of the best materials possible.

The king of Tyre is pleased by Solomon's message and request (1 Kings 5:7). We can't say if Hiram is a believer, but he certainly seems to have respect for the God of Israel—perhaps due to David's godly influence. He sets a plan in motion.

Solomon offers Hiram whatever he wants as payment for the timber to build the temple. The arrangement is for Hiram to send logs by sea in exchange for payment and food.

In 5:10–12 the two leaders enjoy peace and a good business arrangement leading to a treaty.

📄 **5:13–18**

SOLOMON'S LABOR FORCE

Solomon's wisdom is evident in the way he employs this great workforce. First, in verse 14, he wisely delegates responsibility to men like Adoniram. Second, instead of making the Israelites work constantly away from home, he works them in shifts, as described in 5:13–14.

In addition, verses 15–18 seem to suggest that those who carry burdens and quarry stone are Canaanite slave laborers.

Three hundred from the chiefs of Solomon's deputies form the middle management team, administrating the work of building the temple.

The fact that the stones are quality shows that Solomon is determined to use the best materials, even in the temple's foundation where the stones cannot be seen.

The men of Gebal (5:18) may refer to the inhabitants of Biblos, north of Sidon, on the coast of the Mediterranean Sea.

Take It Home

Solomon's use of quality stones in the foundation of the temple speaks to the way we should work for God. We don't work for appearance only, but also to excel in the deep and hidden things.

It also speaks to the way God works in us. He works in our hearts, when others are concerned with appearances. It also speaks to the way God builds the church. He wants to do a work of strong foundations instead of a work a mile wide but an inch deep.

1 KINGS 6:1–38

THE CONSTRUCTION OF THE TEMPLE

Setting Up the Section

Solomon begins to build the temple four hundred years after the Israelites began worshiping God at His tabernacle. Solomon uses only the very best skills, men, and materials of his day.

📖 6:1–10

BASIC DIMENSIONS AND STRUCTURE

According to the first verse of chapter 6, Solomon begins to build the temple in the fourth year of his reign. This shows just how long Israel lived in the promised land without a temple. The tabernacle served the nation well for more than four hundred years. The temple being built, then, was prompted more from divine instruction than out of absolute necessity.

The actual construction begins in the second month of the fourth year, but Solomon probably began organizing the work right away, building on the preparation his father David had already completed. There is some evidence that it took three years to prepare timber from Lebanon for use in building. If Solomon began the construction of the temple in the fourth year of his reign, he probably started organizing the construction in the very first year of his reign.

The work is carefully organized and planned even before Solomon becomes king. In fact, 1 Chronicles 28:11–12 reveals that David gave Solomon the plans for the temple that the Holy Spirit had given him. They included plans for the vestibule, treasuries, upper chambers, inner chambers, the mercy seat, the courts, and the chambers. Everything was planned.

Demystifying 1 Kings

The temple's length is 60 cubits, its width 20 cubits, and its height 30 cubits. Assuming that the ancient cubit was approximately 18 inches (perhaps one-half meter), this means that the temple proper was approximately 90 feet (30 meters) long, 30 feet (10 meters) wide, and 45 feet (15 meters) high. This was not especially large as ancient temples go, but the glory of Israel's temple was not in its size.

Allowing for the outside storage rooms, the vestibule, and the estimated thickness of the walls, the total size of the structure was perhaps 75 cubits long (110 feet, 37 meters) and 50 cubits wide (75 feet, 25 meters).

The dimensions of the temple tell us that it was built on the same basic design as the tabernacle, but twice as large. This means that Solomon meant the temple to be a continuation of the tabernacle. The difference, however, is that the temple was a permanent structure. The last of the internal enemies of Israel had been conquered, and the people were permanently established in the land.

Take It Home

During the temple's construction, no hammer or chisel or any iron tool was heard at the site itself (6:7). The stones used to build the temple were all cut and prepared at another site. The stones were only assembled at the building site of the temple.

This speaks to the way God wants His work done. The temple had to be built with human labor. Yet Solomon did not want the sound of man's work to dominate the site of the temple. He wanted to communicate, as much as possible, that the temple is of God and not of man.

6:11–38

GOD'S PROMISE AND SOLOMON'S BUILDING

At some point during the building, the word of the Lord comes to Solomon (6:11–13). We might say that there is nothing particularly new in this promise. These are essentially the same promises of the old covenant made to Israel at Sinai. But this is an important reminder and renewal of previous promises.

God says that if Solomon walks in His statutes, He will fulfill His promises to David through Solomon. Notice it is conditional.

God promises an obedient Solomon that he will reign and be blessed, fulfilling the promises God made to David about his reign (2 Samuel 7:5–16). He also promises that His special presence will remain among Israel as a nation. He seems to be careful to not say that He will live *in* the temple, the way pagans believe their gods live in temples. He will dwell among the children of Israel. The temple is a special place for people to meet with God.

In 6:14–38, we learn of the beautiful finishing touches Solomon installs. For example, he panels the temple with beams and boards of cedar; these are some of the finest building materials available. The impression is of a magnificent building.

He also builds side chambers against the entire temple. This describes the rooms adjacent to the temple, surrounding it on the north, west, and south sides. These side chambers are built in three stories.

The inner sanctuary is 20 cubits long, 20 cubits wide, and 20 cubits high: Special attention is given to the Holy of Holies, or Most Holy Place. It is a 30-foot (10 meter) cube, completely overlaid with gold. It also has two large sculptures of cherubim (15 feet or 5 meters in height), which are overlaid with gold.

It is mentioned that gold chains are hung across the veil separating the Holy Place from the Most Holy Place, accentuating the idea that the Most Holy Place is inaccessible (6:21).

The two cherubim—angels—made of olive wood are large sculptures inside the Most Holy Place, facing the entrance to this inner room, so as soon as the high priest enters he sees these giant guardians of the presence of God.

There is gold everywhere in the temple. The walls are covered with it (6:20–22), the floor is covered with it (6:30), and gold is hammered into the carvings on the doors (6:32).

The walls all around the temple, both the inner and outer sanctuaries, are carved with figures of cherubim, palm trees, and open flowers. This is modeled after the pattern of the tabernacle, which had woven designs of cherubim on the inner covering. The curtain was a deep blue with cherubim—the person who saw it would know that they were in heaven on earth

In 6:36 we see the inner court is the court of the priests, where the altar and laver are set and sacrifices conducted. Outside it is the great court, where the people come to pray.

Critical Observation

It must always be remembered that under the old covenant, the temple was not for the people of Israel; it was only for the priests to meet with God on behalf of the people. The people gathered and worshiped in the outer courtyard.

Demystifying 1 Kings

The writer of 1 Kings never tells us exactly where the temple was built, but the writer of 2 Chronicles tells us it was built on Mount Moriah (2 Chronicles 3:1), the same place where Abraham went to sacrifice Isaac, and—on another part of the hill—where Jesus would be sacrificed.

It takes Solomon and his thousands of workers seven years to finish the temple (6:38). It is a spectacular building. It is easy for Israel to focus on the temple of God instead of the God of the temple. Yet without continued faithfulness to God, the temple's glory quickly fades. This glorious temple will be plundered just five years after the death of Solomon (14:25–27).

1 KINGS 7:1–51

SOLOMON'S PALACE AND THE TEMPLE FURNISHINGS

The Construction of Solomon's Palace	7:1–12
Huram Makes the Temple Furnishings	7:13–51

Setting Up the Section

Solomon may have taken seven years to build the temple, but he puts almost twice that into building his palace. Meanwhile, a skilled bronze worker crafts the temple's furnishings.

📄 7:1–12

THE CONSTRUCTION OF SOLOMON'S PALACE

The writer notes in the first verse of 1 Kings 7 that it takes Solomon almost twice as long (thirteen years) to build his palace as to finish the temple. The temple is glorious, but it seems that Solomon wants a house that is more glorious than the temple.

Its magnificence is described in verses 2–12. Noteworthy is the prevalence of cedar wood from Lebanon—so much so that the structure comes to be known as the Palace of the Forest of Lebanon. Walking in the richly paneled walls of the palace is like walking in a forest. The roof is cedar also (7:3).

Critical Observation

First Kings 10:16–17 says that five hundred gold shields hang in the House of the Forest of Lebanon. Isaiah specifically calls this building an armory in Isaiah 22:8.

At the end of the detailed, magnificent description of Solomon's palace, the writer mentions that some of the great architectural features of the palace are also used in the house of the Lord.

Take It Home

The magnificent cathedrals of old Europe were mostly built hundreds of years ago at great labor and cost to poor people who could never dream of living in such spectacular places. When their most magnificent buildings were churches, it said something about their values. When Solomon made his palace more spectacular than the temple, it said something about his values.

📄 7:13–51

HURAM MAKES THE TEMPLE FURNISHINGS

In verse 13, Solomon hires the best bronze craftsman in the business: Huram from Tyre, who is half Israelite and half Gentile. Huram makes the needed furnishings for the temple after the pattern of the tabernacle furnishings.

Critical Observation

Huram from Tyre casts two pillars of bronze (7:15), structures so impressive that they are given names: *Jachin*, meaning "He shall establish" and *Boaz*, meaning "in strength." Some take this to mean they are a reminder that kings rule by God's appointment and with God's strength. They're mentioned also in 2 Chronicles 3:17.

Others believe that the pillars are meant to remind Israel of the twin pillars from the Exodus. The pillar of fire by night and the pillar of cloud by day are constant reminders of the presence of God in the wilderness.

Regardless, every time someone comes to the house of the Lord in the days of Solomon, they are reminded of these truths and put in the right frame of mind to worship God.

Huram makes the sea of cast bronze, 10 cubits from one brim to the other. The huge laver is more than 15 feet (5 meters) across and is to be used for the ceremonial washings connected with the temple. In addition, Huram makes ten identical lavers of bronze, with each laver containing forty baths. It is significant that the sea was a symbol of chaos, and here God has tamed chaos.

On the golden table sits the bread (7:48). Second Chronicles 4:8 says there are ten individual tables of showbread, though here they are referred to as one.

All these great works of art and articles of great value go inside the temple. This includes the ten carts and the shovels, bowls, and other needed utensils for sacrifices.

When all is finished Solomon brings in the silver and gold furnishings that his father David already had dedicated. God told David that he could not build the temple, but David was still able to collect furnishings and treasures for the temple that his son would build (1 Chronicles 29).

1 KINGS 8:1–66

THE DEDICATION OF THE TEMPLE

Setting Up the Section

In what must have been a celebration on the scale of our modern installation of a new pope, Solomon assembles the elders of Israel, the heads of the tribe, and the chiefs of the families for the dedication of the temple.

📄 **8:1–21**

THE ARK OF THE COVENANT IS BROUGHT TO THE TEMPLE

Solomon chooses the seventh month (8:2) for the dedication, eleven months after the temple is finished (6:38). This may have been because it was the time for the Feast of Tabernacles.

By making it clear that the priests are the ones who carry the ark, the author of 1 Kings shows how Solomon is carefully obeying what God commanded about transporting the ark of the covenant. He will not repeat the error of his father David in 2 Samuel 6:1–8.

The ark, which David had already brought up to Jerusalem (2 Samuel 6), is the most important item in the temple—it represents God's presence—but it is not the only item. The book of Exodus records God's instruction about the items kept in the tabernacle (Exodus 30:25–29). The priests bring these other items into the temple: the lamp stand, the table of showbread, and the altar of incense.

Demystifying 1 Kings

First Kings 8:9 says that the ark holds nothing but the two tablets of stone that Moses put there at Horeb. Yet earlier in Israel's history the ark held the golden pot that had the manna (Exodus 16:33) and Aaron's rod that budded (Numbers 17:6–11), as well as the tablets of the covenant (Exodus 25:16). We don't know what happened to the golden pot of manna and Aaron's rod, but they are not in the ark when Solomon sets it in the Most Holy Place.

The description of sacrificing so many sheep and cattle (8:5) sounds as if Solomon goes overboard in his effort to honor God on this great day.

The reminder of the deliverance from Egypt (8:9) is significant, because there is a sense in which this—some five hundred years after the Exodus—is the culmination of the deliverance from Egypt. Out of Egypt and into the wilderness, Israel, out of necessity, lived in tents—and the dwelling of God was a tent. Now, since Solomon built the temple, the dwelling of God among Israel is a *building*, a place of permanence and security.

After the ark is in place, the priests withdraw from the Holy Place, and the temple fills with the cloud of glory (8:10).

Demystifying 1 Kings

The cloud of God's glory that filled the temple in the Most Holy Place—later called the Shekinah Glory—is hard to define. We might call it the radiant outshining of His character and presence. It's so intense that the priests have to stop performing their service.

This glory remained at the temple until Israel utterly rejects God in the days of the divided monarchy. The prophet Ezekiel sees the glory depart the temple (Ezekiel 10:18).

Take It Home

We know that God is good and that God is love—why should an intense presence of goodness and love make the priests feel they could not continue? Because God is not only goodness and love, He is also *holy*. And the holiness of God made the priests feel that they could no longer stand in His presence.

The intense sense of the presence of God is not a warm and fuzzy feeling. Men like Peter (Luke 5:8), Isaiah (Isaiah 6:5), and John (Revelation 1:17) felt *stricken* in the presence of God. This is not because God forced an uncomfortable feeling upon them, but because they simply could not be comfortable sensing the difference between their sinfulness and God's holiness.

In his response in 8:12–13, Solomon senses that the cloud means that God dwells in the temple in a special way. It is good to recognize a special place to come meet with God, as long as it doesn't turn into something superstitious.

Solomon goes on to make a short speech in which he recognizes that the temple is the fulfillment of God's plan, not David's or Solomon's. They were just the instruments of God's work.

In verse 16 Solomon presses the remembrance of the Exodus. Though it happened five hundred years before, it is just as important and real for Israel as the day it happened.

📄 8:22–53

SOLOMON'S PRAYER

Solomon does not dedicate the temple from *within* the temple. It would be inappropriate for him to do so, because he is a king and not a priest. The Holy Place and Most Holy Place are only for chosen descendants of the high priest.

As Solomon prays he spreads out his hands toward heaven. This is the most common posture of prayer in the Old Testament. Solomon recognizes God is unique and incomparable, and the maker and keeper of promises. He thanks God for His past fulfillment of promises. Then he calls upon God to keep the promises that He made.

In 8:27–30, Solomon recognizes God as transcendent and asks God to dwell in this place and honor those who seek Him here. From statements in verses 12–13 we might think Solomon had a superstitious idea that God actually lived *in* the temple. That makes his comments here even more important. God cannot be restricted to a structure built by human hands—even heaven itself is not big enough for Him.

He asks God to forgive in verses 28 and 30. Next, Solomon asks God to incline His ear toward the king and his people when they pray from the temple. For this reason, many observant Jews still pray facing the direction of the site of the temple in Jerusalem.

He also asks that God hear when the people take an oath at the temple.

Take It Home

This is the great secret to power in prayer—to take God's promises to heart in faith and then boldly and reverently call upon Him to fulfill the promises. This kind of prayer takes possession of God's promise. Just because God made promises doesn't mean we possess them. Through believing prayer like this, God promises and we appropriate. If we don't appropriate in faith, God's promise is left unclaimed.

Demystifying 1 Kings

The temple grounds were used as a place to verify and authorize oaths. When a dispute came down to one word against another, Solomon asked that the temple would be a place to properly swear by.

In 8:33–40, Solomon asks God to hear when the people are defeated, whether due to their own sin, attack from enemies, or during plague and famine.

Take It Home

Solomon recognizes that some plagues are easily seen, but other plagues come from the heart. Solomon asks God to answer such a plague-stricken person when he or she humbly asks, since God knows the heart. A person does not have to be sinless or righteous to have prayer answered. The guilty can find a gracious God if He is sought in humble repentance.

Solomon doesn't forget the people outside Israel who seek God. In 8:41–43, he asks God to hear the prayer of the foreigner out of a missionary impulse. He knows that when God mercifully answers the prayers of foreigners, it draws those from other nations to the God of all nations.

Critical Observation

The temple was in Israel, but it was always intended to be a house of prayer for *all* nations (Isaiah 56:7). The first-century temple included a court of the Gentiles to be a place where the nations could come and pray.

The violation of this principle made Jesus angry in Matthew 21, when He came to the temple and found the outer courts—the only place where the Gentile nations could come to pray—more like a swap meet than a house of prayer. He drove out the money changers and the merchants.

Solomon states in 1 Kings 8:46 what Paul reiterates in Romans 3:23: All human beings sin and fall short of God's glory.

Solomon wraps up his magnificent prayer by asking God to hear Israel's prayer in war and to recognize their sin and offenses in defeat.

🖹 8:54–66

SOLOMON BLESSES THE PEOPLE

Solomon praises God for past fulfillment of promises and asks Him to be with Israel now and forever—that all the people of the earth may know the Lord.

As part of the feast surrounding the dedication of the temple, Solomon offers a staggering amount of sacrifice (8:62–66). It is such a great amount of sacrifice that they just specially consecrate the area in front of the temple to receive sacrifices, because the bronze altar is too small.

Demystifying 1 Kings

The sacrifice of 22,000 cattle and 120,000 sheep and goats is enough to feed a vast multitude for two weeks. It appears that the celebrations are followed by the regular observance of the Feast of Tabernacles.

The dedication of the temple ends where the story of the temple begins: with David, not Solomon, with the people glad in heart for what the Lord had done for His servant David and His people Israel (8:66). The writer remembers that it was David's heart and vision that started the work of the temple (2 Samuel 7:1–3 and following).

1 KINGS 9:1–28

GOD'S WARNING TO SOLOMON

God Appears to Solomon Again	9:1–9
The Ways and Means of Solomon's Building Projects	9:10–28

Setting Up the Section

God again visits Solomon and gives him a promise and a warning. Meanwhile, the king negotiates with his old friend and neighbor, King Hiram of Tyre, and we are told of the forced labor for his other major projects.

📄 **9:1–9**

GOD APPEARS TO SOLOMON AGAIN

Approximately twenty-four years after Solomon came to the throne, he has finished his greatest accomplishments: the temple and the palace in Jerusalem. Some experts comment that the verb in verse 1 conveys a desire like a bridegroom toward his bride, and this obsession may have been the start of Solomon's fall.

God's second appearance to Solomon is more crucial. (The first is in 3:5–9.) He assures Solomon in verse 3 that He heard his great prayer at the temple dedication. God also confirms that He consecrated the temple. The building was Solomon's work, done in the power and inspiration of God. The consecration of the building was God's work. Solomon can build a building, but only God can hallow it.

But then God turns to Solomon himself. God's answer to Solomon's previous prayer has a great condition (9:4–5). If Solomon walks before God in obedience and faithfulness, he can expect blessing on his reign and the reign of his descendants, and the dynasty of David will endure forever. God does not demand perfect obedience from Solomon. David certainly did not walk perfectly before the Lord, and God tells Solomon to walk before Him as his father David walked. This is not out of reach for Solomon.

God warns Solomon (9:6–9) if the condition is not met. If Solomon or his descendants turn from following Him, God promises to correct a disobedient Israel.

God's previous answer to Solomon's prayer in 1 Kings 8 was not an unqualified promise to bless the temple in any circumstance. With such a glorious temple, Israel will be tempted to forsake the God of the temple and make an idol of the temple itself. Here God makes it known that He will never bless this error. He will cast it out of His sight if the kings of Israel forsake Him.

Critical Observation

Under the old covenant, God promised to use Israel to exalt Himself among the nations one way or another. If Israel obeyed, He would bless them so much that others can't help but recognize the hand of God upon Israel. If Israel disobeyed, He would chastise them so severely that the nations would know that the Lord has brought all this calamity on them.

9:10–28

THE WAYS AND MEANS OF SOLOMON'S BUILDING PROJECTS

Solomon next makes a new arrangement with his old friend and neighbor, King Hiram of Tyre, who had supplied him with cedar and pine and gold for the temple and palace. Tyre, the prominent city of the land just north of Israel, in what is now modern Lebanon, was noted for its fine wood.

The twenty settlements Solomon mortgages to Hiram do not please the king. Hiram nicknames the cities *Kabul* or *Cabul*, which literally means "good-for-nothing." It's not clear why, but they appear to be fairly insignificant towns. Solomon, apparently a shrewd dealer, receives a large amount of gold in return, an estimated four tons (9:14).

The forced labor described in verses 15–24 came from remnant Canaanite peoples. Solomon gathered the workforce to complete massive building projects. Archaeology is a witness to the ambitious and successful building projects of Solomon.

This is another apparent compromise by Solomon. God strictly commanded that the remnants of these tribes be driven out of the land, not used as slave laborers in Israel. Solomon doesn't make Israelites forced laborers, but he uses them to oversee the remnants of the Canaanite tribes.

Demystifying 1 Kings

Hazor, Megiddo, and Gezer were three prominently fortified cities in the days of Solomon. Hazor controlled the north, and Megiddo was the great fortress that controlled the major passes from the Plain of Sharon on the coast into the Valley of Jezreel through the Carmel range. (It figures in prophecy as the staging area for Armageddon, in which Christ will defeat the forces of the Antichrist.) Gezer, on the great north-south trade route, was given to Solomon as a wedding gift by Pharaoh to his daughter.

The reference in verse 25, describing that Solomon offered burnt offerings three times a year, may have been a transgression by Solomon. It may be that he took upon himself the exclusive duties of a priest. But it also could be that the phrase refers to him initiating the ceremonies through a priest properly. The three festivals likely are Passover, Pentecost, and Tabernacles (Exodus 23:14–17; Deuteronomy 16).

Solomon also builds ships (1 Kings 9:26–28), perhaps under the influence of Hiram, who sends him sailors. The fleet sails to Ophir and brings back 420 talents of gold.

Critical Observation

No one knows where Ophir was located. Suggestions have included southern Arabia, the eastern coast of Africa, and India.

1 KINGS 10:1–29

THE QUEEN OF SHEBA VISITS SOLOMON

The Queen's Visit	10:1–13
Solomon's Great Wealth	10:14–29

Setting Up the Section

The queen of Sheba travels thousands of miles to see Solomon's riches and wisdom for herself, and indeed the reader of 1 Kings 10 is given a taste of his vast wealth and possessions.

📄 10:1–13

THE QUEEN'S VISIT

The queen of Sheba visits Solomon and Israel at their material zenith. But Solomon's kingdom is famous not only for its prosperity but also for the king's great wisdom. The queen comes to test him with hard questions (10:1). She travels in the manner of queens—with a large royal procession, heavily laden with gifts and goods for trade (10:2).

Demystifying 1 Kings

Sheba, also known as Sabea, was where modern day Yemen is today in southern Arabia. We know from geography this was a wealthy kingdom, with much gold, spices, and precious woods. History also tells us that they were known to have queens as well as kings.

The trip to Israel was long, about 1,500 miles, or 2,400 kilometers. The queen probably came as part of a trade delegation, as implied in 10:2–5, but there is no doubt that she was highly motivated to see Solomon and his kingdom.

The queen challenges Solomon with questions, perhaps diplomatic and ethical in nature, which Solomon answers fully (10:2–3). That, and all that the queen sees of his kingdom, is overwhelming (10:5).

She obviously is familiar with the world of royal splendor and luxury. Yet she says Solomon's court is twice as magnificent as she expected (10:7). Not only that, but she notices that his staff and servants are happy (10:8).

Then she draws the connection to Solomon's God in verse 9. It is fair to ask if this is a true confession of faith, expressing allegiance to the God of Israel. Taken in context, her beautifully phrased language may only be a diplomatic response to the astonishing blessing evident in Solomon's Jerusalem.

Critical Observation

The queen of Sheba's reaction to God's blessing on Solomon and Israel is an example of what God wanted to do for Israel under the promises of the old covenant. God promised Israel that if they obeyed under the old covenant, He would bless them so tremendously that the world would notice and give glory to the Lord of Israel (Deuteronomy 28:1, 10). If Israel did not obey, then God would speak to the nations through a thoroughly disciplined Israel.

Take It Home

If we take the queen of Sheba as an example of a seeker, as Jesus did in Matthew 12:42, we see that Solomon impressed her with his wealth and splendor and also impressed her personally. But she returned home without an evident expression of faith in the God of Israel. This shows that impressing seekers with facilities, programs, and professionalism isn't enough.

Yet, if the queen of Sheba sought Solomon and the splendor of his kingdom so diligently, how much more should people today seek Jesus and the glory of His kingdom?

She acknowledges how Solomon was chosen by God (10:9). This statement is especially meaningful because Solomon is not necessarily the most logical successor of his father David. There were several sons of David born before Solomon.

📄 **10:14–29**

SOLOMON'S GREAT WEALTH

Solomon is an extremely wealthy ruler (10:14–15). The 660 talents of gold itself is a vast amount of gold even by today's standards.

The writer of 1 Kings gives a warning here. He assumes that we know of the instructions for future kings of Israel in Deuteronomy 17:14–20, specifically verse 17. In that passage God tells rulers not to multiply silver and gold for themselves.

God blesses Solomon with great riches, but Solomon allows that blessing to turn into a danger because he disobediently multiplies silver and gold for himself.

In 1 Kings 10:16–26, we are given examples of Solomon's wealth and prosperity. He is so rich that silver holds no value (10:21, 27). In fact, verses 24–25 imply he is the richest man on earth, and the whole earth wants an audience (and is willing to bring gifts to get one).

His golden shields are beautifully displayed in the House of the Forest of Lebanon, Solomon's palace, but they are of no use in battle. Gold is too heavy and too soft to be used as a metal for effective shields. This shows Solomon in the image of a warrior king, but without the substance.

Solomon still recognizes the need for a strong defense, despite not being a warrior. In verses 26–29 we are told of his immense collection of chariots, horses, horsemen, stables, and fortresses.

Critical Observation

When we think of Solomon's great wealth, we also consider that he originally did not set his heart upon riches. He deliberately asked for wisdom to lead the people of God instead of riches or fame. God promised to *also* give Solomon riches and fame, and God fulfilled His promise.

We also consider that Solomon gave an eloquent testimony to the vanity of riches as the preacher in the book of Ecclesiastes. He powerfully showed that there was no ultimate satisfaction through materialism. We don't have to be as rich as Solomon to learn the same lesson.

Demystifying 1 Kings

In 10:28–29, Solomon's horses are imported from Egypt, in direct disobedience to Deuteronomy 17:16, which prohibits it. Yet, perhaps the importation of horses from Egypt began as trading as an agent on behalf of other kings. From this, Solomon could say, "I'm importing horses from Egypt, but I am not doing it for myself. I'm not breaking God's command." Many examples of gross disobedience begin as clever rationalizations.

1 KINGS 11:1–43

SOLOMON'S DECLINE AND DEATH

Solomon's Apostasy	11:1–13
Two Foreign Adversaries	11:14–25
Jeroboam—A Special Adversary	11:26–43

Setting Up the Section

Solomon's love of foreign women leads to his downfall, and adversaries begin to rise as he approaches death.

📖 11:1–13

SOLOMON'S APOSTASY

The writer of 1 Kings confronts two obvious problems in verse 1: Solomon loves foreign women who worship other gods—from nations God specifically told Israel not to intermarry with (11:2)—and Solomon loves many women, rejecting God's plan from the beginning for one man and one woman to become one flesh in marriage (Genesis 2:23–24; Matthew 19:4–6).

Critical Observation

Seven hundred wives, princesses, and three hundred concubines is an almost unbelievable number of marriage partners. Solomon had so many marriage partners because he followed the bad example of his father David, who had many wives and concubines himself (2 Samuel 5:13–16). Why would he do that? It is likely a combination of two types of lust, sexual and the lust for power. In those days a large harem was a status symbol.

Solomon's wives turn him away from God. Age does not make Solomon wiser. He seems to be wiser in his youth, and old age has hardened the sinful tendencies that were present in his younger days. Age and experience should make us more godly and wise, but they do not automatically do so.

Not only does Solomon wander from the Lord, but he participates in worship of the false gods of the day: Ashtoreth, the goddess of the Sidonians, and Molech of the Ammonites (11:5, 7). Probably Solomon does not see this as a *denial* of the Lord of Israel. In his mind, he probably thought that he still honored God and just simply added the honor of these other gods to it. But this is never acceptable to God. He demands to be the *only* God in our life.

Take It Home

If this apostasy was the case with the wisest man who ever lived, then what hope do we have to remain faithful, apart from constant dependence upon Jesus Christ? Let the example of Solomon drive you to greater dependence and abiding with Jesus.

God's judgment comes to Solomon (11:9–13). God has special reason to be displeased with Solomon: He had appeared to him twice and warned him explicitly, and still Solomon went after other gods. Solomon's sin shows ingratitude and a waste of great spiritual privilege.

The Lord says in verses 9–13 that the kingdom will be divided; part of it will be loyal to the descendants of David, and part of it will be under a different dynasty. God promised the entire kingdom of Israel to the descendants of David forever, *if* they remained obedient. David reminded Solomon of this promise shortly before his death (2:4). Yet Israel could not remain faithful even one generation.

Yet for the sake of the memory of David, God delays this judgment until after Solomon's generation (11:13). Even in this great judgment, God mingles undeserved mercy with deserved judgment.

📄 **11:14–25**

TWO FOREIGN ADVERSARIES

Solomon's reign has been glorious, but God has not allowed it to be without problems. There are adversaries like Hadad and Rezon. Rezon is mentioned in 11:23–25. He causes problems out of Aram in the north country.

We are not told specifically how the two warriors attack Solomon, only that they trouble his reign.

📄 **11:26–43**

JEROBOAM—A SPECIAL ADVERSARY

Jeroboam is a fellow Israelite, which sets him apart from the previously mentioned adversaries. In fact, Solomon himself had chosen him (11:28) to oversee the labor force from the tribes of Ephraim and Manasseh (the house of Joseph) during the major projects listed in 11:27.

It is not immediately apparent why these construction projects cause Jeroboam to rebel against Solomon. But it is obvious from the comments from his visitors in verses 1–3 that the oppression of these projects was a reality.

Jeroboam receives a prophecy from Ahijah, perhaps a newly appointed prophet (wearing a new coat). Ahijah, in an acted-out prophecy, shows Jeroboam that he will lead ten tribes of a divided Israel after the death of Solomon.

God promises to make a lasting dynasty for Jeroboam *if* he will do what is right in the sight of the Lord (11:35). An obedient Jeroboam has the opportunity to establish a parallel dynasty to the house of David. Both Jeroboam and David are appointed by God to follow after disobedient kings. David waited upon the Lord to make the throne clear, and God blessed his reign. Jeroboam does not wait on God and makes his own way to the throne, and God does not bless his reign.

Solomon seeks to kill Jeroboam. This is more startling evidence of Solomon's decline. God specifically says the breakup of the kingdom will happen *after* the death of Solomon and in *judgment* of Solomon's apostasy. Solomon doesn't want to hear it, so he seeks to kill Jeroboam. Solomon thinks he can defeat God's will in this, but he is unsuccessful. God's word through Ahijah proves true.

In verses 41–43 we learn of Solomon's death. Many commentators believe that Solomon became king when he was about twenty years old and died around 932 BC, after forty years (a generation) of reign. This means that Solomon did not live a particularly long life. Some scholars also believe that Solomon wrote the book of Ecclesiastes at the very end of his life as a renunciation of his fall into vanity.

1 KINGS 12:1–33
REHOBOAM AND JEROBOAM

Setting Up the Section

Solomon's son, Rehoboam, is made king and opens the door for the breakup of the kingdom. His opponent, Jeroboam, begins his idolatrous rule over the northern kingdom.

📄 12:1–24

REHOBOAM AND THE DIVISION OF ISRAEL

After Solomon dies, the leaders of Israel gather at Shechem to make Rehoboam king (12:1). This is the logical continuation of the Davidic dynasty. Solomon succeeded David; now his son shall succeed him. Although Solomon had a thousand wives and concubines, we read of only one son by name, Rehoboam, and unfortunately he is a fool.

Demystifying 1 Kings

Shechem is a city with a rich history. Abraham worshiped there (Genesis 12:6). Jacob built an altar and purchased land there (Genesis 33:18–20). Joseph was buried there (Joshua 24:32). It was also the geographical center of the northern tribes. Having to meet the ten northern tribes on *their* territory instead of demanding that representatives come to Jerusalem is a weak start for Rehoboam.

Naturally, since God tells Jeroboam through a prophet that he will rule over a portion of a divided Israel when Solomon dies, he returns from Egypt when he hears of the gathering in Shechem. He was in Egypt hiding after Solomon sought to kill him. He joins the elders who address Rehoboam in 12:3–7.

Solomon was a great king, but he took a lot from the people. Israel seeks relief from the heavy taxation and forced service of Solomon's reign, and they offer allegiance to Rehoboam if he agrees to this.

Sadly, the elders of Israel make no spiritual demand or request on Rehoboam. Seemingly, Solomon's gross idolatry and apostasy doesn't bother them enough to seek a change.

Rehoboam sends the group away for three days (12:5-6) and consults with his father's advisors. Their response would be valuable for any ruler, but they also know that Rehoboam is not Solomon and cannot expect the same from the people that Solomon did. Rehoboam has to relate to the people based on who *he* is, not on who his father was. If he shows kindness and a servant's heart to the people, they will serve him forever.

Unfortunately, Rehoboam does not listen. He turns to the young men he grew up with. By turning to those likely to think just as he does, it shows that Rehoboam only asks for advice for the sake of appearances.

The younger advisors' response in 12:10-11 suggests a harsh approach—to make Rehoboam more feared than Solomon. That's how Rehoboam responds in verses 12-15, setting up destruction. God of course knew beforehand what would occur (12:15) but did not *make* Rehoboam take this unwise and sinful action. God simply left Rehoboam alone and allowed him to make the critical errors his sinful heart wanted to make.

Rehoboam's foolishness makes Israel reject him and the entire dynasty of David. They reject the descendants of Israel's greatest king.

Apparently, Rehoboam does not take the rebellions seriously until his chief tax collector, Adoniram, is murdered by an angry crowd and he himself barely escapes (12:18-19). Adoniram was the wrong man for Rehoboam to send. He was famous for his harsh policy of forced labor (4:6; 5:14). Rehoboam probably sent him because he wanted to make good on his promise to punish those who opposed him. His tough-guy policy doesn't work.

Demystifying 1 Kings

From this point (12:19) on in the history of Israel, the name *Israel* refers to the ten northern tribes, and the name *Judah* refers to the southern tribes of Benjamin and Judah.

There was a long-standing tension between the ten northern tribes and the combined group of Judah and Benjamin. There were two earlier rebellions along this line of potential division in the days after Absalom's rebellion (2 Samuel 19:40-43), which developed into the rebellion of Sheba (2 Samuel 20:1-2).

Now Israel turns to Jeroboam and makes him their king (12:20-24). At the time the prophecy of Ahijah (11:29-39) was made, it seemed unlikely that Jeroboam would prevail; but here we see God's word fulfilled.

Demystifying 1 Kings

King Jeroboam is sometimes called Jeroboam I to distinguish him from a later king of Israel also named Jeroboam, usually known as Jeroboam II (2 Kings 14:23–29).

Rehoboam makes plans to reunify the nation by force, but God speaks through a prophet, Shemaiah, and stops him. To his credit, or perhaps due to a lack of courage, Rehoboam listens to God this time.

📄 **12:25–33**

JEROBOAM'S IDOLATRY

In his first acts as leader of the northern kingdom, Jeroboam makes Shechem his capital, because Jerusalem is in the territory of Judah and Benjamin. Then he builds the strategic defensive town of Penuel across the Jordan River.

But instead of following Ahijah's prophecy, in which God promises him an enduring house if he follows God's ways, Jeroboam next promotes false religion to serve his purposes (12:26–29).

The fact that the kingdom is divided does not mean that the northern tribes are exempt from their covenant obligations; they are still under the Law of Moses as much as the southern tribes. Jeroboam fears the *political* implications of yearly trips down to the capital city of the southern kingdom of Judah. So he appeals to a natural desire for convenience in 12:28 and sets up idols in Bethel and Dan.

Demystifying 1 Kings

Jeroboam repeats the same idolatrous words of Aaron about five hundred years before his time: "Here are your gods, O Israel" (Exodus 32:4). It is bad enough for Jeroboam to pervert obedience to the one God Almighty, but it's even more of a sin when the people follow him. He continues to make more places of worship than the main centers at Bethel and Dan. He then goes so far as to establish a priesthood of his own liking, rejecting the commandments of God regarding the priesthood of Israel. He even serves as a priest himself.

Critical Observation

The legitimate priests and Levites who lived in the northern ten tribes did not like Jeroboam's actions. They, along with others who set their hearts to seek God, moved from the northern kingdom of Israel to the southern kingdom of Judah during this period (2 Chronicles 11:13–16). Spiritually speaking, Israel was struck twice: by the ungodly religion of Jeroboam and by the departure of the godly and faithful. There were few godly people left in the northern kingdom.

1 KINGS 13:1–34

THE MAN OF GOD FROM JUDAH

A Prophecy from a Man of God	13:1–10
The Man of God's Disobedience and Death	13:11–34

Setting Up the Section

A prophet comes up from Judah to prophesy against Jeroboam, and then he himself becomes an object of God's judgment.

📄 **13:1–10**

A PROPHECY FROM A MAN OF GOD

As the chapter opens, a man of God comes up from Judah to prophesy at the false altar at Bethel. Apparently, there are no qualified messengers within the northern kingdom of Israel. This is a sad commentary on the spiritual state of Jeroboam's kingdom.

This man of God says a child named Josiah will be born to the house of David (13:2). Addressing the altar, he says Josiah will sacrifice false priests on it. This remarkable prophecy will be precisely fulfilled 340 years later (2 Kings 23:15).

Critical Observation

The man of God's prophecy is more than a pronouncement of judgment against the altar; it also announces that the judgment will come through a ruler of Judah (the house of David). This is a special rebuke and source of concern to Jeroboam, who has always been aware of the threat from his neighbor to the south (1 Kings 12:27).

The man from Judah says the sign to confirm the prophecy will be this: The altar will split and its ashes will pour out (1 Kings 13:3). This will be a direct rebuke to the idolatrous worship at that altar.

Immediately, Jeroboam stretches out his hand and commands his men to seize the prophet. He seeks to silence the messenger rather than respond to the message. What a surprise to see his own hand seize up so that he cannot pull it back. God judges him at the precise point of his most glaring sin: ordering, with illegitimate authority, action against a man of God.

The altar splits as prophesied (13:5), and in the next verse Jeroboam turns not to his golden calf but to the Lord. As the subsequent chapters will show, Jeroboam doesn't really repent here; or if he does, it is only for a moment. Wanting to receive something from God is not the same as repentance.

To his credit, the man of God shows great grace to Jeroboam in verse 6. He quickly moves from being under arrest to being an intercessor for his persecutor. This mercy reflects the great mercy of God, who answers his prayer.

Jeroboam quickly, and naturally, given the circumstances, embraces the man of God as a friend. He wants to refresh and reward him, without any repentance for the sin the man of God denounced. But the man of God refuses the invitation, based on a prior warning from God. To accept Jeroboam's invitation would demonstrate fellowship with his idolatry.

📄 13:11–34

THE MAN OF GOD'S DISOBEDIENCE AND DEATH

An old prophet in Bethel invites the man of God to dinner. Apparently not every godly person has left Israel for Judah; some still remain behind. The old man hears about what the man from Judah did in Bethel and rides to meet him on his way home. He finds him under an oak tree, perhaps tired from fasting and travel.

The old prophet asks the man to come home with him and eat, an invitation he refuses under the same reason he refused Jeroboam—that God had specifically told him to return to Judah without accepting hospitality, and to return a different way.

The old man's deception, that he, too, is a prophet and that an angel told him to bring him home, persuades the man from Judah to give in. Perhaps the angel was a deceiving angel. Satan and his messengers can appear as angels of light (2 Corinthians 11:14–15).

Nevertheless, no matter how natural and enticing this gesture was, it is the duty of the man of God to resist it. He had a word from God to guide his actions and should receive no other word accept through dramatic and direct confirmation by God's Spirit. God does not contradict Himself. His failure at this point ends his usefulness as a man of God.

The man here lives much like Israel, being drawn to the prophets who say what they want to hear, rather than the truth, however harsh.

The old prophet of Bethel will be used for one more prophecy now. At his table God uses him to foretell the man's doom (13:20–22). God judges the man of God far more strictly than He seems to judge Jeroboam or the prophet from Bethel. They are guilty of worse sins (leading national idolatry and a deliberate false prophecy), yet the man of God receives the most severe verdict.

Demystifying 1 Kings

An unburied body is a curse, and it was a disgrace to be buried among strangers, away from family.

The results are swift. In verses 23–25, the old prophet gives the man from Judah his donkey to ride, but he doesn't get far. A lion pounces and kills him, leaving the donkey unharmed. Passersby report the scene in Bethel.

This demonstrates that this is no mere accident, but something unique from God. The lion does not attack the donkey (the donkey stood by it), nor does it attack the men who pass by.

The old prophet hears of the incident in verse 26 and guesses rightly who the victim is. He is sympathetic to the man of God from Judah, even in his disobedience and resulting judgment. The old prophet himself appears not to be a particularly righteous man or good prophet, having used a deceptive prophecy to lead the man of God into sin and judgment. He recognizes the common weakness of this fellow servant of God.

In 13:27–32 the prophet retrieves the body, buries it in his own tomb, and confirms that the judgment is of the Lord. It's not the tomb of the fathers of the man of God, in fulfillment of the previous prophecy. But although he lied to him, led him into sin, and prophesied judgment against him, perhaps the old man from Bethel still respected the man of God, recognizing he had courage to speak against Jeroboam that he himself did not have.

Even after all this, Jeroboam does not repent. Instead he keeps consecrating anyone who wants to be a priest, leading to the destruction of his name from the face of the earth.

Take It Home

Jeroboam had great opportunity, especially in light of the promise of God through Ahijah, recorded in 1 Kings 11:38. But he does not obey God and honor His commandments, and he never fulfills his potential or promise.

The same principle works in servants of God today. We are not called because of our obedience or used out of merit; our disobedience hinders our potential for full use. God uses vessels of honor, separation, usefulness, and preparation to their fullest potential (2 Timothy 2:21).

1 KINGS 14:1–31

THE END OF JEROBOAM AND REHOBOAM

The End of Jeroboam, King of Israel	14:1–20
The End of Rehoboam, King of Judah	14:21–31

Setting Up the Section

In this section we see the end of both Jeroboam and Rehoboam. One started as a populist with a shining prophecy of success and ended terribly, the other governed as a tyrant but humbled himself toward the end (2 Chronicles 12:6–7).

📖 14:1–20

THE END OF JEROBOAM, KING OF ISRAEL

Jeroboam in 14:1–4 sends his wife to the prophet Ahijah to ask him the fate of their son, Abijah. Even kings have troubles common to all people, and consulting prophets was a common practice (2 Kings 1:2; 4:22, 40; 5:3).

This is a familiar pattern for Jeroboam. In his time of need, he turns to the true God and men of God. He knows that idols cannot help him in any true crisis. Yet he also knows that he had rejected God and His prophets, and so he tells his wife to wear a disguise.

Yet he does not tell his wife to pray for the boy or to ask Ahijah to pray. He wants to use Ahijah the prophet as a fortune-teller more than seek him as a man of God.

The woman's disguise and Ahijah's blindness (1 Kings 14:4) don't matter, because God has told Ahijah what is going on. When Ahijah greets the woman, he informs her that though she was sent to Ahijah by her husband, in truth Ahijah was sent by God with a message to her and Jeroboam (14:6). She also learns right away that the news will be bad.

Indeed it is bad news. God recounts in 14:7–11 that Jeroboam could have had a lasting dynasty, but he wasted the promise of God with his unbelief, idolatry, and outright rejection of God. Jeroboam is worse than all who have ruled before him. Saul was a bad man and a bad king. Solomon was a good king but a bad man. Jeroboam is far worse. He has thrust God behind his back, a powerful description of contempt (see Ezekiel 23:35).

In verses 12–16, Jeroboam's wife hears an immediate judgment and a distant one. First, their son will die. Yet his death will be a demonstration of mercy, because at least he will be buried in honor and properly mourned. Such great judgment is coming upon the house of Jeroboam that all will see that, by comparison, this son was blessed in his death.

Second, God will uproot Israel from the land He gave them and scatter them, a judgment that will be fulfilled some three hundred years later. God knew that the root of Jeroboam's apostasy would eventually result in the bitter fruit of national exile.

The immediate judgment is fulfilled in 14:17–18, demonstrating the future prophecy to be true.

The rest of Jeroboam's reign is recorded elsewhere (14:19). According to 2 Chronicles 13:20, the Lord strikes him down, and after twenty-two years of rule, he dies (1 Kings 14:20).

📄 14:21–31

THE END OF REHOBOAM, KING OF JUDAH

Meanwhile, under King Rehoboam's reign, Judah has sinned and angered God. The sins involve idolatry (14:23) and prostitutes associated with the worship of idols (14:24). In fact, the people of Judah have sunk to practicing the abominations of those nations the Lord had cast out. Considering the depth of depravity among the Canaanite nations, this is a strong statement.

The debauchery leads to God's chastisement. Only five years into Rehoboam's rule—not that long from the years of security in Israel—the king of Egypt attacks (14:25). God chastises Rehoboam through Egypt.

No foreign enemy ever did as much against God's people during the time of David and Solomon as during Shishak's aggression in 945–924 BC. Both 2 Chronicles and archaeology confirm it (see 2 Chronicles 12).

Shishak takes the treasures of the house of the Lord and the treasures of the king's house (14:26). Solomon left great wealth to his son Rehoboam, both in the temple and in the palace. After only five years, that wealth is largely gone.

Rehoboam replaces the gold shields of his father Solomon with bronze shields, a perfect picture of the decline under the days of Rehoboam. He places them in the hands of the commanders of the palace guard, hidden away in a protected guardroom until they are specifically needed for state occasions.

The writer of 1 Kings sums up Rehoboam's account by mentioning continual warfare with Jeroboam (14:30) and repeating that his mother is Naamah, an Ammonite—reminding readers that it was Solomon's marriages to foreign wives that started Israel's decline.

1 KINGS 15:1–34

ABIJAM, ASA, NADAB, AND BAASHA

Two Kings of Judah: Abijam and Asa   15:1–24
Two Kings of Israel: Nadab and Baasha   15:25–34

Setting Up the Section

Of the four next kings of Judah and Israel, only Asa does right before God, and God grants him a long reign.

📄 **15:1–24**

TWO KINGS OF JUDAH: ABIJAM AND ASA

In 15:1–8 we learn that the son of Rehoboam, Abijam, rules Judah for three years. The brevity of his reign indicates God did not bless him.

Yet by comparing the 1 Kings 14 account with 2 Chronicles 13, we can tell that Abijam knows something of the Lord and even knows how to preach. But he does not uproot the idolatry and sexual immorality that was introduced by his father, Rehoboam. His heart is not devoted to God, as was David's (15:3). This is his real problem. David sinned during his reign, but his heart stayed loyal to his God.

God allows his rule, not because of the character of David's descendants (15:4), but to preserve David's dynasty.

Demystifying 1 Kings

Second Chronicles 13 fills in more interesting details about the reign of Abijam (called Abijah in Chronicles). It tells us how there is war between Jeroboam of Israel and Abijam of Judah, and how Abijam challenges Jeroboam on the basis of righteousness and faithfulness to God.

Jeroboam responds with a surprise attack, and victory seems certain for Israel over Judah, but Abjiam cries out to the Lord, and God wins a victory for Judah that day.

Abijam's son, Asa, succeeds him and reigns forty-one years. Unlike his father, Asa does right as measured against David and begins a series of reforms (15:12–15).

He banishes the state-sanctioned temple prostitutes who were introduced into Judah during the reign of Rehoboam (14:24). He deposes his own grandmother, Maacah, because she keeps a repulsive pole associated with the fertility cult of Asherah. This demonstrates the thoroughness of Asa's reforms. He is able to act righteously even when his family is wrong.

Asa's heart remains dedicated to the Lord, and in verse 15 he restores to the temple some of the displaced silver and gold.

Meanwhile, the struggle with the northern kingdom of Israel for dominance continues. The current king of Israel, Baasha, gains the upper hand in the days of Asa because he effectively blocks a main route into Judah at the city of Ramah. He hopes this military and economic pressure on Judah will force Asa into significant concessions.

Asa counters by gathering the silver and gold from the palace treasuries to buy the favor of Ben-hadad of Syria so that he will withdraw support from Israel. Apparently, Baasha of Israel could not stand against Judah by himself; he needs the backing of Syria.

The plan works. Ben-hadad moves against Israel, forcing Baasha to withdraw from Ramah. Asa uses the materials Baasha had gathered to rebuild two key towns, Geba and Mizpah. Asa's actions are condemned as he lacked reliance on God.

Critical Observation

Second Chronicles 16:7–10 tells us that God is not pleased by Asa's deal with Ben-hadad. He sends the prophet Hanani to tell Asa this and to prophesy that because of his foolishness, Asa will face wars from that point on.

Sadly, Asa reacts badly and throws the prophet in prison. Asa shows us the tragedy of a man who rules well and seeks God for many years, yet fails in a significant challenge of his faith and then refuses to hear God's correction. (See 2 Chronicles 14–16 for additional details about Asa's reign.)

All in all, Asa is a good man who does not finish well (15:23–24). The last years of his life are marked by unbelief, hardness against God, oppression against his people, and disease.

📄 15:25–34

TWO KINGS OF ISRAEL: NADAB AND BAASHA

In the northern kingdom, the short reign of Nadab, king of Israel (15:25–32), does not go well. This son of Jeroboam does as his father did, continuing in his idolatry and hardness toward God. His assassination by Baasha, and the murder of all his family (15:29–30), effectively fulfills God's prophecy that the house of Jeroboam will be destroyed.

Baasha, the son of Ahijah, becomes king over all Israel (15:33–34) and ushers in a dreadful period for the nation, both spiritually and politically. He does evil in the sight of the Lord and walks in the way of Jeroboam. Though Baasha is not a genetic descendant of Jeroboam (having murdered his family), he is certainly a spiritual descendant of Jeroboam.

1 KINGS 16:1–34

FIVE SUCCESSIVE KINGS OF ISRAEL

Setting Up the Section

Sinful kings come to power in Israel, culminating in Ahab and his wicked wife, Jezebel.

📄 **16:1–20**

TWO SHORT DYNASTIES OVER ISRAEL: BAASHA AND ZIMRI

God's rebuke and judgment of Baasha reveals the behind-the-scenes way God moves, even through the conspiracy of Baasha against Nadab (chapter 15).

Because Baasha is a wicked king after the pattern of Jeroboam, he will face the same judgment as Jeroboam and his house (16:3–4). This has special relevance to Baasha because he is the instrument of judgment God uses to bring justice to the house of Jeroboam. It is considered a special disgrace to have your dead corpse desecrated and be kept from proper burial.

Demystifying 1 Kings

The word of God came by the prophet Jehu. Apparently Jehu had a long career as a prophet. Second Chronicles 19:2 mentions another work of Jehu the son of Hanani. Some fifty years after this word to Baasha, he speaks to Jehoshaphat, the king of Judah.

Jehu also wrote specific books of history regarding kings of Israel (2 Chronicles 20:34). His father, Hanani, is also mentioned in 2 Chronicles 16:7–10, where it describes how he suffered imprisonment because he was a faithful prophet in speaking to King Asa.

Critical Observation

In 1 Kings 16:2, God says that He lifted Baasha out of the dust and set him as ruler over Israel. In doing this God used Baasha to bring judgment upon the house of Jeroboam; yet God did not *cause* Baasha to do this. He rightly judged Baasha even though God used Baasha's wickedness to bring judgment upon Jeroboam.

God did not need to coerce a reluctant Baasha to conspire against and assassinate Nadab the son of Jeroboam. That wicked desire was already in the heart of Baasha. In using Baasha to bring judgment on the house of Jeroboam, God only needed to let Baasha do what he wanted to do. Therefore, it was proper of God to judge Baasha for something that ultimately furthered God's eternal plan.

Next, Elah, son of Baasha, becomes king (16:8–10) for two years. But before we are told much about Elah, a man named Zimri, an officer in the army of Israel, assassinates him. Even as Baasha gains the throne through assassination, so the son of Baasha is assassinated.

Zimri kills all Baasha's household, a common practice in the ancient world (and exactly what Baasha did to the house of Jeroboam in 1 Kings 15:29). David's treatment of the house of Saul was a glorious exception to this common practice. The massacre is an exact fulfillment of the word of God through the prophet Jehi, the son of Hanani (16:2–4).

But Zimri is destined to reign all of seven days (16:15–20). The army revolts and names their commander, Omri, king (16:16). Omri's rise shows that the democratic influence in Israel is greater than many realize. The people—especially the army—simply do not want Zimri to reign as king over them. They therefore reject his authority and appoint Omri in his place.

Omri and the army lay siege to Tizrah, where Zimri is located. The rejected ruler, who walked in the ways of Jeroboam (16:19) even if for a short time, goes to the citadel of the palace, sets it ablaze, and dies.

Critical Observation

Zimri is one of the few suicides in the Bible, along with Samson (Judges 9:54), Saul (1 Samuel 31:4), and Ahithophel (2 Samuel 17:23).

📄 16:21–34

THE FOURTH DYNASTY OF ISRAEL: THE HOUSE OF OMRI

Civil war breaks out as soon as Zimri dies, with half of Israel supporting Omri and the other half supporting Tibni, son of Ginath (16:21–28). Scholars say the conflict continues for five years, until Omri's forces defeat those loyal to Tibni. Tibni dies, presumably killed by Omri, whose rise to full power is the beginning of another dynasty in Israel.

In verse 24, Omri builds a city on the hill, the new capital of the northern kingdom, and calls it Samaria. His aim is to have a capital that is politically neutral (being a new city with no previous tribal associations) and in a strong defensive position (on top of a hill).

In the records of secular history, Omri—the sixth king of Israel since the once-unified kingdom's split—is one of the more successful and famous kings of ancient Israel. But in 16:25–26 it's clear that Omri follows Jeroboam's evil ways. He dies and is buried in Samaria (16:28).

While Asa is ruling for forty-one years in Judah, there are seven different kings in Israel. Omri's son, Ahab (16:29–34), distinguishes himself in being worse than Jeroboam.

Omri is a political and economic success for Israel but a spiritual failure. Ahab picks up where his father left off. Ahab introduces the worship of completely new, pagan gods. In his disobedience Jeroboam said, "I will worship the Lord, but do it my way." Ahab said, "I want to forget about the Lord completely and worship Baal."

Ahab takes as his wife Jezebel, the daughter of Ethbaal, king of the Sidonians (16:31). *Ethbaal* means "with Baal." Jezebel is famous for her hostility and cruelty. Their marriage is also politically expedient, as the alliance with the Sidonians, or Phoenicia, gives Ahab a powerful ally.

Critical Observation

In his later years, King Solomon worshiped pagan gods. Yet Omri and Ahab were far worse in that they *commanded* the worship of idols (see Micah 6:16).

Ahab sets Hiel of Bethel to work (16:34) rebuilding Jericho, in disregard of Joshua's prophecy that anyone rebuilding the city shall lose his firstborn and his youngest (Joshua 6:26). If Ahab does think that he can fortify Jericho without being affected by this curse, he is wrong. Hiel lays its foundation at a cost of losing Abiram, his firstborn; and with his youngest son, Segub, he set up its gates.

1 KINGS 17:1–24
THE EARLY MINISTRY OF ELIJAH

Elijah Experiences God's Provision	17:1–7
God Provides for Elijah through a Widow	17:8–16
Elijah Raises the Widow's Son	17:17–24

Setting Up the Section

The prophet Elijah comes on the scene, challenges Ahab, and then encounters a widow with a dying son.

📄 17:1–7

ELIJAH EXPERIENCES GOD'S PROVISION

At this crucial time in the history of Judah and Israel—when it looks as if the worship of the true God might be eliminated from the northern kingdom—the prophet Elijah suddenly appears (17:1). He will become the dominant spiritual force in Israel during these dark days of Ahab's apostasy.

Demystifying 1 Kings

The name *Elijah* means, "Yahweh is my God." In the days when Ahab's government officially supported the worship of Baal and other gods, even the name of this prophet told the truth.

Elijah confronts Ahab with the dramatic pronouncement that there will be no dew or rain in the next few years, until Elijah gives the word. This is a challenge to the pagan god Baal, who was thought to be a storm god, thus his association with lightning. Elijah is not merely the prophet of this drought; in the sense of prayer, he is the cause. James 5:17–18 makes this clear.

Elijah's bold statement gives us an understanding of the source of his strength. Everyone else lives as if the Lord is dead, but for Elijah, the Lord lives. He is the supreme reality of Elijah's life.

The Lord sends Elijah to Cherith, or the Kerith Ravine, east of the Jordan, for his safety. God is leading Elijah one step at a time. (He does not tell him to go to Cherith until he first delivers the message to Ahab, and He does not tell him to go to Zarephath until the brook dries up.) Elijah follows in faith, practicing dependence upon the Lord (17:5).

Critical Observation

God sends Elijah away, just as he had become famous as an adversary of Ahab, so mighty that his prayers could stop the rain. At the moment, God wanted Elijah to hide and be alone with God. There is a time for the hidden life.

Every bit of food that comes to Elijah is from the beak of an unclean animal (17:6). Elijah has to put away his traditional ideas of clean and unclean or he will die of starvation. Through this, God teaches Elijah to emphasize the spirit of the law before the letter of the law.

Just as He faithfully provided manna for Israel in the wilderness, God provides for Elijah's needs, morning and night. Elijah comes to trust more than ever in the miraculous provision of God.

Elijah stays by the brook until it dries up (17:7), the start of the drought Elijah prayed for. He does not pray for rain to come again, even for his own survival. He keeps the purpose of God first, even when it adversely affects him.

📄 **17:8–16**

GOD PROVIDES FOR ELIJAH THROUGH A WIDOW

Next God calls Elijah to go to Zarephath (17:8–9), a Gentile city in the general region of the wicked Queen Jezebel. He is entering enemy territory. There a widow will supply him with food.

Widows were notorious for their poverty in the ancient world. When He is rejected by His own people, Jesus uses this example of Elijah's coming to the widow of Zarephath as an illustration of God's right to choose a people to Himself (see Luke 4:24–26).

Once in Zarephath (1 Kings 17:10–11), Elijah sees a woman gathering sticks, a sign she is poor. Elijah perhaps thought that God would lead him to an unusual rich widow, but God leads him to a poor Gentile widow.

Critical Observation

God tells Elijah that He commanded a widow to feed the prophet. Yet this woman seems unaware of the command. This shows how God's unseen hand often works. She goes to gather fuel, not meet a needy guest. She is planning to feed herself and her son, not a hungry man. Yet in her obedience, faith, and service she is blessed.

Elijah boldly requests, in faith, water and bread from the woman. Common sense and circumstances tell him that the widow will not give so generously to a Jewish stranger, but faith makes him ask.

She responds in verse 12 with a polite statement, showing that she respects God, yet recognizes that the God of Israel is Elijah's God and not her own. Elijah quickly finds out that she is not only poor, but desperately poor. Elijah encounters her right before she is going to prepare her last morsel of food for herself and her son and then resign themselves to death (17:12).

Elijah makes an audacious request (17:13), after encouraging the widow not to be afraid. He asks the destitute woman to feed him first, perhaps with her last bit of food. But he goes on to prophesy that her source of flour and oil will not be used up.

The widow obeys in faith and is immediately rewarded with food every day (17:16) for both Elijah and her family. God uses her as a channel of supply, and her needs are met as a result.

📄 17:17–24

ELIJAH RAISES THE WIDOW'S SON

This happy time of sustenance is replaced by a dark cloud as the widow's son grows ill and dies (17:17–18). She indirectly blames Elijah and more directly blames herself and her unnamed sin. Whatever her sin is, the guilty memory of it is always close to her.

Demystifying 1 Kings

The death of the son is a double blow to this widow. Not only does she suffer as any mother who loses a child, but she also suffers as one who lost her only hope for the future. The expectation is that her son would grow and provide for her in her old age. Now that expectation is shattered.

Elijah takes the dead son out of the widow's arms (17:19). This vivid detail shows that the widow clutched the dead child tightly in her arms. He takes him to the upper room where he is staying and cries out to God (17:20–21).

Elijah prays with great heart and intimacy with God. He brings the seemingly unexplainable and irredeemable sadness to God in prayer. Since he knows God lead him to this widow, Elijah asks Him to remedy it.

The Lord answers Elijah and raises the boy from the dead. God provides for the widow on every level—not only with the miraculous supply of food but also with the resuscitation of her son.

1 KINGS 18:1–46

ELIJAH'S VICTORY AT CARMEL

Setting Up the Section

Elijah returns to Israel and meets faithful Obadiah in Ahab's court. He arranges the dramatic confrontation on Mount Carmel between Baal's prophets and Elijah, the prophet of the true God.

📄 18:1–17

ELIJAH MEETS AHAB

God tells Elijah to go back to Ahab, and God will end the severe drought which has lasted three and a half years by Elijah's fervent prayer.

Earlier God told Elijah to *hide* himself. Now it is time to *present* himself. There is a time to hide and be alone with God, and there is also a time to make ourselves active in the world.

Ahab had previously summoned a man named Obadiah, a brave believer who stood for God, to work for him (18:3). In fact, he was so brave that while Ahab's wife, Jezebel, was killing the Lord's prophets (18:4), Obadiah was hiding a hundred of them in two caves, secretly supplying them with food and water.

The drought is so bad that the king himself is out searching for pastureland for his horses and mules (18:5–6). Ahab goes one direction and Obadiah goes another. Elijah then encounters Obadiah in verse 7. Obadiah recognizes him and bows, calling him lord.

Reverence turns to fear (18:9–14) when Elijah asks Obadiah to announce to Ahab that he wants an audience. Obadiah knows that King Ahab conducted an exhaustive search for Elijah, to punish him for the drought that his prayers imposed on Israel. Obadiah fears that if he announces that he met Elijah and the prophet disappears again, Ahab will kill Obadiah for letting Elijah get away.

Kindly and wisely, Elijah responds to Obadiah's legitimate fears and assures him that he will meet with Ahab. He will not make Obadiah a martyr for Elijah's deeds.

At their meeting (18:17–19), Elijah and Ahab trade accusations. According to his theology, it makes sense for Ahab to blame Elijah. Ahab believes in Baal, so much so that his government promotes and supports Baal worship and persecutes the worshipers of Yahweh. Ahab believes that Elijah has angered Baal, and therefore Baal withheld rain. Ahab probably thought that Baal would hold back the rain until Elijah was caught and executed.

Elijah challenges King Ahab to gather the idol prophets of Baal and Asherah—those who eat at Jezebel's table, or in other words, are supported by the government of Israel—for a meeting at Mount Carmel.

It is important to confront and eliminate these prophets of Baal before God sends rain to the land of Israel. It is crucial that everyone understands that the rain comes from Yahweh, not from Baal.

ELIJAH'S VICTORY ON MOUNT CARMEL

Ahab obeys Elijah, sending word throughout Israel of the impending confrontation. Perhaps he hoped that the people would be so angry with Elijah for the last three years of drought that they would turn against the prophet.

Elijah addresses the people of Israel in verse 21, asking them how long they will waffle between two worldviews. This is a logical and useful question. The people of Israel want to give some devotion to *both* Yahweh and Baal. But the God of Israel is not interested in such divided devotion.

The people do not answer (18:21). They lack the courage to either defend their position or to change it. They are willing to live unexamined lives of low conviction.

Critical Observation

The appeal of Elijah makes it clear that there is a difference between the service of Baal and the service of Yahweh. Perhaps in the minds of many, there is not a great difference. The only important thing is to have *some kind* of religion, and to be sincere about that, following your heart to whichever god you feel led to follow. Yet Elijah knows it can never be this way; you either serve Baal *or* you serve Yahweh. There is a difference.

In verses 22–24, Elijah says he alone is left as a prophet of the Lord. He knows this is not literally true, since Obadiah had told him of the sheltered one hundred, but perhaps Elijah means the last prophet able to confront Baal in public.

He proposes a test between God and Baal on Mount Carmel. He gives the prophets of Baal the advantage: They can pick which bull to sacrifice—they get to go first. The deities will answer by fire from the sky—another apparent advantage, since it was thought that Baal was the sky-god, lord of the weather and the sender of lightning.

The prophets of Baal take up the challenge and pray for fire from their god (18:25–29). They pray long and with great passion. Yet because they do not pray to a *real* God, their prayer means nothing.

Elijah cannot resist the opportunity to mock the prophets of Baal for their foolish faith, and the prophets work even harder. They cry louder and cut themselves, a common practice to arouse the deity's pity.

Take It Home

The prophets of Baal were utterly sincere and completely devoted to their religion. They were so committed that they expressed it in their own blood. They had zeal, but without knowledge—therefore their zeal profited them nothing.

This is the sad result of worshiping an imaginary god or a god of our own making. We may dedicate great sincerity, sacrifice, and devotion to such gods, but it means nothing. There is no one there to answer.

When it is Elijah's turn to make the sacrifice, he first wants to get the attention of the people. This is for their benefit, not his own or for God. They need to pay attention so they can see that the Lord is the true God, in contrast to the silent Baal.

He repairs a broken altar with twelve stones, one for each tribe of Israel. Elijah is looking to revive something that once was. Then he prepares the altar so that there can be no question of trickery. In wanting to make a deep impression upon the people, Elijah requires more of Yahweh than he does of Baal. Elijah does not even suggest to the prophets of Baal that they wet down their sacrifice once or twice, much less three times. Yet Elijah does this, confident that it is no harder for God to ignite a wet sacrifice than it is for Him to set a dry one ablaze.

Everything is prepared in time for the evening sacrifice. Some fifty years before this, Jeroboam, the king of Israel, officially disassociated the citizens of the northern kingdom from the worship of the God of Israel at the temple in Jerusalem. Nevertheless, Elijah still remembers the evening sacrifice that is offered according to God's commandment every day at the temple in Jerusalem.

In his prayer in verses 36–37, Elijah wants it known that God is God and he is His servant. He also wants the people to know that everything Elijah has done is at God's instruction. Elijah does this according to the Word of God. It isn't prompted because of his own cleverness, because of presumption or vainglory. God led Elijah to this showdown with the prophets of Baal.

Within what appears to be minutes, God answers. Fire falls from the sky, consuming the burnt sacrifice, the wood, the stones, and the dust. And it licks up the water that is in the trench (18:38–40).

Critical Observation

When the fire of God fell, its work was beyond expectation. It would have been enough if only the cut-up pieces of the bull on the altar were ignited, but God wanted more than simple vindication—He wanted to glorify Himself among the people.

The people fall on their faces (18:39). At this moment, the people are persuaded. Asked to choose between Baal and Yahweh, there is no choice to make. Obviously the Lord is the one true God. Tragically, this is only a momentary persuasion. The people are decidedly persuaded, but not lastingly changed.

Elijah has them seize the prophets of Baal, who now face the same fate they promoted for the prophets of Yahweh. They were dealt with according to the Law of Moses (Deuteronomy 13:5, 13–18; 17:2–5; 18:9–22).

📄 **18:41–46**

ELIJAH GOES TO JEZREEL

Elijah knows that once the official worship of Baal has been defeated, the purpose for the drought is fulfilled and rain is on the way. Elijah and Ahab will now each do what they want to do: Ahab will eat and Elijah will pray.

Elijah prays persistently. He sends his servant to look for rain seven times. Elijah will not take "no" for an answer, because he has confidence that God's will is to send rain. Elijah obviously senses this is the will of God, yet it is his fervent prayer that brings the rain. The evidence of the rain comes slowly and in a small way, but out of this small evidence God brings a mighty work.

Elijah sends his servant to tell Ahab to get moving to Jezreel before the rain stops him. This is a word of faith from Elijah to Ahab. Based only on the sighting of a small cloud, he knows a torrent is on the way.

The amazing day ends with dark clouds and heavy rains and a supernaturally empowered fourteen-mile, cross-country run. We don't know exactly why it is important to God for Elijah to reach Jezreel first.

1 KINGS 19:1–21

GOD ENCOURAGES ELIJAH

Elijah Flees to the Wilderness	19:1–4
God's Ministry to the Despairing Elijah	19:5–21

Setting Up the Section

In this famous chapter, we see Elijah go from the high point of winning a contest with the prophets of Baal to the low point of post-traumatic depression. God ministers to him, though, and sends him to anoint a new king and his own successor, Elisha.

📄 **19:1–4**

ELIJAH FLEES TO THE WILDERNESS

Ahab tells his wife, Jezebel, the champion of Baal and Astarte worship in Israel, of all that Elijah has done. She thought so much of these priests that she supported them from the royal treasury—and now they are dead at the hand of Elijah.

So she sends a messenger to Elijah and vows to kill him within twenty-four hours. Elijah's response? He flees in fear (19:4). We cannot say for certain if this is led by God or not. It is clear that God wants to protect Elijah, but we cannot say if God wanted to protect him at Jezreel or by getting him out of Jezreel. Nevertheless, Elijah flees about eighty miles south to Beersheba.

Once at the distant city of Beersheba, Elijah secludes himself even more, lies down, and prays to die. This mighty man of prayer—mighty enough to make the rain and the dew stop for three and a half years, and then mighty enough to make it start again at his prayer—has given up.

Demystifying 1 Kings

Thankfully, Elijah's prayer to die is not answered. In fact, Elijah is one of the few men in the Bible to never die. We can imagine that as he is caught up into heaven, he smiled and thought of this prayer—and the blessed *no* that answered his prayer. To receive a *no* answer from God can be better than receiving a *yes* answer.

In his depression Elijah cannot take any more. The work is stressful, exhausting, and seems to accomplish nothing. The great work on Mount Carmel did not result in a lasting national revival or return to the Lord.

Perhaps Elijah had especially hoped that the events on Mount Carmel would turn Ahab and Jezebel and the leadership of Israel in general around. If so, Elijah forgot that people reject God *despite* the evidence, not *because* of the evidence.

📄 **19:5–21**

GOD'S MINISTRY TO THE DESPAIRING ELIJAH

God rejects Elijah's request to die and ministers to his physical needs (19:5–8). This is not always His order, but physical needs are important.

The angel God sends twice orders Elijah to eat and drink and then sends him on his two-hundred mile journey to Mount Horeb, also known as Mount Sinai. Elijah takes forty days, four times as long as needed for a straight trip. This shows that God does not demand an immediate recovery from Elijah. He allows the prophet time to recover from his spiritual depression.

Once at Horeb, God allows Elijah to vent his frustrations. Elijah goes into a cave, perhaps the cave or cleft of the rock in which Moses hid when God appeared to him (Exodus 33:22).

God asks him what he is doing there. God knows the answer, of course, but it is good for Elijah to speak to the Lord freely and to unburden his heart. So Elijah vents.

Elijah recounts the bad situation he's in and says he's the only prophet left. This is not accurate, but it reflects how Elijah feels. Discouraging times make God's servants feel more isolated and alone than they truly are.

God knows what the depressed and discouraged Elijah needs (19:11–12). He needs a personal encounter with God. There is nothing fundamentally wrong with Elijah's theology, but at the time there is something lacking in his experience.

God brings His presence before Elijah, but first to show where He is *not*. The Lord is not in the wind, He is not in the earthquake, He is not in the fire. Like many others, Elijah probably only looked for God in dramatic manifestations. Certainly, God sometimes appears in such ways, but He often appears in less dramatic surroundings.

Then, after the fire, a still small voice: This final phenomenon is in marked contrast to the previous manifestations. God actually meets Elijah in the quiet whisper of a voice instead of the earth-shaking phenomenon that had gone before. Because he senses the special presence of God, Elijah immediately humbles himself and wraps his face in his mantle.

Take It Home

Elijah perhaps thought that the dramatic display of power at Mount Carmel would turn the nation around. Or perhaps he thought that the radical display of God's judgment against the priests of Baal, following the vindication at Mount Carmel, would change the hearts of the nation. Neither of these worked. This example is important for Christian leaders, especially preachers, today. It shows that displays of power and preaching God's anger do not necessarily change hearts. Instead, the still small voice of God speaking to the human heart is actually more powerful than outward displays of power or displays of God's judgment.

Immediately after ministering to Elijah, God gives him work to do (19:14–15). The prophet needs a task to focus on. He needs to stop looking at himself and his own (admittedly difficult) circumstances. He needs to get on with what God wants him to do.

God sends him to anoint three servants: Hazael, to be king over Aram (19:15); Jehu, king over Israel (19:16); and Elisha, his own successor (19:16).

Critical Observation

Elijah needs a friend; the core of his complaint before God is that he is alone. God lets him know that there is a man ready to learn from the great prophet and be his disciple and companion.

Elijah also needs hope, and since Elisha will be raised up as a successor to Elijah's prophetic office, Elijah knows that his work will continue even after his death.

The three will provide justice by putting to death all who have followed Baal (19:16–17). This is another source of encouragement to Elijah. With this promise he knows that ultimately justice will be carried out, and God will not allow the institutionalized persecution and promotion of idolatry to go unpunished.

The final encouragement to Elijah is God's promise that He has reserved seven thousand in Israel, all whose knees have not bowed to Baal (19:18). Elijah repeatedly bemoans that he is alone among the true followers of God. This assures Elijah that he is not alone and that his work as a prophet has indeed been fruitful. His quiet ministry through the years actually bears more fruit than the spectacular ministry at Mount Carmel.

Elijah finds Elisha at work and commissions him to ministry (19:19–21). The mantle is the symbol of Elijah's prophetic authority. This act signifies that Elijah is calling Elisha as his successor.

Demystifying 1 Kings

We are told that Elijah finds Elisha first, doing what the voice of God told him to do but perhaps in reverse order. Perhaps Elijah believed that he *first* needed a friend and apprentice.

Elisha begs to say good-bye to his parents. It appears that Elijah begrudgingly gives permission. Elisha sacrifices his twelve oxen (having that many indicates his relative wealth), burns his equipment as fuel to cook the meat, and shares it with the community. This demonstrates Elisha's complete commitment to following Elijah. He destroys the tools of his trade in a going-away party for his family and friends.

1 KINGS 20:1-43

ISRAEL'S VICTORIES OVER SYRIA

Ben-hadad Comes Against Samaria	20:1–12
Victory for Israel	20:13–22
A Second Victory over Syria	20:23–43

Setting Up the Section

God gives Israel two victories over the attacking Syrians to the north, and Ahab is condemned for letting the ruler Ben-hadad go free.

📖 **20:1-12**

BEN-HADAD COMES AGAINST SAMARIA

The writer of 1 Kings now turns from Elijah to accounts of war between Israel and Aram. Ben-hadad, king of Syria, rises against Israel (20:1–6) and makes demands. Thirty-two kings are with him, a formidable military force. Though the Israelites are outwardly strong politically and militarily during the reign of Ahab, they are not strong enough to discourage such an attack.

Ahab's response to Ben-hadad (unconditional surrender) fits his general personality. He is a man concerned with the luxuries and comforts of living, and so he does not have the character to stand in the face of such a threat. Indeed, the national and military might of Israel is greatly weakened by the three-and-a-half year drought and famine that had just ended.

Ben-hadad makes further demands (20:5). Officials will come and search Ahab's house and those of his servants, to take away anything valuable. This is a greater demand than what Ben-hadad makes at first.

The king of Israel calls the elders of the land. It would have been wiser for Ahab to seek the counsel *before* he surrendered to the Syrians. Now, in the brief time between the message of surrender and the actual abduction of his women and the plundering of his goods, he seeks counsel.

The elders of Israel rightly see that such surrender to Ben-hadad and the Syrians is the first step to a total loss of sovereignty for Israel. If they want to remain a kingdom at all, they have to resist this threat.

Ahab tells Ben-hadad that he will do most of what he requested, but not all. But to deny a tyrant on one point is to deny him on every point. Ahab could expect a harsh reaction.

Critical Observation

Though it was an uncharacteristically bold speech from Ahab, his response to Ben-hadad (20:11) is a wonderful piece of wisdom. The idea is that you should do your boasting *after* the battle, not before.

📄 **20:13–22**

VICTORY FOR ISRAEL

The two sides prepare for war, and a prophet approaches Ahab (20:13–14). This nameless prophet does not seem to be either Elijah or Elisha. He is one of the seven thousand in Israel who are quietly faithful to Yahweh.

God promises victory, a generous gesture to an idolatrous ruler. Israel's hardened rejection of God deserves divine abandonment. God has every right to leave them alone and let them perish without His help. Yet God is rich in mercy, and He shows His mercy to Ahab and Israel.

Ahab asks who will make it happen (20:14). He is looking around at his army and military leaders and wondering how God can bring a victory against a mighty enemy. Ahab also asks who will lead the battle, and God answers that Ahab himself will. God wants to win this victory by working through the unlikely people Ahab already has on his side.

Take It Home

Whenever a work for God is to be done, we often ask Ahab's question: "By whom?" When many Christian leaders ask God that question, they expect God will answer by bringing someone new to them, a leader or champion that can do the work or at least help with it. However, many times God's way of working is to use those who are already there, even if it seems unlikely.

Israel claims the victory over Ben-hadad, who at the start of the conflict is seen getting drunk at the command post. (In part, he is defeated by his own weak character.)

God blesses the army of Israel and the leaders that Ahab has, even blessing Ahab's own leadership of the army. Despite great odds, they win the battle.

Soon after, the same nameless prophet advises preparation again. The victory over Ben-hadad does not end the conflict between Israel and Syria. He tells Ahab to prepare for a Syrian attack in the coming spring. The prophet knows that God works through the careful preparation of His people.

📄 20:23–43

A SECOND VICTORY OVER SYRIA

The Syrians indeed try again in the spring (20:23–34). They strategize to meet the Israelites on the plains, where they think Israel's God is weakest. The idea of the *localized deity* was prominent in the ancient world. The ancients felt that particular gods had authority over particular areas. Because the recent victory is won on hilly terrain, the servants of the king of Syria believe that the God of Israel is a localized deity with power over the hills, not the plains. The action they recommend is logical, given their theology. Their theological belief directs their advice and action.

Take It Home

Sometimes we pick and choose God's domain as the Syrians did—the God of the hills but not of the plains. At times we think He is the God of the past but not always of this present moment. Some think He is the God of a few special favorites but not of all people. But God is over everything, everywhere, forever.

The armies muster, and Israel routs Ben-hadad in an even more spectacular victory (20:26–30). A casualty count of one hundred thousand Syrian foot soldiers in one day is clearly a miracle, yet it is a miracle working through the existing Israelite army, not by another outside agency. God wants to show that as unlikely as it seems, God *can* work through this outwardly weak and ineffective instrument.

Those who escape to the city of Aphek are killed when a wall falls on them. Ben-hadad hides with his officials. They decide to beg for their lives (20:32).

Ahab feels a kinship toward this pagan king with exceedingly pagan ideas of God. Perhaps Ahab wants Ben-hadad and Syria's friendship as protection against the powerful and threatening Assyrian Empire. If so, he looks for friends in the wrong places. Ahab has no business making a treaty with Ben-hadad, as Israel's victory is the Lord's.

In verses 35–38, a new prophet prepares to confront the king about Ben-hadad.

The prophet prepares himself to become an object lesson. When what appears to be a fellow prophet declines to strike him as requested (20:35–36), the first prophet pronounces God's judgment on him (death by lion).

The prophet disguises himself and waits for Ahab to pass by. He brings God's message through a story. He tells Ahab of a man who was responsible to guard the life of another and proved himself unfaithful. In the story, the guilty man's excuse was that he was busy here and there. But he should have paid attention to the job he had to do.

Ahab rightly judges that the fictional man should be held responsible for his failure to guard what was entrusted to him. That's when the prophet reveals his identity, because Ahab otherwise would not listen.

Now he is forced to hear God's judgment (20:41–42). God intends that Ben-hadad should be utterly destroyed, but He also intends that this happen by the hand of the army of Israel. God is interested in more than the mere death of Ben-hadad; He is interested in the way that death is carried out.

Ahab goes home sullen but not repentant (20:43). He has the sorrow of being a sinner and knowing the consequences of sin, without having the sorrow for the sin itself.

1 KINGS 21:1–29

THE MURDER OF NABOTH

Naboth Is Murdered for His Vineyard   21:1–16
Elijah Confronts Ahab   21:17–29

Setting Up the Section

Ahab and Jezebel arrange the death of Naboth to obtain his land. Elijah strongly condemns the murder.

📄 **21:1–16**

NABOTH IS MURDERED FOR HIS VINEYARD

The account of Naboth and his land begins as an attempted simple real estate transaction. Ahab wants the vineyard near his royal house in Jezreel so that he might have it as a vegetable garden. He says he is willing to trade for the land or pay for it.

Naboth's response is an emphatic *no*. His rejection of the otherwise reasonable offer is rooted in the ancient Israelite idea of the land. They believed that the land was an inheritance from God, parceled out to individual tribes and families according to His will. Therefore land was never really sold, only leased—and only under the most dire circumstances. Real estate offices in ancient Israel didn't do very good business.

Ahab pouts before Jezebel (21:4–7) for being refused this small portion of land. This seems entirely characteristic of Ahab, a man who reacts this way when he meets any kind of adversity.

Jezebel's manner of speech in verse 7 reveals who really exercises authority in the palace of Israel. She begins to plot Naboth's murder with Ahab's collusion, since he allows letters in his name to be sealed with his seal (21:8).

Jezebel lays the groundwork for the idea that some evil or calamity has come upon Israel, and a scapegoat has to be found for the evil. Jezebel intends for Naboth be revealed as the scapegoat. She has him seated in honor, then destroyed.

Two scoundrels accuse Naboth of blasphemy, worthy of stoning. Jesus is charged with similar crimes, accused of offending both God and Caesar. Naboth, just like Jesus, is completely innocent of such accusations and is murdered without cause. The stoning of Naboth over a piece of land for a vegetable garden shows the brutal and immoral character of Jezebel and Ahab.

Demystifying 1 Kings

Second Kings 9:26 indicates that the crime is even worse than this, connecting the murder of Naboth with the blood of his sons. It is likely that the entire family of Naboth was murdered, so no heirs were left to claim his property.

In 1 Kings 21:15–16, Ahab takes possession of Naboth's land, which adds evil to evil. Even with Naboth dead, the land does not belong to Ahab or the royal house of Israel. It belongs to the family of Naboth. Ahab probably claimed the land as a royal right because the crown seized the land of any executed criminal.

📄 21:17–29

ELIJAH CONFRONTS AHAB

God sends Elijah to confront Ahab as he is enjoying his new possession (21:17–24). Elijah does what few other men have the courage to do: confront this wicked, brutal, and immoral king and queen of Israel. He pointedly charges them with the two crimes: murder and theft of Naboth's land.

Notice that Elijah confronts Ahab over the sin of Jezebel and her wicked associates. God clearly holds Ahab responsible for this sin as husband, as king, and as beneficiary of this crime. He predicts that dogs will lick Ahab's blood on the same field on which Naboth died.

God continues to prophesy through Elijah. He tells Ahab that disaster is coming, and He will consume every descendant of Ahab's (21:21–22).

This is a severe judgment against anyone, in particular against a king. A king's legacy is in his posterity succeeding him on the throne, and here God announces an end to the dynasty of Omri (Ahab's father). His dynasty would come to a dead end just like the dynasties of Jeroboam and Baasha.

In addition, the dogs shall eat Jezebel by the wall of Jezreel. Her end will be horrible and disgraceful.

The writer of 1 Kings here summarizes Ahab's great wickedness (21:25–26), likening his sin to the sin of the Amorites. Thus, God prepares the ground for the future eviction of Israel from the promised land. Just as the Amorites were cast out of Canaan for their continued idolatry and rejection of God, the northern kingdom of Israel will meet a similar fate.

For all his wickedness, though, Ahab receives this prophecy of judgment exactly as he should (21:27–29). He understands that the prophecy is in fact an invitation to repent, humble one's self, and to seek God for mercy. However, it's clear that the repentance is outward and superficial, arising from terror and not from sincere belief.

God nevertheless honors Ahab's actions. This shows the power of both prayer and humble repentance. If Ahab did not humble himself in this way, then the judgment would have come in his own day. This shows that God gave the prophecy of judgment as an invitation to repentance, and God opened the door of mercy when Ahab properly responded to that invitation.

There is no record of Jezebel's humility or repentance. Therefore we can expect that God's judgment will come upon her exactly as He first announced.

Take It Home

God's response to Ahab shows us the character of God's mercy: It is given to the undeserving. By nature, the innocent do not *need* mercy. Ahab was a great sinner, but he won great mercy (in this life) through humble repentance. The worst sinner should not disqualify himself from receiving God's mercy if that sinner should only approach God in humble repentance.

1 KINGS 22:1–53
THE DEATH OF AHAB

God Foretells Ahab's Doom	22:1–28
Ahab Dies in Battle	22:29–40
The Reigns of Jehoshaphat and Ahaziah	22:41–53

Setting Up the Section

The book of 1 Kings ends with Ahab's death and Jehoshaphat's reign in Judah.

📄 22:1–28

GOD FORETELLS AHAB'S DOOM

During a visit from Judah's king, Jehoshaphat, Ahab sets his eyes upon Ramoth-gilead in the north (22:1–4).

Previously, the king of Syria promised to return certain cities to Israel (20:34) in exchange for leniency after defeat in battle. Apparently this was a city that Ben-hadad never returned to Israel, and it is in a strategically important location.

Ahab asks Jehoshaphat to help him in this dispute against Syria. Ramoth-gilead is only forty miles from Jerusalem, but there is probably another reason for Ahab's request. It seems clear that Jehoshaphat is in a treaty relationship with Ahab, and Jehoshaphat is the subordinate partner in the alliance.

Jehoshaphat responds by proposing that they seek God in the matter. Considering the generally adversarial relationship between Ahab and the prophets of Yahweh, this is a bold request of Jehoshaphat to ask of Ahab. It isn't surprising that Ahab picks prophets who will tell them what he wants to hear.

Jehoshaphat still wants to hear from a prophet of Yahweh (22:7). Ahab knows of one more, Micaiah, whom he hates because he never says anything good. Yet he is willing to call him when the king of Judah responds that Ahab should listen to Micaiah (22:8).

Demystifying 1 Kings

It was an ancient custom to hold court and make decisions at the gates of the city. There were even thrones for high officials to sit on at the gates of the city of Samaria. Ahab and Jehoshaphat are there, surrounded by the unfaithful prophets (such as Zedekiah) who are prophesying in the name of the Lord, but not truthfully. Perhaps these were true followers of Yahweh who were seduced by Ahab's sincere but shallow repentance three years before (21:27–29). After that, they began to align with Ahab uncritically. Three years later they were willing to prophesy lies to Ahab if that was what he wanted to hear.

The prophet Zedekiah uses a familiar tool of ancient prophets, an object lesson, to convey his prophecy (22:11). He uses horns of iron to illustrate the thrust of two powerful forces, armies that would rout the Syrians. Zedekiah has the agreement of four hundred other prophets (all the prophets prophesied so).

Into this dramatic scene comes Micaiah, the faithful prophet, in rags and chains straight out of prison (see 22:26). The messenger who retrieved him has already told him what's happening and advised him to go along with the basic message (22:13). Micaiah assures him that he will simply repeat what God says to him.

But first he mimics the false prophets (22:15). King Ahab recognizes the mocking tone of Micaiah's prophecy and demands that Micaiah tell nothing but the truth.

Micaiah now changes his tone from mocking to serious. He says that not only will Israel be defeated, but also that their leader (the shepherd) will perish.

Ahab turns to Jehoshaphat with a quick, "See? I told you he never says anything good." Ahab can't handle the truth.

King Ahab and others at the court may have found it hard to explain how one prophet could be right and four hundred wrong. Micaiah goes on to reveal the inspiration behind the four hundred prophets (22:19–23).

He describes the throne of God, with God asking who will entice Ahab to attack Ramoth-gilead and die. Apparently, one of the fallen angels volunteers for this task. Since Ahab wants to be deceived, God will give him what he wants, using a willing fallen angel who works through willing unfaithful prophets.

Zedekiah responds to Micaiah's vision (22:24–28) the way many do when they are defeated in argument: with violence. He slaps and taunts him. And Ahab responds the way tyrants do when they are confronted with the truth: He sends him back to prison.

Micaiah's final appeal indicates that he is willing to be judged by whether his prophecy comes to pass or not (22:28).

22:29–40

AHAB DIES IN BATTLE

So Jehoshaphat and Ahab go into battle. It is easy to understand why King Ahab of Israel attacks; it is less easy to understand why King Jehoshaphat of Judah follows the false prophecy. He should have believed Micaiah and known that the battle would end in disaster and the death of at least Ahab.

Going into the battle, Ahab does not want to be identified as a king and therefore be a special target. Perhaps he thought this would help protect him against Micaiah's prophecy of doom. The fact that Jehoshaphat agrees to go into the battle as the only clearly identified king is evidence that Jehoshaphat was the subservient partner in his alliance with Ahab.

The result? Jehoshaphat is saved and Ahab dies in battle. Ahab's previous mercy to Benhadad does not win any lasting favor with the rulers of Syria.

Finding himself as the only identifiable king in the battle, Jehoshaphat realizes he is in mortal danger. He cries out (22:33) to God and is saved when his attackers see that he is not the king of Israel. Second Chronicles 18:31 makes it clear that the Lord hears Jehoshaphat's cry and rescues him.

Demystifying 1 Kings

After the close escape at Ramoth-gilead, Jehoshaphat rededicates himself to the spiritual reform of Judah. He goes out again among the people from Beersheba to the mountains of Ephraim and brings them back to the Lord God of their fathers (2 Chronicles 19:4).

A bowman at random strikes Ahab, as if the arrow is a sin-seeking missile. God orchestrates unintended actions to result in an exercise of His judgment.

Ahab orders his body propped up in his chariot, facing his enemies, to inspire his troops. All day long he lingers, but by evening he dies, and the battle is over.

The word through the prophet Micaiah proves true. King Ahab never returns to Samaria or Israel in peace.

When they go to wash Ahab's chariot, the dogs lick his blood (22:38). This is almost the fulfillment of God's word through Elijah in 1 Kings 21:19, where Elijah prophesies that dogs will lick the blood of Ahab. This proves true, but not in the place Elijah said it would happen. God relents from His original judgment against Ahab, but because of Ahab's false repentance and continued sin, a very similar judgment comes upon him.

There is another prophecy fulfilled in the death of Ahab. It was the word from the anonymous prophet of 1 Kings 20:42, that Ahab spares Ben-hadad's life at the expense of his own.

By materialist standards, the reign of Ahab was a success. He was generally militarily successful and enjoyed a generally prosperous economy. Yet spiritually his reign was a disaster, one of the worst ever for Israel.

📄 22:41–53

THE REIGNS OF JEHOSHAPHAT AND AHAZIAH

The focus now turns to Jehoshaphat (22:41–50) and his reign. Jehoshaphat, son of the good king Asa, follows in his footsteps and does what is right in the eyes of the Lord.

Jehoshaphat does not take away all the high places, though (22:43), a serious shortcoming.

Jehoshaphat builds ships at Ebion-geber, a territory of the Edomites, who are without a king at the time (22:47). After a disastrous shipping venture, Jehoshaphat is tempted to make an alliance with Ahaziah of Israel, Ahab's successor (22:49), but Jehoshaphat will not. This is to his credit. He learned the lesson of not entering a partnership with the ungodly.

The book of 1 Kings ends with mention of the son of Ahab, Ahaziah, who reigns for two years (22:51–53), walking in the same evil ways as his father and his grandfather, Jeroboam.

With this, 1 Kings ends on a low note. It began with the promise of the twilight of Israel's greatest king, David. It ends with the sad reign of one of the most wicked kings reigning over a divided nation.

2 KINGS

INTRODUCTION TO 2 KINGS

The books of 1 and 2 Kings were originally joined in one book. The narrative covers almost five hundred years, tracing the history of Israel and Judah from the last days of the monarchy under David to the disintegration and capture of the divided kingdoms.

AUTHOR

The author of this book is unknown. While there is a Jewish tradition that points to the prophet Jeremiah as the author, there is more evidence that the book evolved over a long period of time.

PURPOSE

First and Second Kings were written to the people of the southern kingdom of Judah to explain that the fall of the northern kingdom of Israel was God's judgment on their idolatry, to call the southern kingdom to repentance for following Israel's example, and to remind them of the hope promised through the royal—and ultimately messianic—line of David.

THEMES

The book of 2 Kings repeatedly demonstrates the judgment that results from unfaithfulness and idolatry. Over and over, kings and commoners are charged with worshiping false gods or worshiping the true God in false ways.

The book also highlights the way God uses other nations to execute His judgment: Israel falls to Assyria in 722 BC, and Judah falls to the Babylonians in 586 BC.

Along with God's judgment, however, 2 Kings underscores God's patience. He sends prophets to call His people to repentance, warns them over and over of the consequences of disobedience, and hears the prayers of faithful people.

HISTORICAL CONTEXT

The compilation of 1 and 2 Kings began before Babylon invaded Judah in 586 BC, but since the final chapters tell of events that occurred midway through the Babylonian captivity, obviously the book could not have been completed until then.

STRUCTURE

The commentary for this book is laid out by chapters for ease of use, but here is a look at the broader structure of this book of the Bible:

The Divided Kingdom   1:1–17:41
    Elisha's Ministry
    Kings of Israel and Judah
    Israel's Exile to Assyria
The Surviving Kingdom   18:1–25:30
    Kings of Judah
    Judah's Exile to Babylon

2 KINGS 1:1–18

AHAZIAH AND ELIJAH

Setting Up the Section

The book of 1 Kings ends with King Ahab's death and his son Ahaziah's ascension to the throne. The reign of Ahab had been a spiritual disaster for Israel, the northern kingdom, but it was a time of political security and economic prosperity. Moab, the land just south of Israel and west of the Dead Sea, had been under Israelite domination since the days of David (2 Samuel 8:2, 11–12). After Ahab's death, the kingdom of Moab finds a good opportunity to remove their nation from the domination of Israel. This is where the book of 2 Kings picks up the story.

📖 **1:1–9**

AHAZIAH'S INJURY

After Ahab's death, the land of Moab rebels against Israel (1:1). This rebellion of Moab in the days of Ahaziah is significant of the decline of Israel's power and the judgment of God.

King Ahaziah apparently leans against a wooden lattice on a second-floor balcony or room. When the lattice gives way, Ahaziah falls to the ground below (1:2). This is surely an unexpected crisis. Such accidents happen to kings and peasants both. Ahaziah shows that he is a true worshiper of the pagan god Baal-zebub, because he turns to this god in his time of trouble.

Demystifying 2 Kings

The god identified as Baal-zebub was originally named Baal-zebul, "Baal, the prince." This god was believed to have great power. The Israelites used the name Baal-zebub, "lord of the flies," as a jab or parody of this false god. The name stuck however—in the New Testament, Beelzebub is a common name for Satan, or the prince of devils. If the wooden lattice was intended to screen out flies, it would have made sense to Ahaziah to call on this god when the lattice failed.

There is little doubt that King Ahaziah believes that Yahweh lives, but Elijah's question (1:3) points out that Ahaziah *lives* as if there is no God in Israel. He is a practical atheist, and the way he seeks Baal-zebub instead of the Lord demonstrates this.

Since Ahaziah does not seek help from the real God, he will receive no real help. Instead this will be an occasion for God to send a message of judgment to King Ahaziah. When ancients sought their gods about medical issues, the response was considered to be a medical diagnosis. It was as if Elijah said, "Here's your diagnosis Ahaziah: Your condition is fatal and irreversible" (1:4).

Although Ahaziah had sent the messengers to seek a word from the pagan priests of Baal-zebub, the word from Elijah persuades them so much that they do not follow through on their original mission (1:5–6).

Ahaziah clearly suspects it is the prophet Elijah who spoke this word. His suspicion is confirmed when the man is described as being hairy and wearing a leather belt around his waist (1:7–9). The Hebrew words translated *hairy man* literally mean, "possessor of hair." Most likely this description refers to clothing made of hairy animal skins.

Critical Observation

Identifying Elijah by his clothes also connects him to the ministry of John the Baptist, who dressed in hairy skins from animals (Matthew 3:4). When the priests and Levites saw him they asked, "Are you Elijah?" (John 1:19–21).

📄 **1:10–18**

ELIJAH APPEARS BEFORE AHAZIAH

The king sends a captain with fifty men (1:9). This should have been plenty of men to capture one prophet. Clearly, Ahaziah sends more men than are normally required. There are many reasons why Ahaziah wants to arrest Elijah, even though he already heard the prophecy through Elijah. Perhaps he wanted Elijah to reverse his word of doom and was willing to use force to compel him to do it. Perhaps he just wanted to show his rage against this prophet who had troubled him and his father Ahab for so long. Perhaps he wanted to dramatically silence Elijah to discourage future prophets from speaking boldly against the king of Israel.

The captain admits Elijah's righteousness when he calls him a man of God. The implication is that they are wrong in doing this, even though they are following orders from their king.

Elijah puts the issue in stark contrast. If he really is a man of God, then the captain and his men are on an ungodly and immoral mission. Since Elijah cannot bring down fire from heaven without divine approval, he asks God to evaluate these men and the rightness of their actions against God's prophet (1:10). Essentially Elijah says, "You say I am a man of God even though you are not acting like it. Maybe I am and maybe I am not. Let's let God decide by fire."

The captain commands Elijah to come down. The man of God doesn't come down, but the fire of God does (1:11). God brings judgment on these men who act as if Yahweh is not a real God and as if Elijah is not truly His servant.

The second captain repeats the same error as the first captain, but with even more guilt because he knew what happened to the first captain. The judgment upon the first group should have warned this second captain and his fifty men, but the specific request of the second captain ("Come down quickly!") shows that the second captain makes his request even more bold and demanding (1:11).

Elijah leaves the matter in God's hands, and God again responds in dramatic judgment (1:12).

The third captain approaches his mission in a completely different manner. He comes to Elijah humbly, recognizing that he really is a man of God (1:13–14). Perhaps the third captain looked at the two blackened spots of scorched earth nearby before he spoke to Elijah!

The problem isn't that God does not want Elijah to go to King Ahaziah; it is that Ahaziah, his captains, and their soldiers all act as if there is no God in Israel. When the request is made wisely and humbly, Elijah goes (1:15). God assures Elijah that he has nothing to fear from Ahaziah.

Again, Elijah asks, "Is there no God in Israel" to answer your question? (1:16 NLT). This is the same message Elijah gave to the men Ahaziah sent to inquire of Baal-zebub. The message from God does not change just because Ahaziah doesn't want to hear it the first time.

The proof of Elijah's credibility is in the result. Elijah is demonstrated to be a man of God because his prophecy is fulfilled just as spoken. Ahaziah does not recover from his fall through the lattice (1:17).

Jehoram, who succeeds Ahaziah, is also the son of Ahab (3:1) and therefore the brother of Ahaziah. Ahaziah has no descendant to pass the kingdom to, so the throne goes to his brother. The account becomes a little confusing here, because the king of Judah at that time is also named Jehoram (the son of Jehoshaphat).

The Book of the History of the Kings of Israel, referred to in 1:18, is not the books of 1 Kings and 2 Kings, but a nonbiblical book.

2 KINGS 2:1–25

ELIJAH'S ASCENSION

Elijah Ascends to Heaven	2:1–12
The Beginning of the Ministry of the Prophet Elisha	2:13–25

Setting Up the Section

Chapter 1 of 2 Kings relates Elijah's confrontation with King Ahaziah and concludes with Ahaziah's death. Chapter 2 picks up the story at the end of Elijah's ministry and tells the account of his miraculous departure in a whirlwind and of Elisha's succession as prophet.

📖 **2:1–12**

ELIJAH ASCENDS TO HEAVEN

The Lord is about to take Elijah into heaven by a whirlwind (2:1). Apparently, this is somewhat common knowledge. Elijah, Elisha, and the sons of the prophets each knew that Elijah would soon be carried into heaven by a whirlwind (2:2–3); presumably there was a prophecy announcing this that at least some knew.

Elijah knows that God has a dramatic plan for the end of his earthly life, yet he is perfectly willing to allow it all to take place privately, without anyone else knowing. He seems to test the devotion of Elisha by telling him to stay behind (2:2). Since it is known that Elijah will soon depart to heaven in an unusual way, Elisha wants to stay as close as possible to his mentor. Elijah continues to test the devotion of Elisha, and Elisha continues to stay with his mentor until his anticipated unusual departure (2:4–6).

When Elijah and Elisha reach the Jordan, Elijah takes his mantle, rolls it up, and strikes the water. The water divides so that the two of them cross over on dry ground (2:7–8). This is a strange and unique miracle, though it was reminiscent of the crossing of the Red Sea during the Exodus and the stopping of the waters of the Jordan when the Israelites entered Canaan. Elijah walks in the steps of Moses and Joshua as those whom God uses to miraculously part waters.

After testing Elisha and finding him faithful, Elijah is now able to give him whatever he asks for (2:9). When invited to make a request, Elisha asks for a big thing—a double portion of the mighty spirit of Elijah. Elisha sees how greatly the Spirit of God worked through Elijah, and he wants the same for himself.

Demystifying 2 Kings

The idea of a double portion is not to ask for twice as much as Elijah has, but to ask for the portion that went to the firstborn son, as in Deuteronomy 21:17. Elisha asks for the right to be regarded as the successor of Elijah, as his firstborn son in regard to ministry. Yet Elisha has already been designated as Elijah's successor (1 Kings 19:19). This is a request for the spiritual power to fulfill the calling he already received.

Elijah tests the devotion of his protégé one more time by seeing if he will persistently stay with him through these last remarkable hours. If the devotion of Elisha remains strong through the testing, his request to be the successor of the first prophet will be fulfilled (2:10).

As the two prophets walk, a fiery object separates the two of them, and then a whirlwind carries Elijah up to heaven (2:11). This is a strange and unique miracle. Elijah is taken up to heaven in the whirlwind, not in the chariot and horses of fire (2:12). These chariots and horsemen symbolize the forces of God's spiritual presence. In them, Elisha recognizes that the strength of Israel has been that of the presence of the prophet of God. When Elisha himself dies, Joash, the reigning king, has the same vision and cries out the same words (13:14).

Elisha sees it: This fulfills the requirement mentioned in 2 Kings 2:10. Elisha will indeed inherit the prophetic ministry of Elijah. Yet Elisha isn't happy when this happens; he takes hold of his own clothes and tears them into two pieces as an expression of deep mourning (2:12).

🕮 2:13–25

THE BEGINNING OF THE MINISTRY
OF THE PROPHET ELISHA

Elijah takes up the mantle of Elijah that had fallen from him (2:13). Since the mantle is the special mark of a prophet, this is a demonstration of the truth that Elisha truly has inherited the ministry of Elijah.

Take It Home

Think of what it was like for Elisha to pick up that mantle. The mantle did not fall from heaven and rest on his shoulders; he had to decide to pick it up and put it on. He had to decide: *Do I really want to put this on?* Elijah's ministry was one of great power, but also of great pressure and responsibility. What mantles lay waiting for you to pick them up?

When Elisha strikes the water, it is divided (2:14). This shows that Elisha immediately has the same power in ministry that Elijah had. He goes back over a divided Jordan River the same way that he and Elijah first came over the river.

Elisha asks, "Where is the God of Elijah?" Elisha knows that the power in prophetic ministry does not rest in mantles or fiery chariots. It rests in the presence and work of the living God. If the God of Elijah is also with Elisha, then he will inherit the same power and direction of ministry.

The succession of Elisha to the power and office of Elijah is apparent to others (2:15). Elisha doesn't need to persuade or convince them of this with words. God's blessing on his actions is enough to prove it.

The sons of the prophets wonder if the chariot of fire had not merely taken Elijah to another place in Israel (2:16). Elisha knows that it had carried him to heaven, so he is hesitant to give permission for what he knows will be a futile mission (2:17).

At this time Jericho had a poor water supply. This made agriculture impossible and life very difficult (2:19). When the water is purified, it is not because Elisha wants to impress others or because he thinks it will be good to do it. This is a work of the Lord that announces the healing of the water (2:20–22).

The ancient Hebrew word translated *youths*, or *boys*, refers to young men in a very broad sense (2:23). This term applied to Joseph when he was thirty-nine (Genesis 41:12), to Absalom as an adult (2 Samuel 14:21; 18:5), and to Solomon when he was twenty (1 Kings 3:7). These youths are from Bethel, and their mocking shows the continuing opposition to a true prophet in Bethel, the chief center of pagan calf-worship.

The young men mock Elisha both because of his apparent baldness and because of his connection with the prophet Elijah. The idea behind the words *go up* (2 Kings 2:23) is that Elisha should go up to heaven like Elijah did. It mocks Elisha, his mentor Elijah, and the God they serve.

Demystifying 2 Kings

Elisha's baldness isn't the result of old age; since he lived about fifty years after this incident, he must have been relatively young at the time. His baldness may have been all the more noticeable by comparison with Elijah's hairiness.

Elisha leaves any correction of these young men up to God but pronounces a curse on them in the name of the Lord (2:24). In response to the curse of Elisha, God sends two female bears and they maul (cut up, not kill) the young men. Forty-two in all are mauled. The bear attack has the effect of breaking up the gang, while Elisha continues on his way unharmed (2:25).

2 KINGS 3:1–27

WAR AGAINST MOAB

Three Kings Gather against the Moabites	3:1–10
Elisha Speaks for the Lord	3:11–27

Setting Up the Section

King Ahab dies, leaving the throne of the northern kingdom of Israel to his son Ahaziah. When Ahaziah dies without a son, his brother Jehoram (or Joram) succeeds him. There has also been a change in the prophets: Elisha succeeded Elijah after Elijah is carried to heaven in a whirlwind.

📄 3:1–10

THREE KINGS GATHER AGAINST THE MOABITES

King Jehoram (or Joram) comes from a family that is far beyond dysfunctional. His father, Ahab (3:1), was one of the worst kings the northern kingdom of Israel ever knew, and his mother, Jezebel, was certainly the worst queen Israel ever knew. Jehoram is better than his father and mother, but he is still a wicked man (3:2–3). He is the ninth consecutive bad king over the northern kingdom, which never had a godly king.

The sin of Jeroboam that Jehoram perpetuates includes setting up golden calves for the people to worship in Bethel and Dan (1 Kings 12:25–32). Possibly Jehoram tears down the sacred pillar of Baal out of bad motives—either because he is frightened when he remembers the judgment that came against his father Ahab and his brother Ahaziah, or because he wants to impress Jehoshaphat so the Judean king will agree to an alliance. Either way, Elisha isn't impressed with Jehoram's putting away of Baal (2 Kings 3:13).

The Moabites live on the eastern side of the Dead Sea and are under tribute to Israel. The rebellion that began when King Ahab died (1:1) continued under Jehoram (3:4–5). Jehoram asks Jehoshaphat, king of Judah, for help (3:6–7). Jehoshaphat is a godly king (1 Kings 22:41–43), who followed in the godly footsteps of his father Asa (1 Kings 15:9–15).

Yet Asa had fought against Israel (1 Kings 15:16) while Jehoshaphat made peace with the northern kingdom (1 Kings 22:44). Though the kingdom of Israel was long since separated by a civil war, the two nations (Judah and Israel) are now willing to come together to fight this common foe.

Demystifying 2 Kings

The Moabite Stone (also called the Mesha Stele), discovered in 1868, contains a Moabite inscription that confirms many of the events of 2 Kings 3, but it gives a distinctly pro-Moabite spin.

Jehoram of Israel asks Jehoshaphat of Judah for military advice because Jehoshaphat is more experienced in battle than Jehoram. The king of Judah advises Jehoram that they attack Moab from the south, going through the dry desert of the Edomites (2 Kings 3:8).

The combined armies of Judah, Israel, and Edom have to travel a considerable distance to attack Moab from the south, and they find themselves in the wilderness with no water (3:9). Jehoram's guilty conscience convinces him that this calamity is the judgment of God. His own sin makes him think that everything that has happened against him is the judgment of God (3:10).

3:11–27

ELISHA SPEAKS FOR THE LORD

Both Jehoram and Jehoshaphat believe there is a divine element to their current crisis. Jehoram believes that God is to be *avoided* because of the crisis, while Jehoshaphat believes that God should be *sought* because of the crisis (3:11).

The description of Elisha in verse 11 has been translated as "personal assistant." This is a wonderful title for any servant of God. Elisha is the humble and practical servant of Elijah. This is spiritual service that prepares him for further spiritual service.

The kings' decision to go to Elisha (3:12) is encouraging humility on the part of these three kings. Normally, kings demand that others come see them. These three are willing to go to the prophet.

Elisha's call is to continue the ministry of Elijah, and in verse 13 we see that he imitates Elijah's plain speaking to powerful people. Elisha's plain speaking strikes the conscience of the king of Israel. Elisha is willing to speak to these three kings for the sake of Jehoshaphat, the godly king of Judah (3:14).

Elisha wants to become more sensitive to the leading and speaking of the Holy Spirit, so he asks for the service of a musician (3:14–15). This demonstrates the great spiritual power in music. One way to be open to the Spirit is through psalms, hymns, and spiritual songs.

God makes a strange promise: Water will be provided, but not through just any rain or storm. The people must dig ditches in order to catch what God will provide (3:16–17). They must dig the ditches before the water comes so they can benefit from it.

Critical Observation

What many versions translate as the command, "Dig ditches," in 2 Kings 3:16 is in some versions translated as a statement that the valley or streambed will hold water. The injunction to dig, however, is in keeping with the principle that God wants us to prepare for the blessing He wants to bring. Listening to Him, we are to anticipate His working and to get ready for it.

Digging ditches was something the people of God could do. God didn't ask them to do more than they were able to do. When God wants us to prepare for the blessing He will bring, He gives us things that we can really do.

The kings come to Elisha inquiring about water. God wants to give them more than their immediate need. He wants to give them complete victory over their enemies (3:18–19).

It seems that God sends an intense downpour in the nearby mountains, and this causes a flash flood though the desert of Edom (3:20). God meets their need for provision when mysterious water flows through the camp. The water is available only because they are obedient to dig the ditches. The ditches collect the water from the flash flood.

Take It Home

If Israel and Judah had disobeyed God and failed to dig the ditches, then God's blessing would have passed them by. God told them to get ready and prepare to receive and catch His blessing. God often moves us to do things that may or may not make much sense for the moment, but they are things that will prepare us for what He will do in the future.

The measure of water available to these thirsty men is directly connected to how faithful they are to dig the ditches. The more ditches and the bigger the ditches, the more water provided. Though it was hard and unpleasant work, the more they did the more blessing they received.

The ditches are not the blessing, and they are not the victory, though they are essential parts of both the blessing and the victory. Without the miraculous blessing of God, the ditches mean nothing.

The ditches that catch the water and save the armies of these three kings from dehydration are also the means of confusion and defeat to the enemies of the people of God. When they see the sun shining on the water collected in the ditches, they think it is blood from the three kings fighting one another (3:21–23).

When they come to the camp of Israel, Israel rises up and attacks the Moabites, so that they flee before them. God uses the ditches in a completely unexpected way to supply the need *and* to defeat the enemy (3:24–25).

That the king of Moab is willing to sacrifice his own son and heir (3:26–27) shows how desperate he is. He does this to honor his pagan gods and to show his own people his determination to prevent defeat. The radical determination of the king of Moab convinces the kings of Israel, Judah, and Edom that they cannot completely defeat Moab. They leave content with their near-complete victory.

2 KINGS 4:1–44

GOD WORKS MIRACLES THROUGH ELISHA

Setting Up the Section

We are not told precisely when the events recorded in chapter 4 occurred. In contrast to the faithlessness of King Ahaziah and King Jehoram described in 2 Kings 1–3, here we read of simple people with profound faith.

📄 **4:1–37**

MIRACLES CONNECTED WITH A WIDOW AND A BARREN WOMAN

This woman in verse 1, the widowed wife of one of the sons of the prophets, has debts and no means to pay them. The legal system in Israel does not allow her to declare bankruptcy; she has to give her sons as indentured servants to her creditor as payment for the debts.

Elisha makes this woman commit herself in faith to God's provision. To borrow vessels in this manner (4:3–4) invites awkward questions, but she does as the Lord through His prophet commands her (4:5). Elisha tells the woman to take what she has—one jar of oil (*all* that she has)—and to pour that out in faith into the borrowed vessels. As she does this, the oil miraculously continues to pour from the original vessel until all the borrowed vessels are filled. At the end of it, she has a lot of oil—enough to pay the debt and provide for her future (4:6–7).

We notice that Elisha makes *her* do this. Perhaps Elisha was tempted to gather the vessels and pour the oil himself, but he knew that she had to trust God herself.

Take It Home

The miracle is given according to the measure of the widow's previous faith in borrowing vessels; when the vessels are full, the oil ceases. Had she borrowed more, more would have been provided; had she gathered less, less would have been provided.

The oil does not pour out on the ground or simply flow about. It is intended for a prepared vessel. Each vessel had to be prepared by being gathered, assembled, emptied, and then put in the right position. When there are no more prepared vessels, the oil stops.

The principle of this miracle is the same as the principle of the ditches (chapter 3). The amount of one's work with the miracle determines the amount of blessing and provision actually received. God's powerful provision invites our hard work and never excuses laziness.

A remarkable relationship between Elisha and the Shunammite woman begins when the woman seeks to do something for the prophet and offers him a meal (4:8). Elisha doesn't seek anything from this woman; she simply offers her hospitality. The Shunammite woman then seeks to do more for the prophet. With the approval of her husband, they make a room for Elisha to stay in on his frequent travels through the area (4:9-10). Still she asks for nothing in return (4:13).

It is Gehazi, Elisha's servant, who identifies what the woman needs: a son to care for her in her old age (4:14). To this barren woman this promise seems too good to be true. The stigma associated with barrenness was harsh in the ancient world, and this promised son would answer the longing of her heart and remove the stigma of barrenness (4:15-16).

The woman who so generously provides material things for the prophet of God is now blessed by the God of the prophet, blessed beyond material things (4:17).

Yet the son granted by miraculous promise, in reward to the faithful service of the Shunammite woman, tragically dies on the lap of his mother after a brief but severe affliction (4:18-20).

When the woman lays her son on Elisha's bed and prepares to fetch Elisha (4:21-24), she shows her faith. She prepares for the resurrection of the boy, not his burial. Perhaps she heard that Elijah had raised the widow of Zarephath's son to life (1 Kings 17).

The Shunammite woman doesn't want Elisha to learn of her grief through his assistant Gehazi (2 Kings 4:25). She wants the man of God to hear it from her own lips and sense her own grief. Elisha seems mystified that this woman (who he presumably often prays for) is in a crisis that he is not aware of. In this circumstance, Elisha is more surprised that God *didn't* speak to him than if God had spoken to him (4:27).

Instead of going directly himself, Elisha sends his servant Gehazi with his staff (4:29). This seems to follow the previous pattern in Elisha's ministry: He does not do things for people directly but gives them the opportunity to work with God and to trust Him for themselves. God tells the alliance of kings to have ditches dug (3:16). God tells the widow to gather vessels and pour the oil herself (4:1-7).

It may be that the Shunammite woman fails under this test, because she thinks that the power to heal is more connected with Elisha himself, and she refuses to leave his presence (4:30). The child is not healed by the laying on of the staff (4:31), though (hypothetically) the child may have been healed with only the staff if the Shunammite would have embraced this promise with full faith.

God does heal the Shunammite's son in response to Elisha's prayer (4:32-37). He prays after the pattern shown by his mentor Elijah (1 Kings 17:20-23). Elisha prays with great faith because he knew God worked in this way in the life of his mentor Elijah. He also prays with great faith because he senses that God wants to raise this boy from the dead.

Critical Observation

There is a significant contrast between the stretched-out supplication of Elijah and Elisha and the authoritative command of Jesus in raising the dead (as in John 11:43). Elijah and Elisha *beg* God to raise the dead. Jesus *commands* the dead to be raised.

📄 4:38–44

MIRACLES CONNECTED WITH THE PROVISION OF FOOD

The famine mentioned in verse 38 may be the seven-year famine referred to in 2 Kings 8:1–3. Elisha feels a special responsibility to help in this situation because he tells the men to gather ingredients for the stew, and they gather the wild vine that poisons the pot (4:38–40).

Demystifying 2 Kings

It's probable that the poisonous gourds were *colocynth*, also known as wild cucumber. These vines still grow near the Dead Sea. The dried pulp can be used to induce vomiting, and too much of it can be fatal.

There is nothing inherently purifying in the flour Elisha puts in the pot (4:41). The real purification is a miraculous work of God.

The twenty barley loaves are bread of the firstfruits (4:42). Normally anything from the first harvest, like these loaves, is reserved for God (Leviticus 23:20) and the Levitical priests (Numbers 18:13; Deuteronomy 18:4–5). But religious practices had been corrupted under King Ahab and his sons. The farmer probably brings his firstfruits to Elisha because he knows Elisha to be a man of God.

In a miracle that anticipates Jesus' miracle of feeding the five thousand, Elisha commands that a small amount of bread be served to one hundred people, quoting God's promise not only to provide, but to provide beyond the immediate need (2 Kings 4:43). Elisha trusts the promise of God, acts upon it, and sees the promise miraculously fulfilled (4:44).

2 KINGS 5:1–27
NAAMAN THE LEPER

Setting Up the Section

The miracle recounted here in 2 Kings 5 does not occur chronologically between the events described in chapter 4 and those in chapter 6. Rather, this account, grouped with other miracles that Elisha performs, demonstrates his credibility as a prophet of God.

📄 **5:1–8**

NAAMAN COMES TO ELISHA

Naaman is the chief military commander of Syria (translated as Aram in some versions), a persistent enemy to both Israel and Judah. Not long before, in the days of Ahab and Jehoshaphat, Syria had fought and won against Israel (1 Kings 22:35–36). His position and success make him a great and honorable man, and personally he is a mighty man of valor (2 Kings 5:1).

Naaman has a lot going for him, but what he has against him is devastating. He is a leper, which means that he has a horrible, incurable disease that will slowly result in his death. No matter how good and successful everything else is in Naaman's life, he is still a leper.

Demystifying 2 Kings

The disease called leprosy at this time began as small, red spots on the skin. Before too long the spots got bigger and started to turn white, with sort of a shiny or scaly appearance. Pretty soon the spots spread over the whole body and hair began to fall out—first from the head, then even from the eyebrows. As things got worse, fingernails and toenails became loose, started to rot, and eventually fell off. Then the joints of fingers and toes began to rot and fall off piece by piece. Gums began to shrink until they couldn't hold the teeth anymore, so each tooth was lost. Leprosy ate away at the face until literally the nose, the palate, and even the eyes rotted—and the victim wasted away until death.

The girl who serves as a maid to Naaman's wife (5:2) is an unwilling missionary, taken captive from Israel and now in Syria. She was probably raised in a godly home, yet taken from her family at a young age. God allows the tragedy of her captivity to accomplish a greater good, illustrating the mysterious ways God works.

This young girl is an outstanding example of a faithful witness in her current circumstance. She cares enough to speak up, and she has faith enough to believe that Elisha will heal Naaman of his leprosy (5:3).

Considering the record of wars between Israel and Syria described in the previous chapters, it seems strange that the king of Syria would send a letter of recommendation with his general Naaman (5:4–6). It seems that 2 Kings is not necessarily arranged chronologically, so this probably occurred during a time of lowered tension between Israel and Syria.

Naaman took over one million dollars worth of gold, silver, and merchandise with him to Israel. All this together shows how desperate Naaman's condition is and how badly the king of Syria wants to help him.

When the king of Israel (Jehoram) reads the letter, he is understandably upset. First, it is obviously out of his power to heal Naaman's leprosy. Second, he has no relationship with the prophet of the God who does have the power to heal. He thinks the king of Syria seeks a quarrel (5:7).

Elisha gives a gentle rebuke to the king of Israel: "This is a crisis to you, because you have no relationship with the God who can heal lepers. But it is a needless crisis, because you *could* have a relationship with this God." Sadly, Naaman will never know there is a prophet in Israel by hanging around the royal palace. The true prophet in Israel isn't welcome at the palace (5:8).

📄 **5:9–19**

NAAMAN IS HEALED

Naaman takes the trouble to come to the home of Elisha, but Elisha refuses to give him a personal audience. He simply sends a messenger (5:9–10). This is humbling to Naaman, who is accustomed to being honored. The messenger brings simple, uncomplicated instructions. Yet as Naaman's reaction demonstrates, these are humbling instructions. Naaman has it all figured out. In his great need, he anticipates a way in which God will work, and he is offended when God doesn't work the way he expects. Because his expectation is crushed, Naaman wants nothing to do with Elisha. If the answer is washing in a river, Naaman knows there are better rivers in his own land (5:11–12).

Thank God for faithful subordinates who will speak to their superiors as Naaman's men do (5:13). Naaman is obviously angry, yet they are bold enough to give him the good advice he needs to hear. They use a brilliantly logical approach. If Elisha had asked Naaman to sacrifice one hundred or one thousand animals to the God of Israel, he would have done it immediately. Yet because his request is easy to do and humbling, Naaman refuses.

Naaman does exactly what Elisha tells him to do (5:14). Therefore, each dunk in the Jordan is a step of faith, trusting in the word of God through His prophet. Naaman's response of faith is generously rewarded. God answers his faithful actions with complete and miraculous healing. Elisha's absence makes it clear that the miracle is from God, not from Elisha.

Before, Naaman expected the prophet to come to him. Now he returns to the man of God and stands before him. The healing, connected with the word of the prophet, is convincing evidence to Naaman that the God Elisha represents is the true God in all the earth. Naaman's desire to give a gift to Elisha is a fine display of gratitude (5:15). We can say that Naaman only means well by this gesture. He feels it is appropriate to support the ministry of this man of God whom the Lord had used so greatly to bring healing. However, Elisha steadfastly insists that he will take nothing from Naaman (5:16).

Like many new believers, Naaman is superstitious in his faith. He holds the common opinion in the ancient world that particular deities have power over particular places. He thinks that if he takes a piece of Israel back with him to Syria, he can better worship the God of Israel (5:17). As an official in the government of Syria, Naaman is expected to participate in the worship of the Syrian gods. He asks Elisha for allowance to direct his heart to Yahweh even when he is in the temple of Rimmon (5:18). Some commentators believe that Naaman asks forgiveness for his previous idolatry in the temple of Rimmon, instead of asking permission for future occasions. Apparently, the Hebrew will allow for this translation, though it is not the most natural way to understand the text.

By generally approving, but not giving a specific answer, it seems that Elisha leaves the matter up to Naaman and God (5:19). Perhaps he trusted that the Lord would personally convict Naaman of this and give him the integrity and strength to avoid idolatry.

📖 5:20–27

THE GREED OF GEHAZI

As Gehazi hears Naaman and Elisha speak, he is shocked that his master refuses to take anything from such a wealthy, influential, and grateful man. He figures that someone should benefit from such an opportunity, and he takes the initiative to run after Naaman and take something from him (5:20–21).

Gehazi may have thought that God was blessing his venture. After all, he asks for one talent of silver, and Naaman is happy to give him two talents (5:22–23). The fact that he hands them to two of his servants shows that this is a lot of silver. But the fact that Gehazi deliberately hides the silver from Elisha (5:24–25) suggests that he knows that he has done wrong.

Elisha knew what Gehazi had done (5:26). We don't know if this was supernatural knowledge, or simply a familiarity with Gehazi's character. At any rate, all Gehazi's attempts to cover his sin fail.

It seems that Elisha had no absolute law against receiving support from those who were touched by his ministry. Yet it is spiritually clear to Elisha, and should have been clear to Gehazi, that it is not appropriate at this time and circumstance (5:26). Obviously, Gehazi does not bring home all of the things Elisha lists: vineyards, cattle, and servants. Yet he wants all of these things, and Elisha exposes his greedy heart.

Gehazi receives a severe judgment (5:27), but as a man in ministry he is under an even stricter judgment. When he allows himself to covet what Naaman has, he thinks only in terms of the money. God allows him to keep the riches, but also gives him something else Naaman has—severe leprosy.

2 KINGS 6:1–33
GOD'S PROTECTION OF ELISHA

Setting Up the Section

Chapter 6 of 2 Kings deals with needs both great and small. The recovery of a lost ax head is a miracle of provision. The miracle of protection from the Samarian army is a dramatic demonstration of God's invisible but very real power. Chapter 6 concludes with a situation even graver: a siege that threatens to destroy the population of an entire city.

📄 6:1–7

THE RECOVERY OF THE AX HEAD

At this time Elisha has a significant impact on the nation. The old facility for housing the sons of the prophets is not large enough to meet the needs of all those who want to be trained in ministry (6:1–2). Elisha does not initiate or lead this work of building a new center for training the prophets, but it cannot happen without his approval and blessing (6:3).

Losing the iron ax head in the water (6:4–5) is a significant loss. Iron was certainly present at this time in Israel, but it was not common enough to be cheap. The man who loses the ax head is rightly sensitive to the fact that he lost something that belongs to someone else, making the loss more acute.

This is an obvious and unique miracle. There is no trickery in the way Elisha puts the stick in the water; it is simply an expression of his faith that God honors (6:6).

Conceivably, God could have arranged a way for the ax head to appear right in the man's hand without any effort on his part. But this miracle works in a familiar way—God does the part only He can do, but He leaves to man the part that he can do (6:7).

📄 6:8–23

GOD PROTECTS ELISHA FROM THE SYRIANS

Elisha does not support the corrupt monarchs of Israel, but he knows that it is even worse for Israel to be conquered and subjugated under Syria. Therefore, he gives the king of Israel information from divinely inspired espionage (6:8–10).

The king of Syria is naturally mystified by the way the king of Israel knows all of Syria's plans beforehand. He is convinced there is a traitor among them, until one servant reveals that Elisha, the prophet in Israel, knows and reveals these things (6:11–13).

When Elisha's servant sees the horses and chariots and the great Syrian army that has come to seize Elisha, he is naturally afraid (6:13–15). He knows that there is little chance of escaping or surviving an attack from so many. But Elisha says not to fear, for they have more men (6:16). This is not empty hope or wishful thinking; it is a real reason for confidence, even if the servant cannot see it. This seems unbelievable to Elisha's servant. He sees the horses, the chariots, and the great army surrounding them. He cannot see anyone who is with himself and Elisha.

Elisha does not pray that God will change anything in the situation, nor does he try to persuade the servant of the reality of those who are with them. His only request is that his servant can actually see the reality of the situation (6:17). When a person is blind to spiritual reality, only God can open his or her eyes.

When his eyes are opened, the servant sees what he could not see before. He sees that there really are more with him and Elisha than those assembled against them.

The previous lack of perception on the part of Elisha's servant does not make the reality of the spiritual army any less real. If there are fifty people who do not see something, it doesn't invalidate the perception of one who does see.

Critical Observation

Horses and chariots were the most sophisticated and mighty military instruments of the day. But the invisible army of God had literally more firepower than the horses and chariots of the Syrians. The spiritual army had chariots of fire all around Elisha.

The Syrian soldiers could not see the spiritual army, so they do not hesitate to approach Elisha. But just as he previously prayed that God would give sight to his servant, he now asks God to strike this people with blindness. God answers this prayer, just as He previously answered the prayer to give perception to the servant (6:18).

When Elisha tells the army to follow him, he tells a technical truth but certainly intends to deceive. He does in fact bring them to the man whom they seek (when their eyes are opened, Elisha is there with them). However, he leads them back to Samaria—the capital city of the kingdom of Israel and an unfriendly place for a group of Syrian soldiers (6:19–20).

Elisha commands the king of Israel to treat the soldiers with kindness and generosity (6:21–22). This practice of answering evil with good successfully changes the policy of freelance raiders from Syria, and the bands of Syrian raiders no longer invade the land of Israel (6:23).

📖 6:24–33

THE SIEGE OF SAMARIA

Though the kindness of Elisha and the king of Israel changes the heart of the Syrian raiders, it does not change the heart of the king of Syria. He launches a large, full-scale attack against his neighbor to the south (6:24).

Demystifying 2 Kings

The king of Syria used the common method of attack on securely walled cities: He besieged Samaria. A siege was intended to surround a city, prevent all business and trade from entering or leaving, and eventually to starve the population into surrender.

The siege strategy successfully starves Samaria, and there is a great famine. The famine is so bad that a donkey's head or dove droppings become so expensive that only the rich can afford them. Their price of five shekels of silver is more than a month's wages for a laborer. Mothers are so hungry that they even eat their own children (6:25–29).

The king is deeply grieved and angry—but not with himself, with Israel, or with their sin. The king is angry against the prophet of God—and with God Himself (6:30–33).

Critical Observation

Deuteronomy 28 contains an extended section where God warns Israel about the curses that will come upon them if they reject the covenant He made with them. Part of that chapter describes the horrors fulfilled in this chapter (see Deuteronomy 28:52–53).

2 KINGS 7:1–20

GOD'S MIRACULOUS PROVISION FOR SAMARIA

God's Promise and What the Lepers Discover	7:1–9
The Plundering of the Syrian Camp	7:10–20

Setting Up the Section

Chapter 7 of 2 Kings picks up the account of the Syrian's siege of Israel's capital, Samaria.

📖 **7:1–9**

GOD'S PROMISE AND WHAT THE LEPERS DISCOVER

Though the king of Israel blames God for the calamity that came upon Israel and Samaria (6:33), God still has a word for the king and the nation—and it is a good word. God's promise through Elisha is that in twenty-four hours the economic situation in Samaria will be completely reversed. Instead of scarcity, there will be such abundance that food prices will radically drop in the city (7:1).

By the standards of that time, the prices listed were not cheap, but they were nothing compared to the famine conditions associated with the siege.

The king's officer doubts the prophecy, and his doubt is based on several faulty premises (7:2). First, he doubts the power of God. If God wills it, He can drop food from the sky. Then he doubts God's creativity, that He can bring provision in a completely unexpected way. Finally, he doubts the messenger of God who has an established track record of reliability.

Through Elisha, God pronounces a harsh judgment upon the king's doubting officer. He will see the word fulfilled, but he will not benefit from its fulfillment.

The four lepers introduced in verse 3 stay at the entrance of the gate because they are not welcome in the city. Their leprous condition makes them outcasts and untouchables. Their logic is perfect. They will soon die from the famine if they stay in the city. If any food becomes available, they will certainly be the last to receive it. So they decide that their chances are better if they surrender to the Syrians (7:4).

When they come to the outskirts of the Syrian camp, to their surprise, no one is there. This huge army surrounded the city of Samaria for many months, and the camp was the home and supply center for thousands of men. When the lepers come upon it that morning, they discover an empty army camp—fully supplied. The words translated "to the outskirts of the camp" (7:5 NASB) imply that they came not only to the edge of the camp, but that they walked around to the furthermost part of the Syrian camp, the part away from the city. They came to the camp as someone from afar would approach, not as someone from Syria. They figured that this was their best chance, coming as if they were not from the besieged city and to the least fortified positions of the camp.

Israel is powerless against this besieging army, but God isn't powerless. He attacks the Syrian army simply by causing them to hear noises of an army (7:6-7). Perhaps God does this by putting the noise into the air; perhaps He simply creates the perception of the noise in the minds of the Syrian soldiers. The same God who struck one Syrian army so they could not see what was there (6:18) now strikes another Syrian army so that they hear things that are not there. As a result, the siege for Samaria is over—even though no one in the city knows it or enjoys it.

Everything is left behind, leaving the unlikely lepers to spoil the camp. They go into one tent and eat and drink. After the long period of famine, this is the answer to every hope and prayer they had. They know that their discovery of the camp can't remain secret forever, so they hide some of the valuables so they can profit from them even when the camp is discovered by others. After enjoying it all, the lepers realize their responsibility (7:8-9).

📄 7:10–20

THE PLUNDERING OF THE SYRIAN CAMP

The lepers call to the gatekeepers of the city (7:10). Since the lepers are not welcome in the city, they can only communicate with the gatekeepers. There are many people they cannot speak to, but they are faithful to speak to the ones whom they can speak to. The good news from the lepers is communicated in the simplest way possible. It goes from one person to another, until the news reaches the king himself (7:11), whose officers go to check the accuracy of the report (7:12-15). This is the sensible reaction to the good news that started with the report of the lepers. The report might be true or it might not be; it only makes sense to test it and see.

When the good news is found to be true, there is no stopping the people. Because they know their need, they are happy to receive God's provision to meet that need (7:16-17). Through Elisha, God had announced the exact prices in the Samarian markets, and the prophecy is proven to be precisely true (7:18).

The officer who earlier had said provision would never come (7:2) has to personally supervise the people responding to that provision. Not only does the prediction about the prices come true, but so does the prediction Elijah made about the officer himself (7:2). Because of his unbelief, others enjoy God's blessings, but he does not (7:19-20).

2 KINGS 8:1–29

NEW KINGS IN SYRIA AND JUDAH

Setting Up the Section

The story of the kings of Judah pauses at 1 Kings 22:50, where Jehoshaphat the son of Asa ends his twenty-five-year reign and his son Jehoram comes to the throne. This chapter picks up the story of Jehoram again. But first we read of the king of Israel and the assassination of Ben-hadad, king of Syria.

📄 8:1–6

THE RESTORATION OF THE SHUNAMMITE'S LAND

Second Kings 4 describes Elisha's previous dealings with the woman mentioned in 8:1. She and her husband are godly, generous people who help the prophet. Through Elisha's prayer they are blessed with a son, who is also brought miraculously back to life.

On the advice of the prophet, the woman and her family leave Israel because of a coming famine. In the land of the Philistines, they are spared the worst of the famine (7:2). When she returns, she appeals to the king for the return of her land (7:3).

Demystifying 2 Kings

Upon leaving Israel and going to the land of the Philistines, the woman forfeits her claim to her ancestral lands. To regain them requires intervention from the king.

The king is talking with Gehazi (8:4). This is the same servant of Elisha who was cursed with leprosy (5:20-27). It seems strange that a severely afflicted leper would be a counselor to a king, so it seems that either Gehazi is granted healing from his leprosy or that this actually takes place before the events of 2 Kings 5. Of course, it is still possible that the king has this conversation with Gehazi when he is a leper and the king simply keeps his distance.

The woman comes to make her request at the exact time Gehazi tells the king about the miracles associated with her life (8:5). This is perfect, God-ordained timing. The king understands that if God is obviously supportive of this woman, then it also makes sense for him to support her and to answer her request (8:6). In the end, her obedience to God is not penalized by losing her land.

📄 **8:7-15**

A NEW KING IN SYRIA

The leaders of Syria had at one time tried to capture or kill Elisha. But since God has miraculously delivered the prophet so many times, he is now respected and welcome in the courts of the Syrian king. He is especially welcome on account of the king's illness (8:7). Wanting to know the outcome of his present illness, the king of Syria asks the prophet—and with his extravagant gift does whatever he can to prompt a favorable message (8:8-9).

God gives Elisha insight into more than the health of the king of Syria. He also sees the inevitable and ultimately God-ordained political machinations that will unfold. Elisha rightly says that the king will certainly recover from his illness, and he does (8:10). However, Elisha also sees that the same servant he speaks with at that moment will engineer an assassination and take the throne. This is how Elisha's statement is true. The king certainly does recover from his illness, and he really does die soon—but not from the illness.

This is a dramatic, personal confrontation between this prophet and the high official of the king of Syria. Elisha stares at him because he has prophetic knowledge of future events and of how this man will trouble Israel in the future. God tells Elisha more about the coming situation than he wants to know. He shows the prophet that the messenger of the king (Hazael), after he takes the throne from the present king of Syria, will do evil to the children of Israel (8:11-12). Elisha's prophetic calling and gift is at times more of a burden than a blessing. He can clearly see what will befall Israel through Hazael, but he is powerless to prevent it.

Perhaps Hazael had planned this assassination and simply pretends to be ignorant at Elisha's announcement (8:13). Perhaps he has not yet planned it and does know the evil capabilities in his own heart. Either way, his offence is inappropriate. He should have taken this warning as an opportunity to confront himself and to do right, instead of turning an accusation back upon Elisha.

Hazael takes an evil inference from Elisha's prophecy and seizes the throne (8:14-15). Instead of taking the prophet's announcement as a warning to check his own heart, he acts on that evil—and is fully responsible for his own actions.

📄 8:16–29

TWO NEW KINGS IN JUDAH

The fact that Jehoram followed the example of the kings of Israel (8:16–18) is not a compliment. While the southern kingdom of Judah had a mixture of godly and wicked kings, the northern kingdom of Israel had nothing but evil, God-rejecting kings. The wickedness of Jehoram is not a surprise, considering how much he allows himself to be influenced by the house of Ahab. Arranged by his father, Jehoram marries the daughter of Ahab and Jezebel—her name is Athaliah. In order to consolidate his throne, he murders his many brothers and many other leaders (1 Chronicles 21:1–6). Perhaps his marriage to Ahab's daughter makes sense politically or socially, but it is a spiritual calamity for Judah.

Demystifying 2 Kings

It is easy to confuse the variation between Jehoram and Joram in verses 21–23, but in this case, they are two variants for the same name. On the other hand, it's also easy to confuse Jehoram of Judah with the King Jehoram of Israel, mentioned in 2 Kings 3. That Jehoram is called *Joram* in 8:16.

Yet God will not destroy Judah, for the sake of His servant David (8:19). The implication is that Jehoram's evil is great enough to justify such judgment, but God withholds it out of faithfulness to his ancestor David.

The Edomite revolt against Judah (8:20–22) is evidence of the weakness of the kingdom of Jehoram. He thinks that the marriage alliance with Ahab and the kingdom of Israel will make Judah stronger, but this act of disobedience only makes them weaker.

Critical Observation

According to 2 Chronicles 21:12–15, Elijah writes Jehoram a letter, condemning him for his sins and predicting that judgment will come upon him and disaster upon the nation. At the age of forty, Jehoram is struck with a fatal intestinal disease, and he dies in terrible pain (2 Chronicles 21:19).

The short life and reign of Jehoram (he reigns only eight years and dies at age forty) should have warned his son Ahaziah. His brief reign (one year) shows he was even less blessed than his father (8:25–26). His close association with the wicked house of Ahab develops into a war alliance with Israel against Syria. His connection with his mother's family (she is a daughter of Ahab and Jezebel, 2 Kings 8:18) is so strong and sympathetic that he pays a visit to the injured and sick King Joram of Israel (8:27–29).

2 KINGS 9:1–37

JEHU TAKES THE THRONE OF ISRAEL

Setting Up the Section

After the account of kings Jehoram and Ahaziah of Judah in chapter 8, the story shifts back to the northern kingdom of Israel in chapter 9. Joram, the king of Israel identified in 2 Kings 3, is king at the time the events of this chapter take place.

📄 **9:1–13**

JEHU IS ANOINTED AND DECLARED KING

Elisha summons a young man from the association for training prophets in Israel (9:1–3). We might imagine that Elisha gives him this duty as a class assignment. Though Israel has abandoned God, God has not abandoned Israel. He still has the right to interfere among them. He will appoint and allow kings as He chooses, either to bless an obedient Israel or to curse a disobedient nation, according to the terms of His covenant with them at Mount Sinai.

So the young man, the servant of the prophet, goes to Ramoth-gilead. There he finds the captains of the army and Jehu, a commander in the army of Israel, under King Ahab and his son, King Joram (9:4–5). Jehu is anointed but is not to take the throne immediately (9:6). Both Saul and David were anointed as king over Israel before they actually possessed the throne.

Critical Observation

Jehu had previously been anointed as a future king of Israel who would overthrow the dynasty of Omri and Ahab (1 Kings 19:16–18). But that was a long time ago, and now he is anointed again to show that the time of fulfillment of the previous prophecy is at hand.

The young prophet's message about the destruction of Ahab's family (9:7–10) is more than Elisha tells this man from the school of prophets to say (9:1–3). Either Elisha told him to say this and it was not recorded previously, or he came under the inspiration of the Spirit when he did what Elisha told him to do and spoke this in spontaneous prophecy to Jehu. Clearly, God intends to use Jehu as a tool of judgment against the royal house of Ahab.

When Jehu emerges from the tent with his head drenched with oil, it is easy to think that the man who did it is a madman (9:11). It is easy for both Jehu and his associates to think of any God-honoring man as demented. Yet Jehu knows—and the others soon do also—that the man is a true prophet of God. When Jehu repeats the prophet's message, they take his word seriously and proclaim the reluctant Jehu as the king of Israel (9:13). This shows the sense of dissatisfaction they have with Joram.

📄 **9:14–37**

JEHU BRINGS GOD'S JUDGMENT TO THE HOUSE OF OMRI

Upon seeing the company of Jehu approaching, King Joram wants to know if this mysterious group comes in peace (9:14–17). As he waits to recover full strength in Jezreel, Joram is fundamentally insecure in his hold on the throne and easily suspects threats. Jehu's reply (9:18) means that the soldier should not regard this as a time of peace, but a time of conflict—a time to violently overthrow the throne of Joram and the dynasty he comes from. When two messengers do not return but instead join the company of Jehu (9:19–20), it shows that he enjoys popular support among the troops of Israel, and King Joram does not.

Jehu is such an intense man that his personality can be easily seen in the way he drives a chariot (9:20).

The property of Naboth the Jezreelite (9:21) is the land that Ahab and Jezebel had so wickedly obtained by murdering the innocent owner of the land (1 Kings 21:1–16). On this very land—which, as far as God is concerned, still belongs to Naboth—the dynasty of Omri will meet its judgment.

The wicked, compromising Joram wants peace with Jehu (9:22). But none of the dynasty of Omri wants peace with God; nor do Ahab and Jezebel want peace with Naboth.

Jehu's condemnation of Jezebel shows that he takes his previous anointing by Elijah (1 Kings 19:16–17) and his more recent anointing by one from the school of the prophets seriously. Jehu's words as he has Joram's body dumped on Nabal's property confirm that Jehu sees himself as a fulfiller of God's will in bringing judgment on the house of Ahab (9:25–26).

Take It Home

Jehu's mind is not filled with thoughts of political gain and royal glory. He acts for the honor of God, as a conscious executor of divine judgment against the house of Ahab. While we today are not likely to be called to execute kings, we are called to do everything not for our own gain, but for the glory of God (1 Corinthians 10:31).

Jehu receives no direct command or commission from God to bring judgment upon the king of Judah, but he does anyway. Consciously or unconsciously, he is guided by God and he kills Ahaziah. Ahaziah is happy to associate himself with the northern kingdom of Israel and their wicked kings. Therefore he dies in the same judgment that came upon the king of Israel. Ahaziah is also a blood relative of Ahab (Ahab is his grandfather), therefore making him liable under the judgment that came upon Ahab and his descendants (9:27–29). When

Ahaziah is killed in battle, they give him a dignified burial—not for his own sake, but only because his ancestor Jehoshaphat was a godly man (2 Chronicles 22:9).

Jezebel compares Jehu to Zimri (2 Kings 9:30-31), who assassinated King Baasha of Israel (1 Kings 16:9-12) when Zimri was also the servant of Baasha, a commander in his army. It is her way of calling Jehu a despicable rebel. It is also an implied threat, because the brief reign of Zimri is ended by Omri, who is the father of Ahab and the father-in-law of this same Jezebel. By implication, Jezebel says "The dynasty of Omri will defeat you just like it defeated Zimri."

The eunuchs at the window probably work for Jezebel, but they quickly respond to Jehu's command to throw the queen down. In ancient Near Eastern cultures, the desecration of the dead body—Jezebel's body being trampled under the horse's hooves—was a fate worse than death. Yet Jehu is completely untroubled by the ugly end of Jezebel; he eats and drinks after trampling over her dead body and passing over the pavement splattered with her blood (9:32-35).

Verses 36 and 37 record Jehu's conviction that God's promise against Jezebel and the house of Ahab is exactly and righteously fulfilled (1 Kings 21:19, 23-25).

2 KINGS 10:1–36

THE REFORMS OF JEHU

Jehu Executes the House of Ahab	10:1–17
Jehu Strikes against Baal Worship	10:18–31
A Summary of Jehu's Reign	10:32–36

Setting Up the Section

Jehu, anointed king of Israel at God's command, has executed the wicked queen mother, Jezebel, her son, Joram, who is Israel's king, and her son-in-law, Ahaziah, who is Judah's king—all in fulfillment of the judgment the Lord had sworn against them. But seventy sons of King Ahab, the patriarch of this idolatrous family, remain alive.

📄 **10:1–17**

JEHU EXECUTES THE HOUSE OF AHAB

Ahab's seventy sons are a significant danger to the anointed King Jehu. First, they are the descendants of Ahab and have a great interest in battling to keep the throne of Israel among the dynasty of Omri. Second, they are in Samaria, the capital city of Israel—meaning they are away from Jehu, who killed King Joram in Jezreel. Jehu challenges any partisans of the house of Omri to declare themselves and prepare to fight for their master's house (10:1-3).

Instead, terrified, they send a message back to Jehu, promising not to put any of the princes on the throne as king (10:4-5). Jehu's letter—and his previous bold action against Joram and Ahaziah—powerfully persuades the leaders of Israel to execute the sons of

Ahab on behalf of Jehu. The nobles are so afraid of Jehu that they send grim evidence of their obedience: the princes' heads in a basket (10:6–7). Jehu has the heads piled at the gate of the city (10:8).

Demystifying 2 Kings

Jehu doesn't ask for the severed heads on a whim. It is the custom at the time to display the heads of rebels at the city gate as a public warning against rebellion.

When the people see the severed heads of seventy descendants of Ahab, they fear that judgment has gone too far and they will be punished for it. Jehu assures them that they have done right and that none have the right to accuse him, because he acted at the command of God (10:9–11).

On his way to Samaria, Jehu meets relatives of Ahaziah, king of Judah. This is to the great misfortune of these men. Since Jehu is committed to execute all those connected with the house of Ahab, these men are also targets of judgment. Ahaziah is a descendant of King Ahab through his mother (who is the daughter of Ahab and Jezebel). Therefore, their mention of the queen mother does not help them. None of them escape (9:12–14). This is characteristic of Jehu—whole-hearted and energetic obedience.

Next Jehu encounters a man named Jehonadab. Jehu wants to know if Jehonadab is on his side (10:15). Jehonadab is optimistic about this energetic reformer, and Jehu is hungry for the approval of this popular religious leader and reformer. It isn't too cynical to think that Jehu wants to use Jehonadab to add legitimacy to his reign as king.

Jehu's zeal is evident in his complete and energetic obedience to the Lord, to the disregard of his own safety and comfort (10:17). Yet he seems to boast of his dedication (10:16), revealing a dangerous root of pride.

Demystifying 2 Kings

Jehonadab, the son of Rechab (10:15–16), was the mysterious founder of the Rechabites, a reform movement among the people of God protesting the immoral and impure lives of many in Israel and Judah. In Jeremiah 35, God uses the Rechabites and the memory of Jehonadab as an example of faithfulness and obedience to rebuke His unfaithful and disobedient people.

📖 10:18–31

JEHU STRIKES AGAINST BAAL WORSHIP

Jehu feigns devotion to Baal to lure the priests and worshipers of Baal into a trap. The priests of Baal believe the deception (10:18–21). Jehu gathers all the Baal-worshipers in one temple and makes certain that all the worshipers of the true God are put out of the place (10:22–23).

Jehu chooses to offer the sacrifice to Baal first and then to call for the execution of the worshipers of Baal. Ahab had built this temple for his wife Jezebel (1 Kings 16:32); Jehu tears it down. He works to completely eliminate the worship of Baal from Israel, making him a unique king among the other rulers of the northern kingdom (10:24–28). However, he promotes the false worship of the true God after the pattern of Jeroboam, who set up the golden calves that were at Bethel and Dan (10:29).

Critical Observation

Beginning with the first king of Israel—Jeroboam—Israel was steeped in idolatry. Jeroboam began with false representations of the true God (the golden calves described in 1 Kings 12:25–33). The successive kings of Israel continued his idolatry (Nadab, Baasha, Elah, Zimri, and Omri) until the reign of Ahab. Under King Ahab, Israel moved from the false worship of the true God to the state-supported worship of Baal (1 Kings 16:29–34). The son of Ahab (Jehoram/Joram) continued this practice until he was assassinated by Jehu, who destroyed the infrastructure of state-sponsored Baal worship in Israel.

Clearly, there was some good in the reign of Jehu—standing against Ahab and driving out Baal worship. For this, he is rewarded with a dynasty that will last four generations (10:30). Yet, Jehu did not obey or serve God with all his heart (10:31).

📖 **10:32–36**

A SUMMARY OF JEHU'S REIGN

Syria captures large portions of Israel's territory. This is the work of God. For hundreds of years before this—since the time of the entry into the promised land more than six hundred years before—Israel held substantial portions of land on the eastern side of the Jordan River. This land was held by the tribes of Gad, Reuben, and Manasseh. Now this land is taken by the enemies of Israel because of their sin and unfaithfulness to the covenant. These neighboring rulers and their kingdoms are prompted and made successful by God (10:32–33).

Though incomplete in his own goodness, this man is the best of a bad group. Jehu's goodness is rewarded with a twenty-eight-year reign (10:34–36). This is a long reign, but notable only at its beginning. Jehu has the energy and influence to truly turn the nation back to God, but his half-commitment to God leaves that potential unfulfilled and points to a lack of any real relationship with the Lord.

2 KINGS 11:1–21

THE YOUNG KING JOASH

Setting Up the Section

King Ahaziah of Judah has been executed by Jehu, as recorded in 2 Kings 9:27–29. We don't know how many sons he leaves as heirs, but Ahaziah's mother has plans of her own for the throne of Judah.

📄 11:1–12

THE PRESERVATION OF JOASH

Athaliah uses the occasion of her son's death to take power for herself. Athaliah is from the family of Ahab, and Jehu has completely destroyed all of Ahab's descendants in Israel. Now, after Jehu's coup, Athaliah tries to save something for Ahab's family by trying to eliminate the house of David in Judah (11:1).

Demystifying 2 Kings

Athaliah is the daughter of Ahab and Jezebel and is given to Jehoram, king of Judah, as a bride. She is a bad influence on both her husband (Jehoram of Judah) and her son (King Ahaziah of Judah).

Jehosheba, a little-known woman, had an important place in God's plan. Through her courage and ingenuity, she preserves the royal line of David through which the Messiah will come (11:2). Evil people like Athaliah will begin their work, but God can always raise up a Jehosheba.

Though Ahaziah is a bad king who makes evil alliances, he is still a descendant of David and the successor of his royal line. For the sake of David, God remembers His promise and spares this one young survivor from the massacre of Athaliah. The line of David is almost extinguished and continues only in the presence of a small boy, but God does preserve that flickering flame.

Like the boy Samuel, Joash grew up in the temple (11:3). Like Samuel, he probably found little ways to help the priests, whatever could be done without attracting too much attention, while Athaliah reigned over the land for six years.

Jehoiada is a godly man who is concerned with restoring the throne of David to the line of David and taking it away from this daughter of Ahab and Jezebel. From the place—the temple—where Jehoiada charges the guards with an oath of loyalty, and from the context of the oath, we learn that the worship of the true God is not dead in Judah. These captains and bodyguards and escorts respond to their responsibility before the Lord (11:4).

It is a dramatic moment when Jehoiada brings out the young prince, Joash, secret heir to David's throne. Jehoiada chooses the Sabbath for the day of the coup, because that is the day when the guards change their shifts, and they can assemble two groups of guards at the temple without attracting attention (11:5–8). It is fitting for these soldiers to use weapons that had belonged to King David himself (11:9–11).

📄 11:13–21

THE DEATH OF THE QUEEN MOTHER ATHALIAH

Athaliah rushes to the temple and sees the newly-crowned king (11:13). For the usurper queen mother, this is a horrifying sight. For six years she ruled because she believed there were no legitimate claimants to the throne of David. Now she sees that one son of Ahaziah—Joash, her own grandson—escaped her murderous intent.

All the people of the land rejoice (11:14). They were obviously weary of the wicked reign of Athaliah.

Athaliah's charge of treason is not unfounded. This is treason against her government, but it is a well-founded and godly treason against a tyrannical, wicked ruler.

The execution of Athaliah is both righteous and prudent. It is a just sentence against this woman who had murdered so many, and prudent precautions are taken so she cannot mount a resistance. As a priest, Jehoiada has a great concern for the sanctity and reputation of the temple, so Athaliah is not executed there but in the place where horses enter the palace grounds (11:15–16).

Then Jehoiada establishes a new covenant. The covenant is between the Lord, the king, and the people. They commit themselves to honor, obey, and serve God. He also makes a covenant between the king and the people (11:17). Both kings and citizens have mutual obligations toward the other; neither have absolute rights over or against the other.

Previously, Jehu had supervised the destruction of the temple of Baal in Samaria (chapter 10). Here the temple of Baal in Jerusalem is destroyed. They don't stop at destroying the building itself; they go on to destroy both the sacred objects dedicated to Baal and to kill Mattan, the priest of Baal (11:18).

Critical Observation

One reason the people resent the worship of Baal in Jerusalem is because, according to 2 Chronicles 24:7, Athaliah had directed that sacred objects from the temple of the Lord be put into the temple of Baal.

After more than six dark years, the rightful king of Judah once again rules over his grateful people (11:19–21).

2 KINGS 12:1–21

THE REIGN OF KING JOASH OVER JUDAH

Setting Up the Section

Chapter 12 of 2 Kings chronicles the reign of King Joash, who comes to the throne at the age of seven (2 Kings 11). The Hebrew text uses the variant spelling *Jehoash*. Some translations use this spelling, while others use the name *Joash*. Both refer to the young king introduced in 2 Kings 11.

📄 12:1–16

JOASH REPAIRS THE TEMPLE

Joash has a long and mostly blessed reign (12:1). Joash falls short of full commitment and complete godliness, but he does advance the cause of God in the kingdom of Judah. Verse 2 implies that when the priest Jehoiada dies, Joash no longer does what is right in the sight of the Lord. Second Chronicles 24:15–23 tells us that he turns to idolatry when Jehoiada dies, and judgment follows.

Joash implements a halfway reformation but not a total reforming of Israel's worship. He does not take on the difficult job of removing the high places of worship (2 Kings 12:3).

There is a regular income coming into the temple from several different sources—census (Exodus 20:13), assessments or taxes (Leviticus 27:2), and voluntary gifts. King Joash wants to put that money toward a particular purpose: repairing the temple (12:4–5). The temple needed restoration because it had been vandalized by Athaliah and her sons (2 Chronicles 24:7). It is natural for Joash to have a high regard for the condition of the temple, because it was his home as a young boy (2 Kings 11:3).

King Joash has to wait a very long time until the damages of the temple are repaired. The work is going far too slowly (12:6); the priests and the Levites have taken the money for their own use (12:7). Under the direction of King Joash, the priests give the people the opportunity to give (12:8–9).

King Joash gets to the heart of the problem—poor administration and financial mismanagement. Through Jehoiada the priest, he implements a system where the money will be set aside, saved, and then wisely spent for the repair and refurbishing of the temple (12:10–13). Through good administration of the project, they are able to find men who can be trusted to use the money wisely and honestly (12:14–15). In the end, the project succeeds without taking anything away from the priests. They still receive money from the trespass offerings and from the sin offerings (12:16).

THE DECLINE OF KING JOASH

At this time, the kingdom of Syria attacks Judah (12:17). Instead of trusting God, Joash trades prior blessing—the sacred treasures of the temple—to protect his capital and kingdom against the attacking Syrians (12:18). There is no record of repentance on Joash's part. He never comes back to fulfill his early promise (12:19).

The officers' conspiracy against Joash is startling, and it shows that the blessing of God long before vanished from the compromised king who began so well but failed to finish well (12:20–21).

2 KINGS 13:1–25

THE DEATH OF ELISHA

Setting Up the Section

When Jehoahaz, the king who opens this chapter, comes to the throne, it is the beginning of the fulfillment of a promise made to Jehu, recorded in 2 Kings 10:30. God promised him that his descendants would sit on the throne of Israel to the fourth generation. This dynasty—though founded on a violent overthrow of the previous royal house—continues because Jehu came to the throne doing the will of God.

THE REIGNS OF JEHOAHAZ AND JEHOASH, KINGS OF ISRAEL

Jehoahaz follows in the footsteps of both Jeroboam and his father Jehu—two wicked kings (13:1–2). So the Lord delivers the kingdom of Israel into the hand of Hazael, king of Syria (13:3). Israel retains its own name and king, but it is a tributary and subservient nation to Syria.

Demystifying 2 Kings

In the general history of this time, the Assyrian Empire kept the Syrians weak and unable to expand their domain into Israel. But there was a period when internal problems made the Assyrians bring back their troops from the frontiers of their empire, and the Syrians took advantage of this time of Assyrian distraction.

Jehoahaz is an ungodly man, and his prayer does not mark a lasting or real revival in his life. Yet God listens to his prayer because of His great mercy and because of His care for Israel (13:4–5). The identity of the deliverer in verse 5 is unknown.

Though God answers their prayer and sends a deliverer, Israel continues in their false worship of the true God (13:6). Israel's repentance is only halfhearted; they repent because they suffer rather than because they regret their sin (13:7).

After Jehoahaz's death, his son Jehoash becomes king over Israel (13:8–10). He is the grandson of King Jehu, founder of this dynasty. He continues in the same sins as his father and grandfather (13:11).

The reign of Jehoash sees a civil war among the people of God, with the southern kingdom of Judah and the northern kingdom of Israel at war (13:12). On Jehoash's death, his son Jeroboam II becomes king of Israel (13:13).

📄 **13:14–21**

THE DEATH OF ELISHA

Elisha has become ill and will die (13:14). The reaction of King Joash of Israel might seem strange, in light of the sin and evil that marks his reign. However, Joash is not a worshiper of false gods; he is a *false* worshiper of the true God. He has some respect for the true God and therefore some regard and honor for Elisha.

Critical Observation

"The chariots of Israel and their horsemen!" Elisha says these words to Elijah at the end of the elder prophet's days on this earth (2:12). In saying this, he recognizes the true strength of Israel, which is really in the presence of the prophet of God. Now Joash sees the same strength slipping from this earth and mourns it.

Joash is concerned that the true strength of Israel is about to depart from this earth. Therefore, Elisha uses this illustration of the arrow shot through the window to show him that the arrow of the Lord's deliverance is still present, and all Joash has to do is to shoot the arrow in faith (13:15–17). Elisha makes it clear that there is a connection between the shooting of the arrows toward the east and a strike against the Syrians that will bring deliverance to Israel.

The phrase "strike the ground" (13:18) can be used for arrows hitting the ground. Elisha asks Joash to shoot the arrows through the window at no particular target, not to pound them on the floor. Joash timidly receives this invitation. He shoots three arrows and stops, not sensing what he should—that the arrows represent victories in battle over the Syrians. Because King Joash does not seize the strategic moment, Israel will enjoy only three victories over the Syrian army instead of the many more they could have enjoyed (13:19).

Perhaps Elisha expected or hoped that he would be carried up into heaven after the dramatic pattern of his mentor Elijah. Yet that is not God's plan or will for Elisha. Like many others, he simply becomes old, sick, and then dies.

There is little explanation for the resurrection of the corpse that touches the bones of Elisha (13:21). The silence of the record suggests that there is not inherent power in the bones of Elisha to resuscitate others. This seems to be a one-time miracle bringing honor to the memory of this great prophet.

📖 13:22–25

GOD'S MERCY TO ISRAEL

God allows—even plans—King Hazael's oppression of Israel to discipline this wayward nation (13:22). Second Kings 8:12 records Elisha's prior knowledge of the calamity Hazael will bring upon Israel. Israel deserves this discipline, yet God refuses to forsake them. He has given them many blessings and saved them from many problems and will not yet destroy them or cast them from His presence (13:23).

Elisha had promised Joash these three victories over the Syrians (13:24–25). We can suppose that especially after the third victory, King Joash wished he had shot more arrows through the window at the invitation of Elisha.

2 KINGS 14:1–29

THE REIGNS OF AMAZIAH AND JEROBOAM II

The Reign of Amaziah over Judah	14:1–22
The Reign of Jeroboam II in Israel	14:23–29

Setting Up the Section

The parallel and intersecting histories of the southern kingdom of Judah and the northern kingdom of Israel continue in this chapter. Chapter 12 of 2 Kings outlined the reign of Joash in Judah; chapter 13 highlighted the reigns of first Jehoahaz, then Jehoash in Israel. The next chapters relate the reigns of their successors.

📖 14:1–22

THE REIGN OF AMAZIAH OVER JUDAH

Amaziah, son of the great reformer Joash, continues the policies begun by his father. Yet some of those policies allow compromises regarding idolatry. Compared to David, Amaziah does not match up favorably (14:1–4).

Amaziah's execution of the servants who had murdered his father eliminates those who would find the assassination of the king a reasonable way to change the kingdom. It also fulfills God's command to punish murderers with execution, first given in Genesis 9:5–7. It is the standard practice of the ancient world to execute not only the guilty party in such a murder, but also their family. Amaziah goes against the conventional practice of his day and obeys the Word of God instead (Deuteronomy 24:16; 2 Kings 14:5–6).

Amaziah's victory over the Edomites (14:7) shows the military might of Amaziah and that he successfully subdues the weaker nations surrounding Judah.

Critical Observation

Second Chronicles 25:5–16 gives more background to the battle against the Edomites. Amaziah gathers a huge army in Judah to go against Edom (three hundred thousand). He also hires one hundred thousand mercenary soldiers from Israel. But a prophet comes and warns him to *not* use the soldiers from Israel, because God is not with that rebellious and idolatrous kingdom. Amaziah is convinced to trust God, send the mercenaries from Israel away, and accept the loss of the money used to hire them. God blesses this step of faith and gives them a convincing victory over the Edomites.

Proud from his success against Edom, Amaziah decides to make war against the northern kingdom of Israel (14:8). He has reason to believe he will be successful. He had recently assembled an army of three hundred thousand men that killed twenty thousand Edomites in a victory over Edom (2 Chronicles 25:5, 11–12). Jehoahaz seems very weak, having only fifty horsemen, ten chariots, and ten thousand foot soldiers after being defeated by the Syrians (2 Kings 13:7).

The reply of Jehoash, king of Israel, is both wise and diplomatic. He counsels Amaziah to glory in his previous victory over Edom but then to stay at home (14:9–10). Instead, Amaziah provokes a fight he should have avoided and does not consider the effect his defeat will have on the whole kingdom (14:11–18).

The embarrassing loss against Israel undermines Amaziah's support among Judah's leaders. He flees to Lachish, but he meets a similar end to that of his father—assassination (12:20–21; 14:29–30).

This signals the start of the illustrious reign of Azariah (also known as Uzziah). He is the greatest king of Judah after David (14:21–22).

📄 14:23–29

THE REIGN OF JEROBOAM II IN ISRAEL

King Jeroboam II of Israel is a wicked king who continues the politically-motivated idolatry of his namesake, Jeroboam the son of Nebat (14:23–24). During his reign, the prophets Jonah and Amos spoke for God (14:25). This is almost certainly the same Jonah who is famous for his missionary trip to Nineveh.

Out of great mercy, God shows kindness to a disobedient Israel ruled by an evil king (14:26–27). The reign of Jeroboam II is a time of prosperity for Israel because of God's mercy. Around the year 800 BC, the mighty Assyrian Empire defeated Syria and neutralized this power that hindered Israel's expansion and prosperity. With Syria in check, Israel can prosper (14:28).

Zechariah, Jeroboam's son, succeeds to the throne after his father's death (14:29). It was prophesied that the dynasty of Jehu would continue for four generations—Zechariah is the fourth generation (10:30).

2 KINGS 15:1–38

UNSTABLE MONARCHY IN ISRAEL

Setting Up the Section

This section of 2 Kings 15 begins the story of five kings over Israel and anticipates the final dissolution of the northern kingdom. The kings, families, and dynasties ruling Israel change quickly during this period. Yet there is an amazing continuity of evil through these dynasties. Each is evil and each continues the state-sponsored idolatry in Israel.

📄 **15:1–7**

THE REIGN OF AZARIAH (UZZIAH) OVER JUDAH

The reign of Azariah (also called Uzziah in 2 Kings 15:13 and many other places in 2 Kings, 2 Chronicles, and Isaiah) is largely characterized by the good he does in the sight of the Lord. His godliness is rewarded with a long reign of fifty-two years (15:1–3). As with Jehoash (12:3) and Amaziah (14:4), however, the reforms of Azariah do not reach so far as to remove these traditional places of sacrifice (15:4).

Demystifying 2 Kings

Second Chronicles 26 tells us much more about the successful reign of Azariah:

- He began his reign when he was only sixteen years old (26:3).

- He reigned during the ministry of Zechariah the prophet (26:5).

- He defeated the Philistines and took many of their cities and also kept the Ammonites in tribute (26:6–8).

- He was internationally famous as a strong king (26:8).

- He was an ambitious builder and skilled in agriculture (26:9–10).

- He built up and organized the army, introducing several new items of military technology (26:11–15).

Azariah comes into the temple as an arrogant king, and he leaves—indeed, he hurries to get out, because the Lord has struck him (2 Chronicles 26:20)—as a humbled leper (2 Kings 15:5). And so he is to the day he dies. His son Jotham becomes the next king (15:6–7).

📄 15:8–31

FIVE KINGS OVER THE KINGDOM OF ISRAEL

The reign of Zechariah is both short and wicked, and he continues in the state-sponsored idolatry began by Jeroboam (15:8–9). Zechariah is so despised by his own people that Shallum assassinates him in public. This is the end of the dynasty of Jehu, which began with such potential but ends (as God has foretold) in great darkness (15:10).

Shallum's reign is even briefer—four weeks. The violence that marks Shallum's rise to and fall from power shows that he does not reign with the blessing of God (15:13–15).

When Menahem's enemies fail to surrender, his soldiers rip open the pregnant women (15:16). This brutal act is commanded by Menahem himself—the next king of Israel. Menahem's reign is evil and a continuation of the state-sponsored idolatry of Jeroboam (15:17–18). He puts the kingdom of Israel under tribute to the Assyrian Empire, purchasing the backing of the Assyrian king with money raised from the wealthy people in his kingdom. Therefore he rules with the strength of Assyria supporting him (15:19–21).

The previous two kings of Israel (before Menahem) do not establish any kind of dynasty to pass to a son. Menahem rules well enough to pass the kingdom to Pekahiah (15:22–23). The blessing of God is obviously not on Pekahiah, whose reign ends with assassination after only two years (15:24–26).

For chronologists, the twenty-year reign of Pekah is difficult to place. It perhaps includes time that Pekah rules as an antigovernment rebel in certain regions of Israel (15:27–28). The Assyrian king, unlike in the days of Menahem, will not be paid off by the king of Israel this time. He comes and takes some of the best land of the kingdom and carries the Israelites as captives to Assyria (15:29). This is an official state policy of the Assyrian Empire. Upon conquering a land, if necessary, they relocate by force the best and the brightest of the conquered nation, bringing them to Assyria.

Pekah is another king and another dynasty to end with assassination (15:30–31), as a powerful demonstration of the great instability in the northern kingdom.

📄 15:32–38

JOTHAM'S REIGN OVER JUDAH

King Jotham of Judah does what was right in the sight of the Lord (15:32–34). This stands in strong contrast to the evil done by the previously mentioned kings of Israel. Among the kings of Judah, there are good and godly kings.

Rebuilding in the temple is always a positive sign in Judah (15:35). When kings and leaders are concerned about the house of the Lord, it reflects some measure of spiritual revival. Jotham's father Azariah (Uzziah) had misunderstood the link between the royal house and the house of God, demanding priestly authority (2 Chronicles 26:16–21). Many kings before him wanted no link between the royal house and the house of God. Jotham understands that he is a king and not a priest, yet he wants a good, open link between the palace and the temple. The building of this link between the palace and the temple is one of the chief ways that he prepares his way before God.

At this time, Judah begins to be chastened for their partial obedience. Under the inspiration of the Holy Spirit, the writer of 2 Kings tells us that it is the hand of the Lord that sends these foreign rulers who trouble Judah (15:36–38).

2 KINGS 16:1–20
THE COMPROMISE OF AHAZ

Setting Up the Section

Chapter 15 closes with an account of King Jotham of Judah. Chapter 16 is devoted entirely to the reign of Jotham's son, Ahaz. Ahaz may well have been the worst king of a nation ruled by bad kings.

🔖 **16:1–4**

A SUMMARY OF THE REIGN OF AHAZ

This account briefly describes the reign of an unfaithful king of Judah. Whereas many previous kings fall short in some area or another (typically, allowing idolatry), of Ahaz it is simply said that he does not do what was right in the sight of the Lord.

Ahaz not only rejects the godly heritage of David, he embraces the ungodly ways of the kings of the northern kingdom of Israel. The southern kingdom of Judah had a mixture of godly and ungodly kings; the northern kingdom of Judah had only ungodly kings, and Ahaz follows their pattern. Ahaz participates in the worship of Molech, which includes child sacrifice (16:3–4).

Critical Observation

In Leviticus 20:1–5, God pronounced the death sentence against all who worship Molech.

One of the great crimes of the northern tribes of Israel was their worship of Molech (17:17). King Manasseh of Judah gave his son to Molech (21:6). God will bring judgment upon Judah for their continued practice of these sins.

🔖 **16:5–9**

AHAZ MAKES JUDAH A SUBJECT NATION TO ASSYRIA

King Pekah of Israel joins forces with King Rezin of Syria against Judah (16:5). This is part of Pekah's anti-Assyria policy. He thinks that with Judah defeated, Syria and Israel together can more effectively resist the resurgent power of the Assyrian Empire. The combined armies of Syria and Israel are strong enough to capture many cities of Judah but not strong enough to defeat Jerusalem and overthrow the government of Ahaz.

Critical Observation

Judah suffers terrible losses from this attack. King Ahaz loses 120,000 Judean soldiers and 200,000 civilian hostages in these battles with Israel and Syria (2 Chronicles 28:5–8). It is a dark time for Judah, and it looks as if the dynasty of David will soon be extinguished, as so many dynasties in the northern kingdom of Israel had ended.

When this great number of captives is taken to Samaria (the capital city of the northern kingdom of Israel), a prophet named Oded calls on the army to return them to Judah. These leaders in Israel respond, realizing that they have already offended the Lord and risk offending Him even further. So they clothe and feed the captives (who had before this been treated terribly) and return them to Judah (2 Chronicles 28:8–15).

Ahaz sends messengers to Tiglath-pileser, king of Assyria, asking for help (2 Kings 16:7–9). In this way, he surrenders to one enemy in order to defeat another. He refuses to trust in the God of Israel and instead submits himself and his kingdom to an enemy of Israel, making Judah a subject kingdom to Assyria. Ahaz now takes his orders from the Assyrian king, sacrificing the independence of the kingdom of Judah.

Take It Home

What blessing might have come if Ahaz would have surrendered and sacrificed to God with the same energy and whole heart that he surrendered to the Assyrian king? It is true that the Assyrian king answers and delivers Ahaz, but it is short-lived deliverance. He could have really secured his kingdom by surrendering and sacrificing to God in the same way.

📄 16:10–20

AHAZ PERVERTS WORSHIP AT THE TEMPLE

It is unusual for the kings of Judah to make official visits to other kingdoms; they generally stay within the borders of the promised land. Yet Ahaz's trip is much more than a visit—this is an official act of submission to Tiglath-pileser, king of Assyria (16:10). Using the plans sent from Ahaz, Urijah imitates the pagan altar at Damascus and has it ready by the time Ahaz returns from the Syrian capital (16:11). He does this both to please Tiglath-pileser and to incorporate the latest trends in altar design into the national worship of Judah. Of course, Ahaz bears the greater blame in this matter, but the high priest Urijah also bears significant blame in the replacement of the Lord's altar with this one of pagan design.

Ahaz serves as a priest at the altar of his own design, a direct disregard for God's commands regarding priests (Numbers 18:7; 2 Kings 16:12–13). Urijah not only allows Ahaz to do this, he participates.

Critical Observation

Ahaz's grandfather Azariah (Uzziah) dared to enter the temple and serve God as a priest (2 Chronicles 26). Yet at least Azariah falsely worshiped the true *God*. Ahaz falsely worshiped a false god of his own creation.

Ahaz cannot bring in his pagan, corrupt innovations without also removing what had stood before at the temple (16:14–18). This is an ungodly exchange, taking away the good and putting in the bad—including the king's outer entrance built in the days of his father, King Jotham. Collectively, all these things serve to discourage the worship of the true God. All this takes place at the temple Solomon built for the Lord, but the location does not make it true worship.

So ends the reign of an unfaithful king of Judah (16:19–20). Micah—who prophesied during the reign of Ahaz—describes a man who works to successfully do evil with both hands (Micah 7:3). The idea is that the man pursues evil with all his effort. He may very well have had King Ahaz in mind.

2 KINGS 17:1–41
THE FALL OF ISRAEL

Setting Up the Section

Two hundred years and nineteen kings after the time of Solomon (the last king over a united Israel), the northern kingdom of Israel falls. It is not because the God of Israel is unable to help them, but because they have so forsaken God and ignored His guidance and correction that He finally stops actively protecting them and allows them to degrade according to their desire.

📄 17:1–6

THE FALL OF SAMARIA

We last saw Hoshea, in 2 Kings 15:30, as the man who led a conspiracy against Pekah, the king of Israel. After the successful assassination, Hoshea takes the throne and starts his own brief dynasty (17:1). Hoshea is an evil man, but by no means the worst of the kings of Israel (17:2). Sadly, his bloody overthrow of the preceding king and violent ascent to power do not make him unusually evil among the kings of Israel. Yet it is during his reign that the kingdom of Israel is effectively destroyed. This reminds us that judgment may not come at the height of sin. When God judges a nation or a culture, He has the big picture in view. For that reason, the actual events of judgment may come when things are not as bad in a relative sense.

In the pattern of Menaham before him (15:17–22), Hoshea accepts the status of vassal unto the king of Assyria. If he pays his money and does as the king of Assyria pleases, he will be allowed to continue on the throne of Israel (17:3). King Hoshea hopes to find help among the Egyptians, who are in a constant power struggle with the Assyrian Empire. On account of this conspiracy, and the failure to pay the yearly tribute money, Hoshea is imprisoned by the king of Assyria (17:4).

The king of Assyria embarks on a long, dedicated campaign to finally crush the rebellious kingdom of Israel, who had defied the power of the Assyrian Empire. Though it takes three years, it is worth it to the Assyrians (17:5). When Samaria finally falls and the northern kingdom is conquered, the Assyrians implement their policy toward conquered nations. They deport all but the very lowest classes back to the key cities of their empire, either to train and utilize the talented or to enslave the able (17:6).

Demystifying 2 Kings

When the Assyrians depopulate and exile a conquered community, they lead the captives away on journeys of hundreds of miles, with the captives naked and attached to one another with a system of strings and fishhooks pierced through their lower lips. (See also Amos 4:2–3.)

📄 17:7–23

THE REASONS FOR THE FALL OF THE NORTHERN KINGDOM OF ISRAEL

In the following verses, the divine historian explains the fundamental reasons for the conquering and captivity of the northern kingdom. At the root, it is a problem with sin. It isn't geopolitical changes or social causes.

First, they had feared other gods (17:7). In the central act of redemption in Old Testament history, God brought Israel up out of the land of Egypt. Remembrance of this act alone should prompt Israel to a single-hearted commitment to the Lord. Yet they do not remember this and instead they fear other gods, breaking the covenant God made with His people.

Second, they conform themselves to the godless nations around them (17:8). Before Israel occupied Canaan in the days of Joshua, the promised land was populated by degenerate, pagan peoples who practiced the worst kinds of idolatry and human sacrifice. One of the fundamental sins of Israel was that they followed in these ancient Canaanite ways. God cast out the Canaanite nations in the days of Joshua because of these sins. Now He has cast out the northern kingdom of Israel for the same sins. God's judgment is not against the ancient Canaanites because of race or ethnicity; it is because of their conduct.

Third, they practice idolatry both secretly and openly (17:9–12). Rebellion and sin cloud the judgment of people, and clearly the judgment of Israel is affected. Their judgment is impaired enough to think they can sin secretly against the God who sees everything.

Fourth, they reject the repeated warnings from God (17:13–15). In love, God sends prophets to the northern and southern kingdoms. Their message is a warning against the sins that corrupt God's people and separate them from their God. They invite God's people with the theme, "Turn from your evil ways." Nevertheless, the people will not hear. God sends these messengers to help Israel and to spare them the judgment that will come if they do not turn from their evil ways. Yet God's people become more stubborn when God brings this call to repentance, and they sink deeper into sin.

Fifth, they forsake God and serve idols—until judgment finally comes (17:16–23). The two calves mentioned here refer to the infamous sin of Jeroboam (1 Kings 12:26–29). This state-sponsored idolatry does not immediately ruin the kingdom—the northern kingdom of Israel lasts as an independent nation for another two-hundred years following the time of Jeroboam. Yet it certainly was the beginning of the end. The people participated in the abominable worship of the idol Molech, to whom children were burned in sacrifice. They embraced the same occult practices as the Canaanite tribes before them. Collectively, these great sins of idolatry provoke God to anger.

This is the end of the ten northern tribes as an independent kingdom (17:18–23). When they are dispersed by the Assyrians, some assimilate into other cultures, but others keep their Jewish identity as exiles in other lands.

Critical Observation

It is a mistake to think of these ten northern tribes as *lost*, though they are indeed lost as a separate entity. Far back in the days of Jeroboam and his original break with the southern kingdom of Judah, the legitimate priests and Levites who lived in the northern ten tribes did not like Jeroboam's idolatry. They, along with others who set their hearts to seek the God of Israel, then moved from the northern kingdom of Israel to the southern kingdom of Judah (2 Chronicles 11:13–16). So actually, the southern kingdom of Judah contained Israelites from all of the ten tribes.

Spiritually speaking, Judah is more faithful to God than the northern kingdom of Israel. Yet they also begin to imitate their sinful neighbors to the north (17:19). Judah had the lesson right in front of them—the conquered nation of Israel is evidence of what happens when hearts turn from God. Yet they ignore these plain lessons and imitate the sins of Israel.

📖 **17:24–41**

THE RESETTLEMENT OF SAMARIA

The policy of the Assyrian Empire is to remove rebellious, resistant people and to resettle their former lands with people from other parts of the empire (17:24). These newcomers do not fear God, so He sends lions among them (17:25–26). This shows that there is not only something special about the kingdom of Israel, but also something special about the *land* of Israel. God demands to be feared among the people of the land, even if they come from other nations.

These Assyrian officials seem to know what the recently conquered kingdom of Israel does not know—that they have to honor the God of Israel. Yet, any faith in God among these resettled people is founded in simple fear of the lions, leading to an inadequate relationship with God.

The priesthood of the kingdom of Israel was corrupt, but the king of Assyria does not know and is not interested in the pure religion of Israel. Therefore this nameless, corrupt priest teaches the new inhabitants of the land a corrupt religion (17:28). Certainly, it has elements of the true faith in it, but at the same time it is corrupted by the centuries of state-sponsored idolatry that reigned in Israel.

The priest-for-hire brought in by the Assyrians does not tell the new inhabitants of the land that they must *only* worship the God of Israel. He does not teach it because, coming from Israel, he does not believe it. The new residents of Israel give a measure of respect to the God of Israel—after all, they do not want to be eaten by lions. Yet they also serve their own gods and pick and choose among religious and spiritual beliefs as they please (17:29-34). This accurately describes the pagan peoples who repopulate Israel. This accurately describes the northern kingdom of Israel before they are conquered and exiled. This accurately describes common religious belief in the modern world.

This mixed religion first promoted by the Assyrians continues for many centuries in Samaria, existing even until New Testament times.

The writer restates God's covenant with His people (17:35-41) to remind us that if Israel had been faithful—even moderately faithful—to their covenant with God, they would still stand. God would have delivered them from all of their enemies. Instead, they are conquered by the Assyrian Empire after their own self-destruction in sin and rebellion.

2 KINGS 18:1-37

HEZEKIAH'S REIGN; ASSYRIA'S THREAT

The Righteous Reign of Hezekiah	18:1–12
The Assyrian Threat during the Reign of Hezekiah	18:13–37

Setting Up the Section

Hezekiah, the subject of chapter 18, comes to the throne of Judah at the very end of the kingdom of Israel. Three years after the start of his reign, the Assyrian armies lay siege to Samaria, and three years after that the northern kingdom is conquered. The sad fate of the northern kingdom is a valuable lesson to Hezekiah. He sees firsthand what happens when the people of God reject their God and His Word and worship other gods.

📄 **18:1–12**

THE RIGHTEOUS REIGN OF HEZEKIAH

Hezekiah is one of the better kings of Judah and thus has a long and mostly blessed reign (18:1-2). He is one of Judah's most zealous reformers, even prohibiting worship on the high places (18:3–4). These are popular altars for sacrifice set up as the worshiper desires, not according to God's direction. He also breaks apart the bronze snake from the time of Moses.

Critical Observation

Numbers 21:1–9 describes how, during a time of a plague of fiery serpents upon the whole nation, Moses makes a bronze serpent for the nation to look upon and be spared death from the snake bites. This statement in 2 Kings tells us that this particular bronze serpent had been preserved for more than eight hundred years and had come to be worshiped as Nehushtan. Hezekiah, in his zeal, breaks this bronze artifact into pieces and puts an end to the idolatrous worship of this object.

This bronze serpent is a wonderful thing—when the afflicted people of Israel looked upon it, they were saved. It was even a representation of Jesus Christ, as Jesus Himself said in John 3:14–15.

Sometimes good things become idols and therefore must be destroyed. For example, if the true cross of Jesus or His actual burial cloth are to be discovered, and these objects become idolatrous distractions, then it is better for those objects to be destroyed.

Hezekiah is unique in his passion and energy of his personal trust in God and for promoting the true worship of God (18:5). This is even more remarkable when we consider that his father, Ahaz, was one of the worst kings to have reigned in Judah (16:10–20).

Because of Hezekiah's faithful trust in the Lord, God blessed him thoroughly (18:6). This fulfills a long-standing promise to David and his descendants: that if they obey God, their reign will always be secure (1 Kings 2:1–4).

At this time Assyria is mighty enough to completely conquer the northern kingdom of Israel. Yet the kingdom of Judah stands strong, because God blesses the trusting and obedient king (18:7). Hezekiah also finds success in subjugating Judah's aggressive neighbors (18:8). He works for a strong, free, and independent Judah.

The fall of Samaria, the capital of the northern kingdom of Israel, is a sobering experience for the southern kingdom of Judah to see. The cruel devastation brought by the Assyrians shows what calamities can come upon disobedient people of God (18:9–12).

📄 **18:13–37**

THE ASSYRIAN THREAT DURING THE REIGN OF HEZEKIAH

Approximately five years after the fall of Samaria, King Sennacherib of Assyria brings his force against Judah, who had successfully resisted him before (18:7). He captures all of the fortified cities of Judah and needs only Jerusalem itself to completely conquer Judah (18:13).

Demystifying 2 Kings

The mention of Lachish in verse 14 is important historically. Lachish was thirty miles southwest of Jerusalem. Archaeologists have discovered a pit there with the remains of about fifteen hundred casualties of Sennacherib's attack. In the British Museum, you can see the Assyrian carving depicting their siege of the city of Lachish, which was an important fortress city of Judah.

Hezekiah offers tribute money in exchange for peace (19:14–16). This is a clear lack of faith on the part of Hezekiah. He feels it is wiser to pay off the Assyrian king and become his subject than it is to trust God to defend Judah against this mighty king. We can suppose that Hezekiah thought that since the northern kingdom had been recently conquered and all the fortified cities of Judah had been captured, God had demonstrated that He would not intervene on behalf of Judah. Therefore Hezekiah feels he must do something himself. Perhaps this idea is strengthened in Hezekiah when he remembers the wickedness of his own father, Ahaz, and when he considers that, because of their prior sin, Judah deserves such judgment.

Hezekiah hopes that this policy of appeasement will make Judah safe. He is wrong, and his policy only impoverishes Judah and the temple and makes the king of Assyria more bold than ever against Judah.

The word *Rabshakeh* in verse 17 is not a name but a title. It describes the field commander for the Assyrian army, who represents the Assyrian king, Sennacherib, and is translated "chief of staff" in some versions. The Rabshakeh seems to be in complete command of the situation. He is able to walk right into the city of Jerusalem and stand at the crucial water supply—which is Jerusalem's lifeline in a siege attack. As he stands there, three officials from Hezekiah's government come to meet him (18:17–18).

From the perspective of the unbeliever, Sennacherib asks a valid question: "What are you trusting in that makes you so confident?" (18:19 NLT). Instead of trusting the Lord, Hezekiah has put his hope in an alliance with Egypt, and the Rabshakeh wants him to lose confidence in that alliance (18:20–21). In this sense, the Rabshakeh speaks wisely. God wants Judah to have no confidence in Egypt at all. But the Rabshakeh does not do it to bring Judah to a firm trust in God, who can and will deliver them from the Assyrians. He does it to completely demoralize Judah and drive them to despair.

Strangely, the Rabshakeh can see the truth of Egypt's weakness better than many of the leaders of Judah can. Hezekiah's trust-in-Egypt policy will indeed be trouble for Judah.

The Rabshakeh anticipates the response of the leaders of Judah. "Rabshakeh, you say that we can't trust in Egypt. All right, we won't. But we can trust in our God" (18:22). The Rabshakeh knows that King Hezekiah has implemented broad reforms in Judah, including the removal of the high places (18:3–4). Yet in the Rabshakeh's thinking, Hezekiah's reforms displease God, so he should not expect help from the God of Israel. The Rabshakeh will say, "Look at all the places there used to be where people would worship the God of Israel. Now, since Hezekiah came in, there is only one place. More is always better, so the God of Israel must be pretty sore at Hezekiah!"

Take It Home

The Rabshakeh's whole strategy is to make Judah give up. This is the entire reason the Rabshakeh is at the aqueduct, speaking to these leaders of Hezekiah's government. He had the superior army—he could have just attacked Jerusalem without this little speech. But the Rabshakeh prefers Judah to surrender out of fear, discouragement, or despair.

The enemy of our soul uses the exact same approach. Many of us picture Satan as one who is itching for a fight with us. Really, Satan doesn't want to do battle with you. First of all, there is the strong chance you will win. Second of all, win or lose, the battle can draw you closer to God. Thirdly, what God does in your life through the battle can be a great blessing for others. No, Satan would much rather not fight you at all! He would rather you just give up.

We see this exact strategy used against Jesus during His temptation in the wilderness. When Satan promises Jesus all the kingdoms of the world in exchange for Jesus' worship, Satan is trying to avoid the fight and trying to talk Jesus into giving up (Luke 4:5–8). It doesn't work with Jesus, and it shouldn't work with us.

The Rabshakeh mocks Judah's weak army. His basic message is, "We could beat you with one hand tied behind our backs!" (18:23–24). The Rabshakeh saves his best thrust for last: "Admit it, Hezekiah. You know that *your* God is on *my* side" (18:25).

It would have been easy for Hezekiah and his men to believe this. After all, hadn't the Assyrians been wildly successful, and don't they have the most powerful army? Surely, God must be on their side. We can just imagine how difficult this is for these leaders in Hezekiah's government. They must have thought, "It's bad enough we have to hear this. But since he is speaking in Hebrew, everyone will hear, and soon the people will become so discouraged they will rise up against us and make us surrender!" (18:26).

The Rabshakeh doesn't care if the common citizens of Jerusalem can hear him. That is one of his goals. The more fear, discouragement, and despair he can spread, the better. He points forward to what conditions will be like in Jerusalem after an extended siege. He wants this to offend everyone who hears it and magnify their sense of fear (18:27).

Then the Rabshakeh stands and calls out with a loud voice in Hebrew (18:28–33). He can't wait to speak to the people of Jerusalem. His speech is intended to glorify the enemy facing God's people, to make God's people doubt their leaders, to build fear and unbelief in God's people, and to make surrender an attractive option. The Rabshakeh refers to the policies of ethnic cleansing and forced resettlement practiced by the Assyrians. When they conquer a people, they forcibly resettle them in faraway places, to keep their spirits broken and their power weak. The Rabshakeh's speech is intended to make this terrible fate seem attractive.

The Rabshakeh's speech is intended to destroy their trust in God. His message is simple: "The gods of other nations have not been able to protect them against us. Your God can't protect you either" (18:34). For anyone who had the spiritual understanding to see it, Judah could have started planning the victory party right then. It is one thing to speak against Judah, its people, and its leaders; it is another thing altogether to mock the God of Israel this way and count Him as just another god. The Rabshakeh's speech is going well until he simply oversteps his bounds. There is no way God will let him off the hook for this one. He has offended God in a way he will soon regret.

The people don't try to argue with the Rabshakeh. Often, it is useless—if not dangerous—to try and match wits with this demonic logic. It is almost always better to keep silent and trust God, instead of trying to win an argument with Satan or his servants. King Hezekiah is wise enough to make this command, and his officials and the people are wise enough to obey him (18:36).

Though they are silent, they are still deeply affected by this attack (18:37). They have the same experience Paul describes in 2 Corinthians 4:8–9. Times are tough, but the battle is not yet lost.

2 KINGS 19:1–37

GOD DELIVERS JERUSALEM FROM ASSYRIA

Hezekiah's Prayers and Sennacherib's Threats	19:1–19
God Speaks Concerning the Situation	19:20–34
God Defends Jerusalem	19:35–37

Setting Up the Section

Hezekiah's response to the current national crisis reveals a king who was wise enough to seek God's guidance.

📄 **19:1–19**

HEZEKIAH'S PRAYERS AND SENNACHERIB'S THREATS

The tearing of clothes and the wearing of sackcloth (a rough, burlap-type material) are expressions of deep mourning, usually for the death of a loved one. Hezekiah receives this report regarding the Rabshakeh seriously, knowing how dedicated this enemy is to completely conquering Jerusalem (19:1).

Hezekiah's initial reaction is good. He sees the situation for what it really is. Jerusalem's situation is desperate and Hezekiah knows it.

Hezekiah's second reaction is even better. He does not allow his mourning and grief to spin him into a rejection of the Lord's power and help. He knows it is more necessary than ever to seek the Lord at this time, so he goes to the temple.

Demystifying 2 Kings

When verse 1 says that Hezekiah goes into the house of the Lord, that doesn't mean the holy place itself, which is forbidden for all except priests. It simply means that Hezekiah went to the courts, to seek God in the place which was open to him as a man of Israel.

A previous king of Judah, King Uzziah, saw his reign tragically end when he broke this command to stay out of the holy place of the temple (see 2 Chronicles 26:16).

The third thing Hezekiah does is also good. The king seeks out the Word of God, given through His prophet (19:2).

Hezekiah puts the words about childbirth in the mouth of his messengers to Isaiah to express the total calamity of the situation (19:3). This is a proverbial expression for a disaster—a woman so exhausted by labor that she cannot complete the birth, so both mother and child die. Hezekiah knows their only hope is that God will take offense at the blasphemies of the Rabshakeh and rise up against him (19:4).

Without hesitation, Isaiah speaks as if he is speaking for the Lord (19:5–6). How these words must have cheered Hezekiah! We can be sure that Isaiah does not take this lightly. The fate of the nation, and his entire credibility as a prophet, is riding on what he says. Isaiah, speaking for the Lord, is about to make a bold prediction (19:7). His prophecy will be entirely provable. It will either happen or it will not happen. Isaiah will either be known as a true prophet or a false prophet. The Lord assures Hezekiah that He will indeed deal with the Rabshakeh. He has heard his blasphemy and will bring judgment against him.

Significantly, in this initial word from the prophet Isaiah, there is no mention of Jerusalem's deliverance or the defeat of the Assyrian army. God focuses this word against the Rabshakeh personally.

The Rabshakeh leaves Jerusalem, and Hezekiah likely thinks this is the fulfillment of the Lord's promise through the prophet Isaiah (19:8).

The Rabshakeh is not in Jerusalem, but that doesn't stop him from trying to build fear, discouragement, and despair in Hezekiah. He sends a letter to the king of Judah to attack him from a distance. Yet if read with an eye of faith, the words of the letter must have been trust-building to Hezekiah. In counting God of Israel among the gods of the nations, the Rabshakeh again blasphemes the Lord and invites judgment (19:10–13).

Hezekiah does exactly what any child of God should do with such a letter. He takes it to the house of the Lord (to the outer courts, not the holy place) and spreads it out before Him (19:14). In this, Hezekiah boldly and effectively fulfills the later command of 1 Peter 5:7: casting all your care upon Him, for He cares for you.

As Hezekiah prays using the title, "God of Israel," it must have reminded him that God is indeed the covenant God of Israel and that He will not forsake His people (19:15).

Hezekiah sees the great majesty of God. Surely, the One who dwells between the cherubim (19:15) will never allow the Rabshakeh's blasphemies to go unpunished. Hezekiah realizes the most fundamental fact of all theology: God is God, and we are not!

In recognizing God as Creator (19:15), Hezekiah sees that He has all power and all rights over every created thing. We can almost feel Hezekiah's faith rising as he prays this!

Hezekiah knows very well that the Lord did in fact hear and see the blasphemies of the Rabshakeh. This is a poetic way of asking God to act upon what He has seen and heard, assuming that if God has seen such things, He will certainly act (19:16).

In his prayer, King Hezekiah draws the contrast between the living God and the false gods of the nations the Assyrians had already conquered. Those false gods are not gods, but the work of human hands, so they are not able to save them from the Assyrians. But Hezekiah prays confidently that the living God will save them, that all the kingdoms of the earth may know that He alone is God (19:17–19).

📄 19:20–34

GOD SPEAKS CONCERNING THE SITUATION.

The glorious answer that fills the rest of the chapter comes because Hezekiah prays (19:20). What if he had not prayed? Perhaps there would have been no answer, and Jerusalem would have been conquered. Hezekiah's prayer was critically important.

The Lord, speaking through Isaiah, simply says to the Rabshakeh, "Do you know whom you are dealing with?" (19:22). The Rabshakeh obviously does not know. Curiously, this prophecy may have never reached the ears of the Rabshakeh. After all, Isaiah doesn't exactly have free access to him. But perhaps before his terrible end, God finds a way to get this prophecy to him. At the very least, this prophecy would have been hugely encouraging to Hezekiah and all of Judah, even if the Rabshakeh never heard it. Sometimes God speaks to the enemy more for the sake of His people than for the sake of the enemy himself.

The Lord describes the great pride the Assyrians have in their own conquests. But they forget that the Lord is really in charge. Even if the Assyrians don't know it, they owe their success to the Lord (19:19–26).

Verses 27 and 28 make an especially dramatic statement, because this is exactly how the Assyrians cruelly march those whom they force to relocate out of their conquered lands. They line up the captives and drive a large fishhook through the lip or the nose of each captive, stringing them all together. God will do the same to the Assyrians.

The invasion has interfered with planting crops, but the Lord promises that enough will grow on its own to provide for the people until they can plant again (19:29).

As much as the Assyrians would like to crush Jerusalem and Judah, they are not able to. God will preserve His remnant (19:30–31). Although the Assyrian military machine is poised to lay siege to Jerusalem and ultimately crush them, they won't. The king of Assyria will not come into this city because God promised to defend it (19:32–34).

Critical Observation

It is hard for modern people to understand the ancient horror of the siege, when a city is surrounded by a hostile army and trapped into a slow, suffering starvation. King Hezekiah and the people of Jerusalem lived under the shadow of this threat, but God's promise through Isaiah assured them that Sennacherib and the Assyrian army would not only fail to capture the city, but would not even shoot an arrow or build a siege mound against Jerusalem. God promised that they wouldn't even begin a siege.

God would defend Jerusalem, not for the city's sake at all—Jerusalem deserved judgment—but for His own sake and for the sake of David. In the same way, God the Father defends and blesses us, not for our own sake but for His, and for the sake of Jesus Christ.

📄 **19:35–37**

GOD DEFENDS JERUSALEM

Simply and powerfully, God destroys the mighty Assyrian army in one night. At the hand of the angel of the Lord, 185,000 die. Against all odds, and against every expectation, the Assyrian army is turned back without having even shot an arrow into Jerusalem. The unstoppable is indeed stopped, the undefeated defeated (19:35–36).

Between 2 Kings 19:36 and 2 Kings 19:37, twenty years pass. Perhaps Sennacherib thought he had escaped the judgment of God, but he hadn't. He meets death at the end of swords held by his own sons.

2 KINGS 20:1–21

GOD EXTENDS HEZEKIAH'S LIFE

Hezekiah's Recovery	20:1–11
Hezekiah's Reception of the Babylonian Envoys	20:12–21

Setting Up the Section

Chapter 20 is set at the time of the Assyrian invasion of Judah; Jerusalem has not been delivered from the Assyrian threat yet (20:6). The events of this chapter are also recorded in Isaiah 38.

HEZEKIAH'S RECOVERY

We are not told how Hezekiah becomes sick. It may have been through something obvious to all, or it may have been through something known only to God. However it happened, it was certainly permitted by the Lord. God is remarkably kind to Hezekiah, telling him that his death is near (20:1).

Critical Observation

We know from comparing 2 Kings 18:2 with 2 Kings 20:6 that Hezekiah is thirty-nine years old when he learns he will soon die.

Hezekiah is earnest in his prayer. He turns his face toward the wall to direct his prayer in privacy to God (20:2–3). Hezekiah lived under the old covenant, and at that time there was no confident assurance of the glory in the life beyond. Also, under the old covenant Hezekiah would have regarded his fatal illness as evidence that God was displeased with him.

God hears Hezekiah's prayer (20:4–5). By all indications, if Hezekiah had not made his passionate prayer, then his life would not have been extended. This is another demonstration of the principle that prayer matters.

In response to Hezekiah's prayer, God grants him fifteen more years (20:6). In fact, God gives two gifts to Hezekiah: the gift of an extended life and the gift of knowing he only has fifteen years left. This gives King Hezekiah the motivation to walk right with God and to set his house in order.

Because Hezekiah recovers, was God's Word in 20:1 proven false? No. First, Hezekiah does in fact die—just not as soon as God first announced. Second, when God announces judgment it is almost always an invitation to repent and to receive mercy.

The Lord's promise to defend Jerusalem (20:6) is in accord with the previous prophecies of deliverance and dates this chapter as being before God destroys the Assyrian army (Isaiah 37:36–37). The connection of the two promises indicates that one will confirm the other. When Hezekiah recovers, he can know that God will also deliver him from the Assyrians.

Apparently, God uses the medical treatment with the figs to bring Hezekiah's healing (20:7). God can, and often does, bring healing through medical treatments, and apart from an unusual direction from God, medical treatment should never be rejected in the name of faith.

Hezekiah wants a sign that will allow him to go up to the house of the Lord (20:8). This is because he cannot and will not go up to the house of the Lord until he is healed, so the two are connected.

God shows even more mercy to Hezekiah. God is under no obligation to give this sign. In fact, God would have been justified in saying, "How dare you not take My word for truth?" But in real love, God gives Hezekiah more than he needs or deserves. God promises to do something completely miraculous as a confirming sign. He promises to make the shadow on the sundial move backward instead of forward (20:9–11). This is a wonderfully appropriate sign for Hezekiah. By bringing the shadow of the sundial backward, it gives more time in a day—just as God gave Hezekiah more time to live.

📄 **20:12–21**

HEZEKIAH'S RECEPTION OF THE BABYLONIAN ENVOYS

Shortly after Hezekiah's illness, the king of Babylon sends letters and a present to Hezekiah (20:12). Apparently this is a gesture of kindness from the king of Babylon, showing concern to Hezekiah as fellow royalty. Most likely it is also an attempt to bring the kingdom of Judah to the side of the Babylonians against the Assyrians. We can imagine that this is flattering for King Hezekiah. After all, Judah is a lowly nation with little power, and Babylon, while a vassal state of Assyria, was far more powerful.

We can imagine Hezekiah wanting to please these envoys from Babylon and wanting to show them that they have good reason to be impressed with him and his kingdom. So he does everything he can to impress them and shows them the very best riches of the royal household (20:13). As the coming rebuke from Isaiah will demonstrate, this is nothing but proud foolishness on Hezekiah's part. He is in the dangerous place of wanting to please and impress others, especially ungodly men.

Isaiah probably already knows the answer to the questions he asks Hezekiah (20:14–15). It is likely that his questions are guided by God to allow Hezekiah the opportunity to answer honestly (which he does) and to see his error himself (which he apparently does not). There is the flavor that Hezekiah is *proud* to tell Isaiah this.

Hezekiah thinks that this display of wealth will impress the Babylonians. All it does is show them what the kings of Judah have and what they can get from them. One day the kings of Babylon will come and take it all away (20:16–17). This prophecy is fulfilled under the Babylonian king Nebuchadnezzar (24:10–13; 25:11–17).

Worse than taking the material riches of the kings of Judah, the king of Babylon will take the sons of the king of Judah—his true riches (20:18). Some think the word *eunuchs* means simply household servants to the king.

Critical Observation

One fulfillment of Isaiah's prophecy is the taking of Daniel and his companions into captivity. Daniel was one of the king's descendants taken into the palace of the king of Babylon (Daniel 1:1–4). Because of this promise of God through Isaiah, many think that Daniel and his companions were made eunuchs when they were taken to serve in the palace.

Hezekiah welcomes the prophecy about his sons (20:19). This is a sad state of heart in the king of Judah. God announces coming judgment, and all he can respond with is relief that it will not happen in his lifetime. In this, Hezekiah shows himself to be self-centered. All he cares about is his own personal comfort and success.

The pool and tunnel bringing water into the city (20:20–21) is an amazing engineering feat. Hezekiah builds an aqueduct to insure fresh water inside the city walls even during sieges. It was more than 650 yards long through solid rock, begun on each end and meeting in the middle. It can still be seen today, and it empties into the pool of Siloam.

There is no doubt that Hezekiah starts out as a godly king, and overall his reign is one of outstanding godliness (18:3–7). Yet his beginning is much better than his end; Hezekiah does not finish well. God gave Hezekiah the gift of fifteen more years of life, but the added years do not make him a better or a more godly man.

2 KINGS 21:1–26
THE WICKED REIGNS OF MANASSEH AND AMON

The Reign of Manasseh, Son of Hezekiah	21:1–18
The Reign of Amon, Son of Manasseh	21:19–26

Setting Up the Section

After the death of Hezekiah (2 Kings 20), Manasseh takes the throne in Judah. This is about twenty-five years after the fall of the northern kingdom of Israel. The kingdom of Judah will survive one hundred more years, but already an unfaithfulness like that of Israel's is apparent.

📄 21:1–18

THE REIGN OF MANASSEH, SON OF HEZEKIAH

Manasseh is twelve years old when he becomes king (21:1). This means that he is born in the last fifteen years of Hezekiah's life, the *additional* fifteen years that Hezekiah prayed for. Those additional fifteen years bring Judah one of its worst kings. Manasseh's reign is both remarkably long and remarkably evil. A long career or longevity is not necessarily evidence of the blessing and approval of God.

Manasseh imitates the sins of both the Canaanites and the Israelites of the northern kingdom (21:2). Since God brings judgment on these groups for their sin, casting them out of their land, then similar judgment against an unrepentant Judah should be expected.

Manasseh opposes the reforms of his father Hezekiah and brings Judah back into terrible idolatry (21:3). This shows that repentance and reform are not permanent standing conditions. Manasseh does not want to imitate his godly father. Instead, he imitates one of the worst kings of Israel: Ahab. He embraces the same state-sponsored worship of Baal and Asherah (honored with a wooden image) that marked the reign of Ahab. Manasseh not only brings back old forms of idolatry; he also brings new forms of idolatry to Judah. At this time the Babylonian Empire is rising in influence, and they have a special attraction to astrological worship. Manasseh probably imitates this.

It is bad enough for Manasseh to allow this idol worship in Judah. Worse, he corrupts the worship of the true God at the temple and makes it a place of idol altars, including those dedicated to his cult of astrological worship (20:4–5). He sacrifices his own son to the Canaanite god Molech, who is worshiped with the burning of children (21:6), and he invites direct satanic influence by his approval and introduction of occult arts.

He even sets a carved image of Asherah in the temple (21:7). Asherah is the Canaanite goddess of fertility, worshiped through ritual prostitution. This means that Manasseh makes the temple into a brothel, dedicated to Asherah.

The people of Judah pay no attention to the generous promises of God, promising protection to His obedient people (21:8–9). This describes the basic attitude of the people throughout the fifty-five-year reign of Manasseh. In addition, they are willingly seduced by Manasseh's wickedness and are attracted to do more evil. Manasseh is indeed a wicked king, but perhaps the greater sin is on behalf of the people who accept this seduction willingly. God speaks to both the people and the leader, but they reject His Word (2 Chronicles 33:10).

When the leaders and the popular culture abandon God, He still has a voice to Judah. He speaks by the prophets to His disobedient people (21:10).

Manasseh acts more wickedly than all the Amorites who were before him (21:11). This is a remarkable achievement of evil. The Amorites were among the Canaanite tribes who populated the promised land before Israel captured it, and they were infamous for their violent, immoral, and depraved culture.

If Judah insists on imitating the sins of the northern kingdom, then God will answer their similar sins with a similar judgment. God will cleanse Jerusalem, subjecting them to their enemies (21:12–15).

Manasseh persecutes the people of God (21:16). This puts Manasseh, king of Judah, in the same spiritual family as Ahab, king of Israel. Under both of these kings—among others—the people of God are persecuted by the religion of state-sponsored idolatry. The extent of it is so great that it can be metaphorically said that he filled Jerusalem from one end to another with the blood of his victims.

Second Chronicles 33:11–19 describes a remarkable repentance on the part of Manasseh. Because he and his people will not listen to the warnings of God, the Lord allows the Babylonians to bind King Manasseh and take him as a captive to Babylon. There, he humbles himself before God, and God answers his prayer and restores him to the throne. Manasseh then proves that his repentance is genuine by taking away the idols and the foreign gods from Jerusalem (2 Chronicles 33:16).

This is a wonderful example of Proverbs 22:6. Manasseh was raised by a godly father, yet he lived in defiance of his father's faith for most of his life. Nevertheless, at the end of his days, he truly repents and serves God. In this way, we can say that it is true that Manasseh rests with his fathers (2 Kings 21:18).

📄 21:19–26

THE REIGN OF AMON, SON OF MANASSEH

Amon's unusually short reign (21:19) is an indication that the blessing of God is not upon it. Amon sins as Manasseh had sinned (21:20–22), but without repentance.

This story of conspiracy and assassination seems more like something that would happen among the kings of Israel, not Judah (21:23). Yet when the kings and people of Judah begin to imitate the sins of their conquered northern neighbors, they slip into the same chaos and anarchy that marks the last period of Israel's history.

But the people of the land execute all those who have conspired against King Amon (21:24). This is a hopeful sign. Up to this point, the people of Judah have largely tolerated some fifty-seven years of utterly wicked kings who led the nation in evil. Now it seems that they want righteousness and justice instead of the evil they have lived with for so long.

God gave them the leaders they wanted and deserved. Now, as the people of the kingdom turn toward godliness, God will give them a better king. God does not yet allow Judah to slip into the same pit of anarchy that Israel has. Because of the righteous action of the people of the land, there is no change of dynasty, and the rightful heir to the throne of David receives the throne (21:24–26).

2 KINGS 22:1–20

KING JOSIAH FINDS THE BOOK OF THE LAW

Setting Up the Section

With the death of King Amon, Josiah becomes king in Judah. He is one of the few kings who is obedient to the Lord throughout his reign.

📄 **22:1–10**

THE BEGINNINGS OF JOSIAH'S REFORMS

The young king Josiah comes to the throne at eight years of age (22:1). This is because of the assassination of his father, Amon. Josiah does what is right in the sight of the Lord (22:2).

Critical Observation

It is possible that Josiah is motivated to rebuild the temple after hearing (or remembering) that this was the workings of King Jehoash many years before (chapter 12). Josiah understood that the work of repair and rebuilding the temple needed organization and funding. He paid attention to both of these needs when he commanded Hilkiah to begin the work on the temple (22:3–7).

The fact that Hilkiah has to find the Book of the Law (22:8) makes it clear that it has been lost. It seems remarkable that this is even worthy of mention—that the high priest finds the Word of God and a scribe reads it. Yet the Word of God is so neglected in these days that this is an unusual event. According to Deuteronomy 31:24–27, there is to be a copy of the Book of the Law beside the ark of the covenant, beginning in the days of Moses. The Word of God was with Israel, but it was greatly neglected in those days. This neglect could only happen because Judah was in prolonged disobedience to God.

Shaphan reads the book before the king (22:9–10). It had been forgotten and regarded as nothing more than an old, dusty book. Now it is found.

KING JOSIAH IS CONFRONTED WITH THE BOOK OF THE LAW

The hearing of God's Word does a spiritual work in King Josiah. It is not merely the transmission of information; the hearing of God's Word has an impact of spiritual power on Josiah. The tearing of clothing is a traditional expression of horror and astonishment. In the strongest of displays, Josiah shows his grief on his own account and on account of the nation (22:11). This is an expression of deep conviction of sin, and a good thing. This conviction of sin is the special work of the Holy Spirit.

Demystifying 2 Kings

Scholars believe that the particular portion of the law that was found and read before King Josiah was the book of Deuteronomy or a portion of it.

King Josiah is so under the conviction of sin that he does not know what to do next. He knew that the kingdom of Judah deserved judgment from God. He could not hear the Word of God and respond to the Spirit of God without seriously confronting the sin of his kingdom (22:12–13).

We know little of Huldah the prophetess other than this mention here (and the similar account recorded in 2 Chronicles 34:22). With the apparent approval of King Josiah, Hilkiah the priest consults this woman for spiritual guidance (22:14). She is not sought out because of her own wisdom and spirituality, but she is recognized as a prophetess and can reveal the heart and mind of God.

Judah deserves judgment, and that judgment will indeed come. Judah and its leaders had walked against God for too long and will not genuinely repent so as to avoid eventual judgment (22:15–17). God's Word is true, even in its promises of judgment. God's faithfulness is demonstrated as much by His judgment upon the wicked as it is by His mercy upon the repentant.

Josiah's heart is tender in two ways. First, it is tender to the Word of God and is able to receive the convicting voice of the Holy Spirit. Second, it is tender to the message of judgment from Huldah in the previous verses (22:18–19). So the Lord promises that Josiah will die in peace before judgment falls on Judah (22:20).

2 KINGS 23:1–37
THE REFORMS OF JOSIAH

Setting Up the Section

Chapter 22 recounts the finding of the Law and Josiah's response to it. Chapter 23 highlights some of the outcomes of Josiah's convictions.

📖 23:1–27

THE COVENANT AND THE REFORMS OF KING JOSIAH

Josiah hears the promise of both eventual judgment (22:16) and the immediate delay of judgment (22:20). He does not respond with indifference or simple contentment that he will not see the judgment in his day. He wants to get the kingdom right with God, and he knows that he can't do it by himself—he needs all the elders of Judah to join in broken repentance with him (23:1).

Josiah is so concerned that the nation hear the Word of God that he reads it to them himself. He stands before the people and publicly declares his commitment to obey God to the very best of his ability. The people take a stand for the covenant in response to the example and leadership of King Josiah. We do not read of any command for the people to do this; they do it spontaneously as they follow the king's example and leadership (23:2–3).

Take It Home

This kind of mass response and commitment to God cannot be commanded, but that does not mean there is no part for people to play. It is clearly the work of God among the people, but God works through the example and leadership of King Josiah.

The fact that this happens among all the people means that this is a special work of the Holy Spirit. The Bible tells us that there are times when the Holy Spirit comes upon people as a *group*, which is a different work than the individual filling of the Spirit (see Acts 2:4; 4:31; 10:44).

Verses 4–7 show just how deep idolatry is in Judah. There are idols dedicated to Baal, to Asherah, and to all the hosts of heaven in the very temple itself. From this account, it seems that Josiah began the cleansing reforms at the center and worked outwards. Josiah's reforms do not only remove sinful things but also the sinful people that promote and permit these sinful things. The idols that fill the temple do not get there or stay there on their own—there are idolatrous priests who are responsible for these sinful practices.

Throwing the ashes of the idols on the graves outside the city is not intended to defile their graves. Any contact with death was believed to be an act of defilement, so scattering the dust on the graves serves to defile the idols.

Verses 8–14 reveal something of the extent of official idolatry in Judah. It is widespread, elaborate, and heavily invested in. Previous kings of Judah had spent a lot of time and money to honor these pagan idols. It takes a long, dedicated commitment on the part of King Josiah to do this work.

King Josiah is so diligent in his reforms that he takes down altars located in the former kingdom of Israel. He removes the pagan altar at Bethel that Jeroboam set up hundreds of years earlier (23:15).

Verses 16–17 record the remarkable fulfillment of a prophecy made hundreds of years earlier. The words of this anonymous prophet are recorded in 1 Kings 13:1–2. Josiah is careful to honor the gravestone of this anonymous prophet, but he executes the pagan priests (2 Kings 23:18–20).

Josiah can't command heart obedience to God, but he can establish a national holiday to observe the Passover. The celebration of the Passover had become so neglected that this was a remarkable observance (23:21–23).

Passover remembers the central act of redemption in the Old Testament: God's deliverance of Israel from Egypt in the days of Moses. Their neglect of Passover proves that they had neglected to remember God's work of redemption for them. It would be like a group of modern Christians completely forgetting the celebration of the Lord's Supper, which remembers Jesus' work of redemption for us.

King Josiah also fulfills the commandment of God to put away those who practice the occult (23:24). His passion is to perform the words of the Law which were written in the book. Josiah is one of the most remarkable kings of Judah, unique in the strength of his obedience and commitment. He stands as a wonderful example of what a leader can and should be (23:25). There were other great kings of Judah and the united kingdom of Israel—such as David and Hezekiah. Yet one thing that makes Josiah unique is his godliness *in his day*. He lived in a remarkably wicked time, so his godliness was remarkable against the backdrop of his times.

Nevertheless, not long after Josiah's reign, Judah is severely judged by the Lord (23:26–27). There is an outward conformity among the people of Judah, yet their hearts are not really turned toward God. God does not turn from His wrath because, despite Josiah's personal godliness and his righteous example and leadership, the people of Judah still provoke Him, loving the sins introduced during the wicked days of Manasseh, Josiah's father.

📄 23:28–37

JOSIAH'S END AND HIS SUCCESSORS

The alliance between Egypt and Assyria is part of the geopolitical struggle between the declining Assyrian Empire and the emerging Babylonian Empire. The Assyrians make an alliance with the Egyptians to protect against the growing power of the Babylonians. When Josiah leads his army against the king of Egypt, he is killed and his body is brought back to Jerusalem for burial (23:29).

The reforms of King Josiah are wonderful, but they are not long-lasting. His own son Jehoahaz does not follow in his godly ways (23:31–32). After the defeat of King Josiah in battle, Pharaoh is able to dominate Judah and make it effectively a vassal kingdom and a buffer against the growing Babylonian Empire. He imposes on the land a tribute, imprisons King Jehoahaz, and puts on the throne of Judah a puppet king, Eliakim, (renamed Jehoiakim), a brother of Jehoahaz (23:33–34).

Jehoiakim is nothing more than a puppet king presiding over a vassal kingdom under the Egyptians. He imposes heavy taxes on the people and pays the money to the Egyptians, as required. Like his brother Jehoahaz, Jehoiakim does not follow the godly example of his father Josiah (23:35–37).

2 KINGS 24:1–20

JUDAH SUBJECTED UNDER BABYLON

Setting Up the Section

As the book of 2 Kings comes to a close, this chapter recounts the reigns of the last three kings of Judah before Judah is taken into exile.

📄 24:1–7

THE REIGN OF KING JEHOIAKIM OF JUDAH

Nebuchadnezzar, king of the Babylonian Empire, is concerned with Judah because of its strategic position in relation to the empires of Egypt and Assyria. Therefore it is important to him to conquer Judah and make it a subject kingdom (his vassal), securely loyal to Babylon (24:1). This happens in 605 BC, and it is the first (but not the last) encounter between Nebuchadnezzar and Jehoiakim. There will be two later invasions (597 and 587 BC).

Demystifying 2 Kings

This specific attack is documented by the Babylonian Chronicles, a collection of tablets discovered as early as 1887 and held in the British Museum. Excavations also document the victory of Nebuchadnezzar over the Egyptians at Carchemish. Archaeologists found evidences of battle, vast quantities of arrowheads, layers of ash, and a shield of a Greek mercenary fighting for the Egyptians.

This campaign of Nebuchadnezzar is interrupted suddenly when he hears of his father's death and races back to Babylon to secure his succession to the throne. He travels about five hundred miles in two weeks—remarkable speed in that day. Nebuchadnezzar only has the time to take a few choice captives (such as Daniel), a few treasures, and a promise of submission from Jehoiakim.

When Nebuchadnezzar has to make a hurried return to Babylon, Jehoiakim takes advantage of his absence and rebels against him.

It might seem that God will honor the Judean independence movement of Jehoiakim, but He does not bless it. God sends against him many adversaries because Jehoiakim is a patriot of the kingdom of Judah, but not a man submitted to God. One of Jehoiakim's great sins is that he persecutes the godly and fills Jerusalem with innocent blood (24:2–6).

The various peoples mentioned in verse 2 are probably allies who are willing to fight with him. In the geopolitical struggle between Egypt and Babylon, Nebuchadnezzar defeats the army of Egypt and then becomes the dominant power in that part of the world (24:7).

Critical Observation

The fall of Jerusalem occurs in stages:

- Nebuchadnezzar's initial subjugation of the city
- Destruction from Nebuchadnezzar's marauding bands
- The siege and fall of Jerusalem under Nebuchadnezzar's main army
- Nebuchadnezzar's return to completely destroy and depopulate Jerusalem

📄 **24:8–16**

THE REIGN OF JEHOIACHIN

Jehoiachin succeeds his father, Jehoiakim. He carries on in the tradition of the wicked kings of Judah (24:8–9).

The previous king of Judah, Jehoiakim, had led a rebellion against Nebuchadnezzar. Now the king of Babylon comes with his armies against Jerusalem, and Jehoiachin hopes to appease Nebuchadnezzar by submitting himself, his family, and his leaders to the Babylonian king. But God allows Jehoiachin to be taken as a bound captive back to Babylon (24:10–12, 15).

On this second attack against Jerusalem, Nebuchadnezzar takes whatever valuables remain in the temple or in the royal palaces of Jerusalem, including the gold from the furniture and the precious things of Solomon's temple. Some ancient traditions tell us that Jeremiah hides the ark of the covenant before this, so that it is not among the things that are cut up and carried back to Babylon (24:13).

Nebuchadnezzar not only takes the material treasures of Judah, but also the human treasures. Anyone with any skills or abilities is taken captive to Babylon (24:14–16). Among these captives is the prophet Ezekiel, who compiles his book of prophecies while in captivity in Babylon.

📖 24:17–20

THE REIGN OF ZEDEKIAH

Since Nebuchadnezzar has completely humbled Judah, he puts a king on the throne whom he thinks will submit to Babylon. He chooses Mattaniah, an uncle of Jehoiachin and a brother to Jehoiakim, and changes his name to Zedekiah (24:17). The name *Zedekiah* means "the Lord is Righteous." The righteous judgment of God will soon be seen against Judah.

Zedekiah, like so many kings before him, does evil in the sight of the Lord (24:18–19). Second Chronicles 36:11–20 tells us more of the evil of Zedekiah, specifically that he does not listen to Jeremiah or other messengers of God. Instead, he mocks and disregards the message. God's patience and longsuffering has finally run its course, and He allows—even instigates—the conquering of the kingdom of Judah (24:29).

2 KINGS 25:1–30

THE FALL OF JERUSALEM AND THE CAPTIVITY OF JUDAH

Jerusalem Is Conquered	25:1–21
Judah and Jerusalem under the Babylonians	25:22–30

Setting Up the Section

The book of 2 Kings opens with Elijah being carried to heaven. It ends with the people of Judah being driven into exile. God's judgment has fallen on His disobedient people.

📖 25:1–21

JERUSALEM IS CONQUERED

When Nebuchadnezzar attacks Jerusalem, he uses the common method of attack in those days of securely walled cities (25:1). A siege was intended to surround a city, prevent all business and trade from entering or leaving, and to eventually starve the population into surrender. After a year and a half, the famine has become severe (25:2–3), and Nebuchadnezzar and the Babylonians are at the point of victory over Jerusalem.

At this desperate point for Judah at the siege of Jerusalem, Zedekiah makes a last-chance effort to escape the grip of the nearly successful siege. He plans a secret break through the city walls and the siege lines of the Babylonians (25:4). The enemy army pursues the king, and they overtake him in the plains of Jericho. This is a considerable distance from Jerusalem. Zedekiah probably thought that his strategy was successful and that he had escaped the judgment that prophets such as Jeremiah had promised. Yet God's Word is demonstrated to be true, and he is captured in the plains of Jericho (25:5).

The Babylonians are not known to be as cruel as the Assyrians, who conquered the northern kingdom of Israel some 150 years earlier, but they are still experts in cruelty in their own right. They make certain that the last sight King Zedekiah sees is the murder of his own sons, and then he spends the rest of his life in darkness (25:6–7).

Critical Observation

Zedekiah's capture fulfills the mysterious promise God makes through Ezekiel regarding Zedekiah shortly before the fall of Jerusalem (Ezekiel 12:13).

The captain of Nebuchadnezzar's guard returns to Jerusalem and sets fire to it (25:8–9). Solomon's great temple is now a ruin. It will stay a ruin for many years, until it is humbly rebuilt by the returning exiles in the days of Ezra. He destroys the walls of Jerusalem—the physical security of the city (25:10). Jerusalem is no longer a place of safety and security. The walls will remain a ruin until they are rebuilt by the returning exiles in the days of Nehemiah.

Then he carries away the rest of the people who remain in the city (25:11–12). This is the third major wave of captivity, taking all the remaining people except for the poor of the land. As the remaining people are taken captive to Babylon, so also the remaining valuables from the temple are taken (25:13–17). Jerusalem is left desolate, completely plundered under the judgment of God.

The last leaders of Jerusalem and Judah are captured and put to death. The king of Babylon has what seems to be complete rule over the former kingdom of Judah. This is the land God gave to His people, the tribes of Israel. They had possessed this land for some 860 years; they took it by faith and obedience, but they lose it through idolatry and sin (25:18–21).

📄 **25:22–30**

JUDAH AND JERUSALEM UNDER THE BABYLONIANS

The king of Babylon has made Gedaliah governor in what remains of Judah (25:22). It seems that Gedaliah is a good and godly man who is a friend of the prophet Jeremiah (Jeremiah 26:24; 39:14). He advises the people to live peacefully and serve the king of Babylon (25:23–24). It seems unpatriotic and perhaps ungodly to do this, but it is the right thing to do. The best they can do under this situation of deserved and unstoppable judgment is to simply accept it from the hand of God. The Babylonians are doing the work of God in bringing this judgment upon the deserving kingdom of Judah. In this situation, to resist the Babylonians is to resist God.

Critical Observation

This situation greatly bothers the prophet Habakkuk. Even though Judah is wicked and deserves judgment, how can God use an even more wicked kingdom like Babylon to bring judgment? Habakkuk deals with these difficult questions in Habakkuk 1:5–2:8.

Because Gedaliah leads the remaining people of Judah to submit to the Babylonians (also called the Chaldeans in some versions), he is assassinated as a traitor to the resistance movement (25:25). Afraid of what the Babylonians will do to them, the people of Judah flee to Egypt (25:26).

King Jehoiachin, mentioned in verses 27–30, is not the last king of Judah; Zedekiah comes after him. Jehoiachin had previously been taken away to Babylon in bronze fetters (24:10–12). These last events of the book of 2 Kings occur after Jehoiachin has been a captive for many years.

The final words of the book of 2 Kings describe small kindness and blessings given in the worst circumstances. Judah is still depopulated, the people of God are still exiled, and the king of Judah is still a prisoner in Babylon. Yet, looking for even small notes of grace and mercy as evidences of the returning favor of God, the divine historian notes that King Jehoiachin begins to receive better treatment in Babylon. This is small, but evidence nonetheless that God is not done blessing and restoring His people, foreshadowing even greater blessing and restoration to come.

CONTRIBUTING EDITORS:

Robert Deffinbaugh grew up in Washington state where he attended Seattle Pacific University. Since then, he graduated from Dallas Theological Seminary and has taught as a national seminar instructor for Prison Fellowship, served on various missions boards, and has taught the Bible in India, Africa, and China. In the 1970's, he helped plant Community Bible Chapel where he has served as an elder and Bible teacher for nearly 30 years. He lives with Jeanette, his wife of 44 years, in Texas. They have 5 grown daughters. Many of Robert's original teaching transcripts can be accessed through Bible.org.

David Guzik is the director of Calvary Chapel Bible College Germany, near Siegen, Germany. David took this position in January of 2003, after serving for 14 years as the founding and Senior Pastor of Calvary Chapel of Simi Valley. He has been in pastoral ministry since 1982.

CONSULTING EDITOR:

Tremper Longman is the Robert H. Gundry Professor of Biblical Studies at Westmont is the Robert H. Gundry Professor of Biblical Studies at Westmont University. He has taught at Westmont since 1998 and taught before that for 18 years at the Westminster Theological Seminary in Philadelphia. Dr. Longman has degrees from Ohio Wesleyan University (B.A.), Westminster Theological Seminary (M.Div.), and Yale University (M.Phil.; Ph.D.). He has also been active in the area of Bible translation, in particular he serves on the central committee that produced and now monitors the New Living Translation.

WITH SPECIAL THANKS TO BIBLE.ORG

Bible.org is a non-profit (501c3) Christian ministry headquartered in Dallas, Texas. In the last decade, bible.org has grown to serve millions of individuals around the world and provides thousands of trustworthy resources for Bible study including the new NET BIBLE® translation.

Bible.org offers thousands of free resources for:
- Spiritual Formation and Discipleship
- Men's Ministry
- Women's Ministry
- Pastoral Helps
- Small Group Curriculum and much more. . .

Bible.org can be accessed through www.bible.org

Watch for All 12 Volumes in the

QUICKNOTES SIMPLIFIED BIBLE COMMENTARY SERIES

ALSO AVAILABLE:

Volume 8: Matthew and Mark
Good News for Everyone
ISBN 978-1-59789-774-7

Volume 9: Luke and John
Life That Lasts Forever
ISBN 978-1-59789-775-4

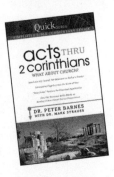

Volume 10: Acts thru 2 Corinthians
What about Church?
ISBN 978-1-59789-776-1

Volume 11: Galatians thru Philemon
Putting Faith into Practice
ISBN 978-1-59789-777-8

Volume 12: Hebrews thru Revelation
Wisdom for Today—and Forever
ISBN 978-1-59789-778-5

Volume 1: Genesis thru Numbers
Where Do We Come From?
ISBN 978-1-59789-767-9

Other Volumes Planned for the Series:

Volumes 3–7: Balance of the Old Testament, 2009–2010

Available wherever Christian books are sold.